The Wapsipinicon Almanac

A Bur Oak Book ❧ Holly Carver, series editor

The Wapsipinicon Almanac

Selections from Thirty Years

EDITED BY

Timothy Fay

University of Iowa Press ❀ Iowa City

University of Iowa Press, Iowa City 52242
Copyright © 2023 by the University of Iowa Press
uipress.uiowa.edu
Printed in the United States of America
Printed on acid-free paper
ISBN 978-1-60938-887-4 (pbk)
ISBN 978-1-60938-888-1 (ebk)
Design by Sara T. Sauers

Cataloging-in-Publication data is on file with the Library of Congress.

COVER ARTISTS: Jim Carpenter, p. 8; Nancy Lindsay, p. 235; Tom Metcalf, p. 238 (top right); Elizabeth Munger, p. 238 (top left); Don Peters, p. xiv (bottom right); Terry Rathje, p. ii; Brian Seger, p. xiv (top right); Will Thomson, pp. xiv (top and bottom left), 238 (bottom left), 246; Chuck Trapkus, p. 238 (bottom right).

FEATURED ARTISTS: Charles Baker, p. 121; Lori Biwer-Stewart, p. 127; Alma Broulik Carlin, pp. xi, 186; Jim Carpenter, p. 32; Kathy Carroll, pp. 46, 100, 103, 109, 115, 164, 244; Dolores Chadwell, pp. 62, 70, 136; Darlene Coltrain, pp. i, 23; Lauren Faulkenberry, p. 247; Laura Jean, pp. xiii, 9, 29, 40, 98, 141, 154, 229; Elizabeth Munger, pp. 57, 250; Kathryn Oliver, p. 214; Terry Rathje, pp. viii, 185, 192, 223; Brian Seger, pp. 176, 188, 198, 253; Will Thomson, pp. ix, 63, 82, 86, 165, 219; Chuck Trapkus, pp. 1, 5, 48, 83, 122, 140; Mary Wolverton, p. 110.

To Floyd Pearce (1927–2019), printer, poet, publisher, mayor

Plant a tree today
for tomorrow!

Only 4 per cent of our
state remains tree
covered. **TREES FOR-EVER** will lead the way
in reforestation and res-toration of Iowa forests
through action oriented
programs and by build-ing public awareness.

For more information,
contact:

5190 42nd St. N.E. ● Cedar Rapids, Iowa 52402

Contents

Introduction

by Timothy Fay

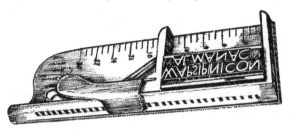

IT'S TAKEN A WHILE for me to realize that the *Wapsipinicon Almanac* is now in the past. This surely hit home earlier this year as I sorted through galleys to disassemble ads, most with mitered borders, many with handset type. Some of these represented that first year, 1988, when a crushing drought baked Iowa.

For those new to this: with ten years of job printing experience and bits and pieces of newspaper and magazine writing under my belt, I began publishing the *Almanac*, a 160-page annual collection of regional essays, fiction, book reviews, various tidbits, and advertisements. I launched the project hoping to offer a journal somewhat out of the mainstream of Iowa journalism.

The *Almanac* met with enthusiasm from various quarters, and this took the venture forward. I tried to stock many libraries in the state with the magazine, and I put together a nice collection of independent bookstores interested in featuring it. These, along with my advertisers (some on board from day one), I'd visit between Thanksgiving and Christmas when I'd head out, solo, with a carload of *Almanacs*—taking my chances with the early winter weather.

Highlights of the year were the various bookstore and radio readings (and accompanying parties) with selected contributors from each hot-off-the-press issue. A fun gig, I'd have to say, and a great way to meet and hobnob with many talented writers, artists, and creative small business proprietors. I'll always relish the memories connected with the thousands of miles and many scenic Iowa backroads I traversed on *Almanac* business. I spent plenty of those hours bouncing along in my thrifty little

Toyota Starlet hatchback. A lifetime of quirky faces, characters, and Main Streets of every stripe populated those wanderings.

I decided I would wrap up things with issue number 25 in late 2018. It was time for smaller projects. Thirty years of road trips, hot metal line casting, and hoisting heavy forms onto a nine-ton flatbed press had been a lot of work. And I wasn't getting any younger (or more open-minded).

Remembering those years in the late 1980s, I can't help but compare that "virtually" internet-less time to now. Contributors mailed me type-written copy. Transactions happened over the phone or in person. Email didn't arrive at the Route 3 Press until 2003. It's good to look to the future and what promise it may hold, but I have to feel some nostalgia for those predigital days. I'd argue that before the internet ruled our existence and handheld devices became more mandatory carry-withs than handkerchiefs, people, especially rural folks, spent more time outdoors, maybe studying the clouds, smelling the flowers, listening to birdsong, or gazing into a starry November night sky.

One thing that can be said about the *Wapsipinicon Almanac* is that our three decades of work offered many fine essays about Iowa's land, our wildlife, our small towns, and other elements that we all now are guilty of readily rushing past. A good deal of work went into producing those letterpress pages, and I am tickled that the magazine's printed volumes will turn up long after we're all gone. Most of the old-time printers I've known throughout my career have passed, and I'll offer the long hours spent producing those past issues as a respectful legacy to their memory.

One hope for me would be for this anthology to plant seeds that would inspire some young writer/editor to start another print publication of essays, fiction, and regional material. The online efforts just don't spark fascination for this old printer.

But back to this volume. My everlasting thanks go out to the University of Iowa Press for pushing for this anthology. It's been difficult trying to choose what to include from what I'd call a lot of good material, and editor/friend Holly Carver proved invaluable through this effort. I regret not having the space to include selections from the "Four Seasons Mini-Almanac," "Cultural News," and (with one exception) the book review sections.

My small town of Anamosa, Iowa, is known in the state as the home of a big prison, the location of a motorcycle museum, and the birthplace of artist Grant Wood. I'm hoping this anthology will enlarge our spot on the map and turn on a few more Iowans and midwesterners to my little publishing effort that ambled along for thirty years here in the rolling hills of eastern Iowa.

I T HAS often been said that printing, as well as other arts, reflects the tastes and tendencies of its time. As life at present is more nervous, self-assertive, and generally disorganized than ever before, it is not strange that our printing should exhibit the same characteristics.

— Bruce Rogers (1943)

The
Wapsipinicon
Almanac

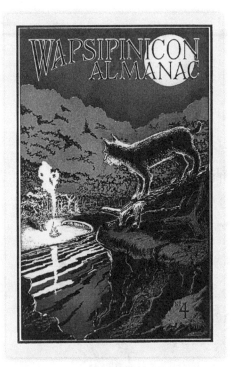

WAPSIPINICON ALMANAC

Number Eleven   Seven Dollars

ROUTE 3 PRESS • NUMBER 14 • EIGHT DOLLARS

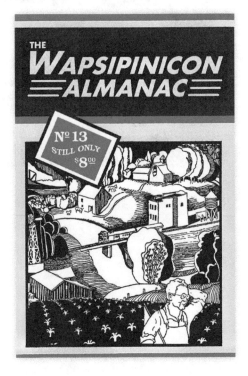

TALK OF THE TOWNSHIP, 1992–2010

Our friend Jim Walters of rural Johnson County, writing in a publication for Iowa bird enthusiasts on middle America's hunger for new, habitat-removing housing developments, notes: "Our modern place names tell us less about what's there than what's lost—Pheasant Ridge (no pheasants), Walden Woods (no woods), Apple Ridge (no apples), Willowbrooke Pointe (no willows, no brook, no point)."

———

Perceptive outdoor types were able to enjoy river skating for a week or so between last year's Christmas and New Year. It's rare that the Wapsipinicon freezes so smooth and snowless—perhaps once every six or seven years. We launched on Buffalo Creek near the new "Ridge Road" bridge by Anamosa. Doubts concerning safety eased as we saw the 3–5" ice could easily support gliding skaters.

Skating on ice over clear, moving water easily tops pond skating. It's spellbinding and even a bit unnerving to watch sand and shredded leaves tumble along with the current. Some stretches of ice glitter in mirror-like clearness unlike the cloudy scratched gray of city rinks.

The half-mile or so down the Buffalo wound interestingly to the Wapsi; there we veered west toward Stone City to the sun sinking behind naked trees.

The next few days found us coursing our way through the Matsell Bridge, Waubeek, and Stone City areas on the Wapsi and near Fremont on the Buffalo.

Bluffs, hawks, wild turkeys, deer, beaver, fish—it all was there to see for a few days. And the quiet—so peaceful on the windless rivers—only the sounds of blades cutting virgin ice.

———

One gentleman we can't help but admire is the ageless Darrell Meredith. His consuming hobby, fueled mysteriously in just the last few years, is planting trees. He's planted well over 100 we're told. Darrell is a retired farmer and former major league pitching prospect. He threw for a while in the Chicago White Sox and Brooklyn Dodger organizations, but these days, at only 86, most of his swinging is via shovelfuls, as he adorns the grounds of his homestead on the Ridge Road between Anamosa and Prairieburg.

We're sure he could outwork any three guys half his age pulled from barstools downtown. He won't be here when those trees reach adult glory, but his example is a strong one, instructing us to begin to plant now so we can enjoy later.

———————

We can't tell you much about the Nelson Products Co. of Sioux Rapids, Iowa. We've dealt only with its "Magic Heat" division. But what we do know is worth mentioning.

A Magic Heat device is simply a blower mechanism that fits into the stovepipe above a heating unit, in our case a woodstove. Warm air is saved from escaping up one's chimney. A good wood-cutting friend presented us with one at Christmas several years back. Eventually, a certain switch wore out and we called the company. At 7:50 a.m. on a Tuesday, a real person answered the phone. We didn't hear a recording offering 10 options that our rotary dial phone wouldn't be able to translate. We weren't put on hold and subjected to lame canned music, or worse, advertising. Yes, a *real* person answered the phone. She *understood* immediately what part we needed and told us it would cost six dollars plus about $1.50 to mail. The part arrived a day or so later. Our call wasn't transferred four times, and our order wasn't strangled somewhere in computer whoop-de-doo-doo.

Why is it that, as more and more communications technology moves its way into our lives, the real business of getting, interpreting, and, if need be, fulfilling the message flounders? Captains of commerce, from both here and across state lines, need to realize that human personal service can constitute a strong selling point.

———————

The most splendid day to be self-employed at home in a rural area is the Tuesday following Labor Day. The mid-morning silence is deafening. Only crickets and a solitary cardinal have spoken recently. All nearby neighbors are off to work in whatever town; their children sit in class-rooms. No tires crunch gravel, no lawnmowers roar their rounds. The hazy summer still is here—but it's not, as the nights have abandoned their sauna personalities. Lush green everywhere, yet the first mover, the buckeye tree, has leaves rapidly browning and dropping.

Today we'll particularly savor that sky blue gaze to the west to see the white spire of the Cass Center Congregational Church reflect its brightness two miles away.

The countryside is emptied today of human activity. Not many farm-ers even left around here, which is a pity sociologically, but the silence is a treat for anyone alone and loving it on a golden early fall morning.

———————

Who says you can't have fun in rural Iowa? Some wags would argue that dancing is the most fun you can have with your clothes on, and several towns in our area still feature ballroom dancing with live music. Little Walford near Cedar Rapids offers the Ponderosa Ballroom and a sched-ule of dances. Also, there's Guttenberg's Lakeside Ballroom and others.

My lovely dancing partner and I look forward to Sunday evening outings at Oxford Junction's Legionnaire Ballroom in southeast Jones County. These are not complicated, competitive, you-really-need-lessons events. I'm talking about two-steps and waltzes in the company of the 60s to 80s age group. Plenty of Howards and Eileens and Ralphs and Lucilles. These folks do travel. I see many out-of-area license plates and familiar faces at different dances in different towns.

I admire anybody of any age group who is willing to rise onto the community platform and move to music. If there was more dancing in this world there'd be less fighting. I especially respect this crowd because I know I'm in close proximity to a bevy of new knees, replacement hips, and creaking joints.

The Legionnaire is subtly decorated and softly lighted. Lyle Beaver and the Brass Notes usually is the featured band. They glide effortlessly through the old standards. I wonder if these tunes and this kind of dancing will fade into history as the older generation passes. Will my only alternative be to flail to loud, bad 1980s rock with the casualties in attendance at Knucklehead's Bar in Anamosa?

It's just good fun to draw close to the strains of "Margie," "Waltz across Texas," or "It Had to Be You." And my partner has clipped a newspaper piece citing a study proclaiming that regular dancing delays dementia. She keeps it well displayed for me to see.

Exercise, romance, simply getting up and going "out"—it's all good. When did you last dance with your sweetheart?

——➤◦◄——

I'd like to congratulate the "Black Art" wizards who've created the Printers' Hall space at Mt. Pleasant on the Old Threshers Reunion grounds. This loose group of letterpress printing enthusiasts has collected and, in most cases, restored tons of machinery that at one time brought forth the printed word. Were it not for their efforts, this long-lived and well-crafted equipment would most likely be rusting in an Iowa scrap yard or en route to a Chinese foundry.

The linecasting machines, presses, paper cutters, and folders became hopelessly obsolete in the 1960s and 70s. We're to a point now in our digital age where much of the offset printing equipment that replaced letterpress is now also obsolete. That must mean we are doubly obsolete at the Route 3 Press.

——➤◦◄——

I fell into a real sweet deal lately. Floyd Sandford, a retired Coe College biology professor, passed on to me a five-pound jar of honey from the Jack Heiken apiary at Scotch Grove. Floyd formerly took his classes to visit Jack's organic farm. Floyd, always thinking ahead, bought all of the basswood flower honey that Jack had for sale in that hallowed year of 1972. A few years have passed, but that honey still works its magic on whatever needs sweetening around here. Not to worry—that jar remained unopened, and the honey smells, tastes, and flows as sweetly as the day Jack bottled it. The honey is dark—its color resembles that of molasses more than the gold hues we're accustomed to seeing on grocery shelves. Different blossoms, different-colored honey. And talk about bottled ambrosia. . . .

The jar holds special significance for me. I knew the Heiken clan, an interesting bunch. I dug and planted trees seasonally in the late 1970s and early 80s with Jack's father Henry at the Scotch Grove Nursery. Henry was past 80 then but still sharpening his spade each morning and heading with me to the fields. I learned a lot from him: both he and Jack lived on little farms back in the gorgeous hills near Scotch Grove and the Maquoketa River. Those guys trapped, farmed, hunted ginseng, and just generally knew most everything about backwoods living. They were quiet, sensible, and polite men who were brilliant fishermen, too. I'd guess either of them, if alive today, could probably manage to hook and reel in a four-pound channel catfish from the Anamosa Dollar General parking lot.

So here's this whopping jar of dark, fine honey from 1972 sitting on my kitchen table. A sweet liquid mass of monosaccharides that require no digestive change before being absorbed into our systems. Thank you, Jack. Maybe I'll try the fishing today out your way.

———※·◦·❁———

My friend Zachary Jack, a highly competent editor, essayist, college instructor, and now novelist, currently is living near Oxford Junction in rural Jones County. Ice Cube Press last summer published his novel *What Cheer, Iowa: A Love Story.* I'd really like to find a copy. Media reports indicate it addresses the phenomenon of a somewhat loveless rural countryside. It seems Zachary laments the shortage of eligible single women to be found in the rural districts. He worries, in this new light and happy fiction work, that single folks his age are to be found only in the cities.

I need to talk to this young (36) fellow. I've lived in rural Jones County for 35 years, and I think the area always has been fairly teeming with single women. I know; I've dated both of them.

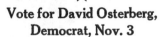

WAPSIPINICON
ALMANAC

A Thinking Man's Look at the "Good Old Days"

A CONVERSATION WITH MEL PEET

1988

We've known Mr. Peet and his family long enough to know that a favorite pastime of Mel's is to chortle away about the colorful life, the wild stories, and the peculiar characters he remembers from his childhood. Born in 1922 on a beautiful farm between Fairview and Viola, in Jones County, Mr. Peet retains both warm and not-so-pleasant memories of a childhood here. He left the area in 1940, returning occasionally to visit his parents, who farmed until the late 1960s. He returned here to live two years ago. We're including this account because a 1920s or 1930s childhood in or around Ana-mosa would be similar to childhood years lived near Manchester, Vinton, Tipton, or any other number of agrarian-based, county seat towns in our region. We find this account particularly fine-edged; this is probably attributable to the fact that he was away for so many years—with much time lived in or around large cities. We've managed to collect this piece in the form of an interview, in which Mel responded to written questions. We think you'll find more than a few strong and candid observations concerning the health, heart, and soul of our region's character.

WA: It's a warm June Saturday night in 1930. You're a lad of 8 or 9, and you are off to town. What do you hear, see, smell, feel?

MP: For a country boy of 8 or 9, going to town on a summer Saturday night in the 1930s was a fabulous journey from a mundane work-a-day world into a realm of mystery and fantasy. It is hard to do justice to the contrast between the two worlds—town and country—that has marked our Western Civilization for over a thousand years, and which impressed itself upon one so strongly back in the 1920s and 1930s around Anamosa. On the farm, everything was done in those days by manual labor or with horses or wind power. In town, electric power reigned, and the automobile. Artificial light on the farm was provided by the dim light of kerosene lamps and lanterns. Most people had also Coleman lamps and lanterns and Aladdin lamps, but I was always dazzled and astonished by the ready availability of bright warm light in town, at the flip of a switch, and the illumination of the streets and intersections by electric lights. It was a cheerful, heart-warming sight on Saturday night to see the crowds of town and country people mingling together on Main Street, in and out of the various businesses, under the handsome streetlights, like great candelabra, along the sidewalks. People who came onto the scene since then, accustomed as they are to the high, cold, industrial night illumination of Anamosa today, could hardly believe the sense of welcome and well-being which that old system of lighting provided.

The country child usually held a nickel or a dime in his or her pocket on a Saturday night, and a large part of the adventure lay in making the choice of on what to spend it. There were items in the five and dime store which could be bought for so little outlay. I can remember buying a Bakelite policeman's whistle, which was a favorite plaything of mine for years. But ordinarily the choice narrowed down to provisions for the stomach. There was then no limit to the amount of pop I could drink when given the chance. Once, Barney Steenhoek, Jim Wild, and I consumed together close to a case of soft drinks in the grandstand at the County Fair while watching the harness races. But that was a few years later when we were clearly provided better with cash. In 1930, nickels and dimes were hard for children to extract from their fathers, and when they were, they were quickly spent on candy, ice cream, or pop. My favorite soft drink was cream soda, and on Saturday nights I usually bought it out of an iced cooler at Ireland's Soda Grill. I would open the bottle on the side of the cooler, and then put my thumb over the open top, shake the bottle up and down, and then squirt a stream of the soda onto the high ceiling overhead.

On these Saturday nights when the weather was good, people of all ages, men, women, and children—most of them dressed in the best and cleanest clothes they owned—pressed up and down the length of Main Street, greeting each other, talking together, and doing their weekly shopping. Bill Ristine might be heard regaling his listeners with the adventure of the week, "Jesus Christ and the cows got out, and God and I was after 'em." The kids were playing tricks on each other and playing impromptu games. The women were exchanging symptoms of the minor illnesses that afflicted them at a time before they had ever heard of gynecology. As these were days of economic crisis in the U.S., and particularly in the farm regions, talk often centered around the bad times. The older people were aware that the social arrangements which they had developed out of the beginnings of their pioneer ancestors were being doomed by industrialization and the big cities.

WA: Who are the merchants your parents will trade with tonight? Are they serious, humorous, staid, or just busy?

MP: There were as many as 10 or 12 grocery stores in Anamosa when I was a child—including an A & P store. But my parents did business exclusively with Tyler & Downing. When we went to town on Saturday night, we usually had a case, made out of wooden slats, of eggs, which were traded at T & D for bread, meat, sugar, flour, salt, or cheese or indeed any item which my parents considered that we could afford. My father had attended high school in Anamosa in the same class with Bud Downing, and they remained good friends throughout their lives. T & D was a unique business establishment conducted with a perpetual air of fun and good-natured harassment of the customers. Dignified matrons were often goosed as they leaned over to examine encased or low-lying merchandise. Smart-alecky kids were teased and tormented by the proprietors and clerks. Off-color jokes were aimed at and fabricated about the young girl who ran the business office, and who was usually too innocent to comprehend them. Once my maternal grandmother complained to Mr. Downing about some mice who were feasting upon a wheel of longhorn cheese standing uncovered upon a butcher block.

"Why Mrs. Eckerman," he replied, "that cheese won't hurt those mice!" Children loved T&D because they could buy a big sack of candy for only a nickel. Most people failed to realize that in this way T&D was attracting customers for future years when these children would be grocery buyers. Some people reasoned that if they could get a big sack of candy for a nickel, then they'd get twice as much for a dime. But the fact was that whatever amount you gave the clerk—5 cents, 10 cents, 25 cents—you always got just the same amount of candy.

Many businesses went bankrupt in the early 30s. One of these, which my father always visited on Saturday night as long as it was solvent, was Hartman's Implement Company. It occupied the building on East Main Street now owned by Graver. It was a favorite store with me because there were always on display there the latest models of McCormick-Deering tractors, manure spreaders, cultivators, harvesters, plows, disk-harrows, and other farming implements. Once, on the eve of an early-1930s Fourth of July, Bob Hartman gave me a huge box of fireworks that had not been sold that year. My cousin Ann Dandridge and I had a marvelous time that 4th, shooting off all the crackers, bombs, rockets, pinwheels, worms, snakes, and sparklers that were in that box.

My father always made it a point to stop in at Nick Hanson's clothing store, John Goodman's hardware store, and Clyde Chipman's appliance store. Nick Hanson had a mordant wit. Once, my aunt Meda Bowdish, who was none too good a driver, almost bounced her 1929 two-door sedan Model A Ford over the curb and into his store window in the process of trying to diagonal-park in front of his shop. He happened to be standing in the doorway of the shop at the time, and he said to her as she sought to recover from the shock and fluster of her unexpected and unintended impact, "Come on in, Mrs. Bowdish, come right on in!" The merchants and clerks of Anamosa were in those days a very much more varied lot than nowadays. The society of that time produced a much richer variety of character types, and the people were willing to display and enjoy unusual qualities and temperaments to an extent that would be inconceivable now.

WA: You've described Anamosa as the "capital city of the surrounding region." Explain.

MP: Today, Anamosa has faded into relative insignificance compared to its resources and offerings of 50 to 70 years ago. Then, all the farmers and villagers gravitated to this "capital city," on a daily, weekly, and year-round basis. It was a financial center, with three banks. At one time in the 1930s, it had two movie theaters, with six or seven separate programs weekly, plus a family night and a bank night. It had two newspapers—one Republican and the other Democrat. That is to say, it had *newspapers*. When a town has only one newspaper, it has, in effect, really no news-paper at all. Two railroads served Anamosa, providing daily passenger and freight facilities to all points of the outside world. Since World War II, the Middle West has become an abandoned region transportation-ally. But this was not true in the 1920s and 30s. Furthermore, Anamosa had real bus service back then. There was daily morning service to both Cedar Rapids and Dubuque. People in Anamosa could go to either city in the morning, shop, and return home in time for supper. And there was a bus station. Passengers could *buy a ticket*—right here in town. And they could sit and wait for their bus in comfort, instead of standing miserably, as they must do now, for the bus to come. There were shops and businesses of every description in Anamosa in those days. And the stores were staffed by clerks who knew their stock and business, and who were eager to serve and please the customers. The ordeals of self-service and the check-out counter were virtually unknown then. Anamosa de-veloped its own electric power in those days. It had its own telephone system. There was a municipal system which delivered delicious, pure water. There were factories, and an office and school supply company. There was an ice company, a creamery, a depot, an annual fair, and fre-quent circuses, including Ringling Bros. and Barnum & Bailey. And in the strict sense, Anamosa was a regional capital because of its library, and its superior school system, and above all because of the State prison and the County government.

Any kind of capital has to have pleasant and refreshing places of public resort. Private entertainment, no matter how fine, cannot take the place of public and communal enjoyment. Television has drawn a large proportion of people from the soda fountains, cafes, taverns, and bars. User-fees and stickers have virtually killed the Wapsipinicon State Park as a place of easy public entertainment. Main Street used to be a sort of well-lighted public living room, alive with shops and customers. Now it is a cold and deserted by-way. The people are mostly in moving cars. There are no knots of visiting neighbors—no popcorn or peanut stands. The people on Main Street seem shy of one another, and mutually repelled. When I was a small child, I knew a woman who said, of a dress she had bought, "It's just a little thing to wear down on Main Street in the afternoon." Every capital—even Anamosa—has to be, among other things, a style center. Now, instead of going down to Main Street, people get into their cars and "Go out to Walmart." What a falling off is there!

WA: Do you think farmers trusted businessmen in those days?
MP: No.

After saying that, I'd like to point out that then, as now, farmers *were* businesspeople. If they weren't, they weren't farmers very long. Still, it must be said also that the majority of farmers in those days were *subsistence* farmers, not businesspeople operating for short-term profits.

But the fact remains that the dichotomy between town and country which I experienced in my childhood between Anamosa and the farms is the modern version of the medieval division between burg and manor. They represent two distinct, antagonistic, but interdependent civilizations. The burghers have won hands-down, in the interval between 1920 and 1988. The 1950s saw the capitulation of the farms, and those who were born then and since cannot know at firsthand what I am talking about. It is hard now to realize the antagonism that existed between farm and town.

As a final remark on this question, I'd say that in those days the businesspeople of town and country distrusted each other as much as was possible without open warfare.

WA: Tell me about a trip that next winter, let's say, with your father to the village of Viola. What do you experience at the general store?
MP: Viola was a much livelier town in the 20s and 30s than it is now. The school was new, and I went to it several times at night with my father, who played basketball in the gymnasium with a group of young men his age who had already graduated from high school. The fact is that my dad actually finished high school at all solely because of his love of this game. Many of my early memories of him are closely connected with athletics and the sports of hunting and fishing. In winter, we usually went to Viola either to pick up something at the depot or at one of the

two or three small general stores that were in the town then. Viola was also the central office of the cooperative telephone company to which the people along our road belonged. My mother used to call up the Viola central girl to find out the exact time or to learn the facts about some local news event to which she would be certain to be privy. In winter, the trip to Viola was often made on a bobsled, if there was enough snow. The road in those days was still an ungraded country track, with bushes and weeds growing right up to the edge of the roadway. When it was first graded up in the early 1930s, it was surfaced with gravel taken from a pit that can still be made out by the discerning eye just west of the Wilcox Cemetery, on the south side of the road. This gravel was mostly of a fineness suitable for road surfacing, but it was also mixed with smoothly rounded chunks of the size of the fist or the head. And these were a menace to wheels, hooves, feet, and tires. My grandmother Peet got me and my cousin Ann Dandridge to go up and down the road with a coaster wagon and gather up these attractive chunks of conglomerate for her to use in building her rock garden.

One of the Viola stores was owned and operated by Frank Benton—a man of immense bulk and strength. My father told an incredible story about him. It seems my father was returning from Viola one late morning on horseback, when he met Frank Benton returning to town from an old barn he was dismantling. He was carrying a high pile of foot-wide, inch-thick boards on his shoulder. The boards he was carrying were so long that they almost dragged on the ground ahead of and behind him. My father engaged him in talk for a long time, for Frank Benton was a match with father in marathons of idle talk. But, father had to give up and go on. Mr. Benton never put down or even shifted his load, but stood there talking, apparently unaware of the heavy burden he was bearing on his shoulder.

Lettie Brown had a store in Viola. I remember being driven through Viola as a small child by my cousin Don Bowdish. He was driving my uncle Robert's Whippet coupe. Don had four cents with him, and he stopped and went into Brown's store and bought four vanilla creams. He gave me two of them. This still stands for me as an example of unparalleled generosity.

One winter day, when several horses were tethered at the curb outside, as well as my father's bobsled and team, I heard a discussion around the potbellied stove at the back end of Smeltzer's general store. A group of men sat around the hot stove and regaled each other with tall stories about the heaviest loads they had ever carried. The last person, of course, told the biggest story, in keeping with age-old tradition. He said, "Well, I've never carried any very *heavy* loads, but the *unhandiest* load I ever carried was a cow and a calf and a cord of wood." After that, there was nothing left but for all of the assembled to leave and go home. Which we did.

WA: Of course these communities could never have existed without the surrounding farms. We can comprehend the physical and mechanical changes farms have undergone. But how would you, who grew up on a farm between Fairview and Viola, describe the countryside's cultural metamorphosis?

MP: Quite apart from the physical and mechanical changes that the farms around Anamosa have undergone, I would say that the region has lost entirely the sense of bright destiny and unique potentiality which it had 60 to 70 years ago. Each farm and each family had its individual ethos. This was a massive fact which we then all experienced and took for granted. Not only was it an adventure of the spirit to go to town, it was also one merely to go to somebody else's *place.* Nowadays, both country and town lie under the homogenizing influence of the government, with its programs, and the mass media, which eradicate human individuality and replace it in the souls of the people with the sterile and artificial caricatures of the television and the movie screen and the garbage of the papers and magazines at the supermarket check-out counter. It would be mistaken to hold that culture of any great depth or richness ever existed in Anamosa or the areas surrounding it. But what there was back in the days of my youth was a veritable Renaissance Spring compared to the flatness and emptiness of today.

In those days, the spirit which fired the great pioneer effort to possess the region west of the Mississippi River for the United States was still very much alive. My grandmother told me Indian stories which were very vivid and exciting to me, because by my day no Indians were in view. Both at home and in school, we were imbued with the mythos of the New England settlements and progressive expansion westward. The French and Indian wars, the Revolutionary struggle with Great Britain, and the war of the Federal Union against the southern slave power were as fresh, important, and alive to us as the stories brought back to us by our fathers from the battlefields and No-Man's-Land of eastern France in 1917 and 1918.

To my mind, the major aim of the early pioneer settlements around Anamosa was to create a permanent agrarian social order in which material security from the land would sustain an unchanging human life cycle of devotion to the Protestant Christian way of life. Farm work and the pleasures of sport and field were to be supplemented by a light and easy program of business education, fairs, circuses, courtships, marriages, families, and occasional ancillary vocations such as teaching, medicine, or law, from cradle to grave. The feeling was that in this middle section of the North American continent, the goal of a thousand generations of ancestors had been nearly reached. It was the contrast between this dream (for mere dream it ever was) and the ruthless destruction of the society and its vision, which set in in the 1940s and 1950s and has nearly reached its end today.

It was inevitable that I should lament this—even while I know that the dream was in most ways shallow and meager—incapable of enlisting or retaining the devotion needed for preserving and completing it. But the dead hand which lies on the land today shocks me. Even I am unable to resist the use of chemicals in my amateur forest management. The Wapsipinicon River is polluted. Rhoten Creek, once alive with minnows, crawfish, turtles, snakes, frogs, and toads, is almost dead. The ground water is contaminated, and the rich soil is saturated with chemicals, overfarmed and overfertilized. Suburbanite households line the roadways. It is the deep twilight of a once bright and hopeful day.

WA: I spent many hours canoeing the Wapsi and walking the woods with your late father (b. 1899). Could you briefly describe him, and try to compare him with a "typical" (if such a thing exists) Fairview township agribusinessman of today?

MP: My father was an unusual man on many counts. He was very good-looking in a blond, Nordic kind of way. Very strong, physically, and capable of great feats of bodily prowess and endurance. While he enjoyed leisure, and was capable of neglecting his work in favor of hours-long bouts of chat and gossip with anyone and everyone willing to spare the time, he performed work on a monumental scale—much of it onerous and disagreeable in the extreme. He was fond of all kinds of athletic sports and games. He loved and was loved by women. He had a reverence for them which was to my experience a rare example of chivalry in our post-medieval world. He loved all aspects of nature, the fields, the flowers, the animals, the birds, the woods, rivers, lakes, sky, and landscapes. As he grew older, he became deeply religious without any of the false piety, self-righteousness, and hypocrisy that frequently attend ordinary religiosity. He loved music, and sang and whistled beautifully at his work and play throughout his life.

He had neither the training nor the disposition of a businessperson. He hated all thoughts and calculations of profit and loss, and until the end of his life he was incapable of keeping records, or of writing his checkstubs, or balancing his books. Without the help and vigilance of my mother, his unbusiness-like ways would have landed him in disaster. The true family religion was the blind worship of money and property, and while father paid due respect to these tutelary deities, he had no real regard for them. His true faith was his devotion to the whole organic way of life which had been worked out in Fairview by his forebears and delivered to him by his parents and their community. I well remember the fervency of his conservatism in this respect. After WWII, the harvesting procedures of threshing began to give way to combining and baling. He was intransigently opposed to this trend. On many occasions, he said that he would *always* thresh—he would *never* combine his oats or bale the straw. He said that he would even go to the extreme of owning his own threshing machine and of doing all the work himself rather than change to the newer way of harvesting. Of course, he was unable to keep this somewhat pathetic oath. The larger, remorseless, historic, annihilating forces of greed and technological innovation swept away his moderate and humane conservatism, producing the deadly and future-destroying processes of present-day farming.

To my observation, the typical agribusiness person of today is a soulless automaton of materialistic power, possession, exploitation, quick profits, and vulgar display. My father was the very antithesis of this. In only one respect did he conform to the norm of local character—he was wholeheartedly non-intellectual. He passed relatively unscathed through the processes of grade and high school. He acquired a mass of facts, but they were rendered trivial by their lacking systematic organization. He carried in his heart a small treasury of memorized poetry of which a passage from *The Vision of Sir Launfal* stood as his favorite. When he was old and sick and confined to his house and his chair, he remembered having learned in his youth Milton's sonnet *On His Blindness*. But the poem's syntactical and grammatical complexities kept him from completely mastering it.

WA: You obviously cherish having grown up near a small Upper Midwest town. What did you sense, though, were the drawbacks to life here when you left in 1940 to attend college?

MP: What you say is true. I have lived most of my life in the sphere of big cities, such as New York, Beirut, and Washington, D.C. My divine vocation turned out to be college-level teaching in some of the oldest and most venerable disciplines in the curriculum—literature, history, philosophy, and religion. The people I have met who did not have the rural, farming childhood that I had have always seemed to me to lack awareness of some of the most important facts of life. Most people simply do not know how nature works. They do not know where the good things they use constantly—food, clothing, and shelter, for example—come from. They don't know how, with what effort and suffering, they are produced. They know little or nothing of the labor, the willed endurance, the frustrations and disappointments—but also the achievements, the victories, and the satisfactions—of the old farm-life, which all unsuspectedly was drawing to a close in the 1920s and 1930s.

To my mind, there is nothing inherently anti-cultural or anti-intellectual about the farming-business symbiosis that had flowered around the turn of the century and then began to decline and vanish in the 1920s and 30s. Nevertheless, all of the vital and spiritual advantages of a college or higher education *that can enrich rural life* have in practice been perversely foregone. They have been neglected in favor of the sheer power of a higher education, of any kind, to release people from menial work and raise the comfort and convenience of their lives. Thus, in effect, to go to college has meant to leave the rural life, the life of fruitful farming work, altogether.

I was virtually forced to leave the farm by a weak physical constitution and a chronic illness, asthma, which was exacerbated by the close contact with pollens and dusts emanating from the plants and animals of the farm. But, I have to acknowledge that I see my illness as the mere negative side of a longing to escape from the narrow province of rural life and to enter into the richness of the cosmopolitan sphere of high culture. The esthetic, emotional, and spiritual poverty of rural life drives many of the people who are confined to it to mental cripplement, eccentricity, and even insanity. I have seen a number of instances of this, and could name locally recognizable names, if I chose. The best construction I can put on the dream of the pioneers was that they wanted to produce in the Middle West a life of simple material security, devoid of spiritual depth and challenge. To the extent that this dream was realized (and it *was* realized to a remarkable extent), the rural way of life became first a notorious backwater, and then a forgotten anachronism. It became an unreal world disconnected from the most vigorous and vital developments of the modern age.

It was only when I went to college that I began to live the rich cultural life that is uniquely possible for the mass of the people in our age. This is the chief value of democracy—that it opens up this possibility to everyone. Art, literature, poetry, history, philosophy, and religion simply did not, and still do not, exist as viable procedures of mental conduct in the rural world. This is the principal drawback to life in and near the small towns. It is also the principal failure of democracy, and the reason why it must fail on all counts. These things are not only not cultivated there. They are determinedly put down, hated, extirpated, and ridiculed. Thus, for the cultivated person, life in the country, where life could be most delightful, is a Persephone-like entombment in an underworld. The image is complete when we realize the ruler of the nether world is Pluto—god of lucre.

WA: You lived for a time near a small town in Maryland. How did it differ from our area?

MP: The area between Frederick and Harpers Ferry where we lived—near the village of Jefferson—is largely given over to dairy farming. Our landlord milked 80 head of Holsteins, and tilled his 400 acres to feed and bed these cows and their ancillary herd. Socially, rural Maryland is more complex than Fairview Township. English and Southern traditions of aristocracy are deeply rooted in western Maryland, and the underlying population is largely made up of "rednecks" and the descendants of slaves. To my eye, 16 years of living in that area gave me no clearer vision of life among those people than wealth, power, and ostentation—the brutal material dream that is widely known simply as "the American dream." Superficially, farm life in Maryland in the 1920s and 1930s seems to have been pretty much what it was in Iowa—given the very real differences of climate, topography, and soil composition. In Maryland, no utopian ideal seems ever to have spread its glow over the mundane quality of rural life, the way it quite palpably and measurably did in the Middle West. For another thing, Iowa has no large cities to disturb steady compass needles of country mentality. In Maryland, Baltimore and Washington, D.C., severely upstage and revitalize the otherwise eternal-seeming verities of the country mind-set. Finally, the Midwest is virtually homogeneous ethnically. In Maryland, you will find, among other diverse elements, a large, repressed black population. The social mix in Maryland is very complicated. No—70 years ago, life in Iowa felt itself much more promising and progressive than it did in Maryland. Today, the exact opposite is true. It is much easier to get rich in Maryland than it is in Iowa, and now, that is all anybody lives for.

WA: Of course you visited your family here many times over the years. But what was it like to actually return here to live in 1986? Having known this area for more than a few decades, would you say there was a time when we "peaked" and was there a decade or an era when we "crashed"?

MP: I looked upon our move to Anamosa in 1986 as a real homecoming. I had retired from an intense 32-year period of teaching, and looked forward to being "back," and to being near my mother and woods. Certainly, I'd agree with you that our area "peaked" (as you put it) in the first and second decades of this century. Very likely the 20s and 30s, which I remember as so wonderful, were in truth a merely silver age. The "crash" began immediately after WWII. Farming then began to cease to be a way of life, and became a route to cash profits, like mining and oil drilling. To me, the face of the land of Fairview Township in the late 1980s is a sterile moonscape compared to its bloom and luxuriance 50 to 60 years before. What I dislike is the deadness of the land now, compared to then. And I miss the big manure piles, the outhouses, the windmills, the fields full of teams of work horses plowing, cultivating, mowing, raking. I miss the old processes of hay-making, and the big hay mows full of loose, not baled, hay. I miss the sounds of the corn harvest as they were then—with the ears of corn cracking against the bang boards as pickers, teams, and wagons slowly crossed the fields of stalks. I lament the loss of the fresh, healthy life of the streams, the rivers, and creeks. I hate the dumps one sees about the area—piles of old cars, farm machinery, and worst of all, the piles of not-quite-empty plastic pesticide and herbicide containers. I list the power lawn mower along with the bulldozer and chain saw as one of the worst tools ever to have been put into the hands of the common person. The mindless mania for endless lawn mowing has reduced whole roadways and areas to uniform stretches of monotonous greensward every growing season. The lawn mower does to the landscape what the television industry does to the collective national mind—reduces it to a living room carpet of dreary, sterile, healthless uniformity.

In closing, I might add that the period of the 1920s and 1930s was also an age of Isolationism, Prohibition, the Florida Land Boom, the Depression, and the era of the big gangsters. Fairview Township keenly felt these movements, and submitted to their influences more than people would be now inclined to think.

One of my fondest memories is Grant Wood's summer art colony that flourished for a summer or two in Stone City, a couple of miles north of our farm. The bohemian life-style of the student artists was a bit of a scandal in the area, and the fields/woods of the region seemed full of bereted, bearded, unkempt workers with easels, paints, canvases, palettes, pens, pencils, and drawing pads. For a time, a certain Emmet Peacock kept a sinister-seeming and mysterious beer joint in the Old Columbia Building in Stone City. And bona fide racketeers from Chicago were reputed to haunt the place when the heat of police repression was on in the Windy City. Compared to the moral quality of life now, the decades of the 20s and 30s were an age of light. But there were dark places and deep shadows even then, and many of those were premonitions of evils which we experience so massively today.

The Last Days of the Schultz Brothers Variety Store

BY OSHA DAVIDSON

1988

G RACE COUNTRYMAN suspected something was up the day Verne Abbott, the store's manager, got the phone call from headquarters.

"Well, the girls figured maybe that was it," says Countryman, a short, pleasant woman in her 60s who has punched the cash register keys at the Tipton Schultz Brothers Variety Store for over 14 years. "And then a salesman came in and said he had to pick up some stuff because he got the word that we were going out of business. They tried to cover that up. 'Oh, no,' they said. '*That's* not it.' Then we really knew it was over."

Countryman punctuates each sentence was a small laugh that sounds more like a cough. She laughs when she tells how she found her job here back in 1975 through her daughter, who worked at the store part-time after school; when she recalls how friends would drop in on rainy afternoons to buy a dishtowel or some nylons and stay and chat with her about nothing in particular; about the irony that places the store's closing on April Fool's Day. She even laughs as tears fill her eyes, and she talks about the future.

"Oh, I'm sure I'll feel real let down when it closes," she says. "I hope I can find anything, really. My husband retired just last month—we didn't know this was coming. So, you see, we were sort of counting on my wages here. I'm older than some of the girls, and I know it'll be a little more difficult for me to find something." She looks down at the floor so that her eyes are hidden and laughs.

But after a decade and a half of working at Schultz Brothers, the hole that will be left by the store's closing is simply too large to be filled by small, dry laughs.

Schultz Brothers Variety Store has occupied the first floor of the yellow-brick Cobb Block Building just north of the grass lawn and wooden benches of Tipton's town square for 58 years. To the left of the glass door entrance stand racks of clothing; school supplies, household goods, toys, and hardware line shelves and displays to the right. The familiar smell of Spic and Span is everywhere.

But the signs of change are unmistakable throughout the store. Some literal: hand-written notices declaring "No Lay Aways, No Refunds, No Checks" are posted every few feet. Large yellow and green letters hanging slightly askew in the front window declare with an unemotional simplicity typical of Iowa and its people: "Goodbye Tipton."

Some signs are not spelled in words, but they are just as plain. Broken-down shelving lies in stacks to the rear of the store, separated from what's left of the merchandise by a rope like those used by the police to cordon off accidents. In fact, the growing heaps of metal and glass strewn over the floor make the store look like an accident in progress. Each day, the rope that separates the store's empty future from its full past moves a few feet forward.

Verne Abbott, Schultz Brothers' 31-year-old manager, is in charge of the closing-up operation. He hustles down the aisles, like a ball boy at center court, Wimbledon, rearranging the dwindling stock, moving signs, slashing prices. Abbott is the only one of the store's employees who will stay with the company. After April 1, he will become co-manager of the Iowa Falls Schultz Brothers store. (Many people in Tipton were surprised to learn that Schultz Brothers is a chain, albeit a small one. With headquarters in Lake Zurich, Illinois, the company operates over 62 variety stores throughout the Midwest—eight of them in Iowa. The Tipton store is one of 12 in the chain that will close over the next few months.)

"Frankly, I was shocked when I got the phone call," says Abbott, who is small and delicately boned, with heavy dark-rimmed glasses that make him look very much the store manager he has been for four years—two of them in Tipton, another two at the Schultz Brothers store in Anagal,

Wisconsin ("Home of the Metz fishing lure," he adds with a high-pitched laugh that is difficult to decipher).

He is seated in a cluttered crows-nest office, a loft tucked into the back of the store. "That's probably the best way to put it: I was shocked. The employees were shocked when I told them. When the rest of the town found out, they were shocked, too."

Not that it hadn't been a long time in coming. Sales had been dropping for several years as farm income declined. Other stores around the square had folded up like mobile homes before a tornado: the bridal shop, a couple of restaurants, a jewelry store.

Then, two years ago came the coup de grâce. The giant discount chain, Walmart, bought some land just north of town. Within weeks, a parking lot ten times bigger than the Schultz Brothers store obscured the former corn field.

"Well, *that* didn't help us any," says Abbott with a laugh as bleak as Countryman's. "No store can compete with them the way we tried. We cut our prices to the bone. And I mean to . . . the . . . bone." Abbott taps out the words with his forefinger on the desktop before him as though in Morse code. He leans back in his chair and sighs, running his hand through straight dark hair.

"But they have over 1,000 stores. They advertise on TV all the time. There was just nothing we could do."

Even so, Abbott and his staff tried it all. They instituted a children's ID program in cooperation with the county sheriff's department. Walmart advertised its full garden line of shrubs, flowers, saplings, starter plants, topsoil, Ph analyzer kits, gloves, spades, pitchforks, and pruning shears (electric and manual).

Schultz Brothers supplied candy and the bunny suit for the annual Easter Egg hunt at the local senior home. Walmart dashed out a $1,000 check for the home to buy a new whirlpool.

Abbott ran sales constantly, special-ordered virtually anything a customer wanted, started issuing weekly circulars in the local paper, refunded money cheerfully and without question if customers decided there weren't enough holes in their new saltshaker or that they didn't look as good in red at home as they had at the store.

But how do you compete with a store that offers 100 different kinds of shampoos and conditioners, all selling for less than the eight or ten brands you carry, and that does the very same thing with dishes, motor oil, diapers, ratchet wrenches, batteries, sunglasses, paper clips, romance novels, licorice, aspirin, wrist watches, charcoal briquets, boots, T-shirts, and everything else you stock (and a thousand things you don't) and then advertises the hell out of their "low-low-everyday" prices on TV and the radio and in the newspaper?

"You don't," states Abbott flatly. "You can't."

Conn Meade, a reporter with the *Tipton Conservative Advertiser*, has seen it happen just like this before, in his native Ireland.

"It's the very same thing. It's scary," says the 23-year-old Meade, drinking black coffee in a booth at the M&L restaurant, just a block away from Schultz Brothers. Done with school in Dublin, Meade is spending four months in Iowa working as a reporter for the town's weekly paper.

The day is bright and warm, a foretaste of summer. Across the county, the farmers who are left (Cedar County lost 28 percent of its farmers in just 5 years; a better record than many Iowa counties) are out spreading manure, discing, preparing for another season as they and their families have for over a hundred years.

"In the 60s, small farms were wiped off the map in Ireland," Meade says in an accent that draws constant comment in an area where the speech is as flat as the horizon. "Shops closed everywhere. The young people had to move on, just like here. I don't know what's going to happen to the old people who are left in Tipton, with Schultz Brothers closing, I mean. A lot of them don't drive. They're used to meeting there, to popping in for a spool of thread. There's no such thing as popping in to Walmart."

The Walmart store is far from the town center—certainly not within walking distance for this or, for that matter, any other group. If you wish to shop there, you must drive, and soon there will be few other alternatives. Robert Moses, the man who redesigned New York City's transportation system to fit the needs of his beloved automobile instead of people, couldn't have done a better job of it.

"Think what this'll mean to the other stores downtown," says Meade. "People come to shop at Schultz Brothers, and they stroll around the square window shopping, running into friends, maybe coming in here for lunch or just coffee. But all that is coming to an end, I guess."

It is difficult for people in Tipton to say what, exactly, "all that" is, though most would agree that "it" is coming to an end. They talk about their loss (when they speak of it at all) in general terms, concluding merely that "things are changing."

They know, for example, they are losing their young, but few realize the extent and implications of that loss. Between 1980 and 1987, nearly 194,000 more people left Iowa than moved in. Because many of those émigrés were young couples who would have been starting families here, the birth rate has dropped by almost 20 percent. The change is evident simply by walking down the street, where the preponderance of elderly faces might cause you to think you are in a retirement community.

They also know they are losing a lot of jobs, only a few of which are being replaced. But, here again, the extent of the problem is not generally appreciated. To paraphrase George Orwell, some jobs are more equal than others. If Grace Countryman were to find work at Walmart, she would most likely be hired part-time, as are the majority of its employees. That would mean no benefits: no health care, no retirement fund.

The new jobs—which, at any rate, are rare—generally pay far less, too. Between 1979 and 1986, Iowa lost 84,000 middle-class workers, those making $20,000 or more. During the same period, the state saw net employment gains in the service sector of 37,000 lower-class jobs, those paying $11,500.

What all this means is that a rather sizeable portion of the citizenry in this formerly middle-class state is slipping into poverty. Even those who still have (part-time) jobs and (diminished) savings are, as social critic Michael Harrington puts it, "one lay-off, one sickness away from poverty."

We are losing something else, something still harder to define, and, for a people loath to discuss anything more personal than the weather or basketball scores, hard even to talk about.

Timothy Gerard, a personnel officer at Southeastern Community College and a moderator at a panel discussion on the future of small towns, puts it this way: "Given that community is an essential part of our humanity, how important is the kind of community to the quality of our humanity?"

What kind of community will we have, and what kind of people will we have become, when all the Schultz Brothers stores (of whatever name) in all the small towns in Iowa have been replaced by Walmarts, Kmarts, and Targets? When our town squares stand silent and empty? When we have been divided into the few wealthy and the many poor?

It is easy, of course, to idealize small towns, to forget the schisms that have always divided them, to ignore the racism and anti-Semitism, the xenophobia and the homophobia, the many forms of intolerance and bigotry that thrive in rural communities. But destroying the economic and social fabric of small towns certainly won't make them more tolerant, more open-minded; it will only make them less so.

Verne Abbott is preparing to close the doors at Schultz Brothers for good. The first thunderstorm of the season washed through the night before, spawning a couple of minor tornadoes to the west of here, twin adolescent zephyrs that slapped down a rickety barn and rearranged a couple of old roofs before spinning themselves into oblivion.

In the morning, the air was warm and so clear that you felt you could almost make out individual buds on the trees that dot the horizon. By afternoon, giant cumulonimbus clouds had boiled up again, trailing blue-gray curtains of rain as they marched east toward the Mississippi River and the rich fields of Illinois beyond.

"This sure puts a hole in downtown," says Abbott as he looks around the near-empty store. "You know, Schultz Brothers has always been a downtown anchor. Maybe *the* downtown anchor."

His simile is apt. It is easy to imagine the small prairie community as a ship—perhaps because of the ocean of corn and beans that lap like waves against the margins of the town, and because of augers that jut above grain elevators like masts and rigging. The wagons that brought the settlers to this land of tall grass and open skies were called prairie schooners after all.

So it is easy, too, to see Abbott's point about Tipton losing its anchor, and to imagine the town as if drifting, carried off by a tide conceived by distant moons, taking its passengers, stunned and silent at the rail, into unknown waters.

Sit for Awhile and Rock

BY RACHEL FALDET

1989

WHENEVER I WALK INTO her house, I'm welcomed by the warm imperative, "sit for awhile and rock." Whether or not she knew I was coming, my mother-in-law always wants me to settle in, to tell her what I know, to linger in the kitchen. It's her sitting room of sorts—a place to keep track of the world.

In the north corners, across from the cupboards and counters, she keeps two rocking chairs. One is by a spinning wheel, a Red Wing crock full of pine boughs, and a dry sink—an auction find. The other, her favorite, belonged to her father. It is a bentwood oak chair, painted green, positioned in front of a hanging collection of worn wooden spoons. Beside it is a copper tub of magazines, newspapers, and days of mail.

In the mornings, after the radio news and a cup of coffee, she sits in the green rocker and calls her sisters and sister-in-law to see what's happened since yesterday. Maybe she finds out from her sister-in-law Esther that her brother decided to sell a few calves at the sale barn because prices were high. Perhaps her sister Anna says that they had what must have been a weasel in the chicken coop during the night. Sometimes her sister Pearl says she couldn't sleep and so has dough rising for apricot and cinnamon rolls that will be out of the oven around 9.

"I'll bring a pan by. They're mighty good while still warm, you know."

"Then I'll call Anna and tell her to come first thing. She wanted to pick some berries anyway. I know Esther can't come. She's coming into town but has to get back home to take care of the grandkids," my mother-in-law says before hanging up.

On those mornings several times a month, two, three, or sometimes four of them sit and talk at the kitchen table, an oak that often needs leaves. Occasionally they drift to stories of girlhood (times they sang comical songs whose words they now try to remember for fun) but usually they talk of family—Peter's new job at the college, how Kaleb and Kristy are doing with their piano lessons, Richard's health, how Carol and Mark's haying is progressing—and people and goings on in the community.

They've been part of this Iowa community all their lives, marrying men who grew up within miles of them and raising their children within miles of each other. When they sit in the kitchen, they remember past married names, talking of how people and circumstances are connected.

"She used to be an Andersen," one says.

"She's always had it rough being so much younger than her sisters and her mother not having much time for her."

"And now this," another adds, seeing the news of trouble as something from the past.

They talk for a while, parting before the morning gets too far gone. They'll talk on the phone tomorrow.

Within the family, they each are known for their specialties. For the monthly potlucks to celebrate all the birthdays on the Jacobson side, Pearl makes angel food cakes with burnt sugar frosting decorated with roses in July and plastic pilgrims in November. Anna rolls butter cookies in powdered sugar—she calls them mice—for Christmas and sends containers full to nieces and nephews. Esther and her husband make lefse—buttered, sugared, and quartered. My mother-in-law makes honey whole wheat bread and Norwegian milk pudding when the relatives get together.

I remember sitting in the kitchen after a family gathering years ago—before I was married—and asking my mother-in-law how to make bread. She'd put away the leftovers, my future father-in-law and husband were washing the serving pieces, and everyone else had gone home.

"I can't tell you," she said, rocking in her father's chair. "You'll have to watch. That's how I learned."

That Saturday I watched her test the tap water with her finger to see when it was lukewarm.

"Feel this," she said. "You need to know when it is just right. If it's too hot, it kills the yeast. If it's not warm enough, nothing will happen."

While the yeast dissolved in a small bowl, she poured scalded milk over a few tablespoons of butter in a large bowl. After the butter melted, she added some salt, some honey. She never really measured.

"Make sure this has cooled before you add the yeast," she told me while stirring the heat out. "If you're not careful—if you're in a rush—you can still kill it."

When the liquid was lukewarm, she poured in the yeast and a handful of cracked wheat and a bit of bran.

"You never really know how much it will take," she said as she took the flour jars from the shelf. They were squat jars and had "Nash's Toasted Coffee" in script on the lids.

Scooping a mug into one jar, she told me, "Just stir it in like this. A cup of white. A cup of wheat. A cup of white. A cup of wheat. You just keep adding until it is finished. Until you can't add any more."

"But how do you know?" I asked, wondering if I could do this without her as my guide.

"You'll know after you've done it a few times," she assured me.

I watched her knead, her fingers turning the dough over, her palms pressing it down. Her hands had done this for many years, just as her mother's had done. Just as I wanted mine to do.

"Feel this," she said when she was satisfied. "When you push it with your finger and it springs back, it's done."

I tested the dough several times, to make sure I learned the feel. After I thought I could remember it, she put the rounded dough in a waiting bowl, covered it with a white towel, and put it on the counter by the window—a warm place.

"Let's sit for awhile and rock," she said.

We didn't need to hurry into anything, even though there was a box of September tomatoes on the outside steps to be sealed in jars. We'd get to them. The dough had to rise twice before she could show me how to shape it into loaves.

"That's the secret," she said. "Some people just let it rise once. They're in a rush and the bread's just not as good. Pearl lets her dough rise twice and her sweet rolls are the best I've ever eaten."

Now my times with my mother-in-law are fewer than I'd like—my family and I live in another part of the country. It takes us a couple days to drive back to the Midwest. Several years ago I used to be able to drive just a few miles out of town to pick a bouquet of zinnias and a sack full of tomatoes from the garden. To sample a pickle from a jar she just brought up from the root cellar before a chicken supper. To stop by for a visit.

But often when I'm fixing a meal for my husband and daughter, I think of my mother-in-law in her kitchen: a place meant for conversations and preparing food, for thinking through the day, for working and resting. Perhaps she's talking with her sisters and sister-in-law. Or taking bread from the oven and letting the loaves cool before turning them out. Or maybe she's just sitting in her father's rocker, the paint on its arms worn through to the wood.

About Tadpoles, Disasters, and Billy Sunday

BY NORMAN SAGE

1989

T HE SMALL Iowa university I attended invited us to chapel on Tuesdays and Thursdays in such a way that we made it a point to attend rather than subject ourselves to a thousand verbal lashings by the president, who was a very religious man.

I remember two speakers at chapel, of the dozens I went to hear, and they were Rabbi Stephen S. Wise and William Ashley (just call me Billy) Sunday. Rabbi Wise was a quiet and dignified man, imposing in both stature and intellect. His was one of the great theological minds of that or any other time, although I didn't realize it then.

Billy Sunday was, at the time I heard him, famous all over the world as an evangelist and foe of the Demon Rum, and why those two words should be capitalized, I don't know, but when he said them you just knew they were. I must have been about twenty or so at the time, and he was nearing the end of his life, for he died in 1935.

Billy was, for a short time, a professional baseball player, and he used the terminology of the sport again and again in his lectures. "Hit a home run for God!" he'd say. And, "Don't let the devil throw you out at first!" He told us of his youth, that his father had died in service to the North in the Civil War, that he was orphaned shortly after that when his mother died, that he grew up in orphanages and on farms, working as a hired hand, before he became a baseball player. He quit baseball in 1903 and went into YMCA work and eventually into Revivalism, with Homer A. Rodeheaver and his choir as his doo-wah back-up group. He claimed to have saved more than a million souls in his years on the platform. Not altogether coincidentally, he picked up over a million bucks in "freewill" offerings along with the saved souls. His battle-cry was, "Hit the sawdust trail, and put your lives in the hands of God!" I don't have any idea where a "sawdust trail leading to God" came from; I do remember there being sawdust on the floor of our meat market, and of course a lot of dying went on there, so that may have had something to do with it.

I will say this for Billy Sunday: he put on quite a show. After a very flowery introduction by the president of the university, Billy stepped out of the wings, looking very much like a small boy ready for a party—high starched collar, well-pressed gray suit, black bow tie, white shirt. His hair was parted in the middle, and although he was not as big a man, one was somehow reminded of Herbert Hoover, who was, at the time, making his second and unsuccessful run for the Presidency.

Billy began quietly enough, with quotations from the Bible and anecdotes concerning his personal and deprived early years, how he was taken in "a stranglehold by the Demon Rum," and as he talked it seemed his temperature rose, and soon he was shouting like an auctioneer who was sure the people in the back rows were deaf. Soon he was pounding the pulpit, loosening his tie, yanking off his collar and slamming it to the floor—all this to punctuate his point, whatever it was. Then, to our amazement, he also ripped off his suit jacket and threw that into the laps of the Pi Phi girls in the front row, and they were visibly shaken.

He was just warming up. He stood with his left foot on the platform and his right on the apron of the stage, beyond the footlights, and by that time he was screaming at the top of his voice about "the wages of sin" and "the Demon Rum." On that morning, I was suffering from an outsize hangover, and I didn't want to hear this stuff. I turned to Boot Stewart and said, "I've got to get out of here. This guy's a lunatic." Boot shushed me and put his hand on my arm to detain me, so I heard it through to the last.

Aside from what I have just told you, what I remember most about Billy Sunday's sermon that day was that he talked a lot about hell and damnation, fire and brimstone, about the sanctity of home and family, the beauty and modesty of womanhood as a whole (misquoting the Bible frequently to his purpose), and lashing out at bootleggers, petty thieves, and whoremongers. I knew what the first part of that word was, but I wasn't sure what a "monger" was. I had heard of ironmongers, and wondered if, somehow, the two were related. Anyway, he seemed to like that word, and he used it a lot, and I remember that it made us all feel a little uncomfortable. He also, of course, spoke of Heaven (capitalized) and hell (not under any circumstances capitalized), and the Man who ran Heaven and the whoremonger who ran the other place.

At this remote time, I am surprised at how much of what he said is still with me, and in recent months I have found myself pondering the nature of Heaven and hell (whether or not they are capitalized) and whether they exist at all, as described by Billy Sunday, and, before him, the old beards who wrote the Old and New Testaments. I have come to a few strange conclusions, and I am happy to share them with you at no cost. If you feel you *must* send something. . . .

I grew up in a small southeast Iowa town on the outskirts of which was a small stream called Snake Creek. We pronounced it "crick." You have to get into Missouri to hear it pronounced correctly. It wound through the countryside in much the same way the Wapsipinicon does, although Snake Creek is not as clear, and its banks are far less spectacular.

Snake Creek is a muddy creek, because it flows through agricultural land not characterized by rocks or sand. I learned to swim in Snake Creek, at a place we called "the bend," a curve washed out by spring rushes and quite deep on the far side, shallow on the near. The bend was only about a hundred yards or so downstream from the town's sewer outlet, but I didn't know that at the time, and sewage in those days was, I think, not as lethal as it seems now.

Across the Rock Island tracks to the north, and about a half-mile away, my family had a summer place which we called "the shack," because that's about what it was—one room and a screened porch. We spent the hottest days of summer there in that eighteen-acre microcosm. Floyd Rowe kept three Guernsey cows there under a verbal pasture-for-keeping-an-eye-on-the-place agreement with my father.

At the bend and at the shack, my youth (and, I guess, my oldth) was shaped. I developed an appreciation for the ways of the natural world. I discovered that even the lowest life forms displayed qualities of good sense and industry. These natural processes, I learned, demonstrated how things *should* work. It is not their fault that I became a moral disaster—that came about later, when I got into the newspaper business.

The timber-pasture where the shack stood also had a very small stream running through it, and there was a very high sandstone and soapstone bluff rising above it at one of its mindless curves. Downstream from that bluff was where, during a spring and summer, I learned about frogs and trap-door spiders and tumblebugs, and if you don't know about those exciting creatures, you are not an educated person.

I watched the frog eggs, guarded from the tiny fish by either mom or pop and sometimes both, hatch into tadpoles—we called them polly-wogs, and I wonder if they still do—with bulbous heads and short tails, and tiny gills concealed by flaps of flesh. And I watched those pollywogs grow legs, for God's sake, and drop their tails, and turn into frogs! If you haven't seen that happen, you have missed out on one of the most magical transmogrifications Nature has to offer. And the dung-beetle, the tumblebug, that most skillful beetle, related to the royal scarab of ancient Egypt, gathering cow dung and rolling it into marble-sized balls, storing them underground in little vertical holes, where they were cut into quarters, some to eat, some to serve as natural incubators for their eggs. Those little bugs have more sense than most people. And the trap-door spiders—I can hardly believe them, and sometimes think I made them up one sunny afternoon, but I know I didn't, because there they were, right before my eyes, whipping out of their hinged door, grabbing an ant, and plopping back into their hole. They dig the hole in the ground, they bevel the surface edge, and they build a truncated inverted cone of earth and grass and dung, and they hinge it with threads of spider-stuff so thin you can hardly see it, and when it flops down to cover the hole, there is no way to see their little cave unless you know it's there. And they line the whole thing with silk, too.

What went wrong was that I got a job at the local daily newspaper, first carrying papers, then working in the back room, later in an advertising service owned by the paper, and learning, to my eternal sorrow, to be-come a printer—they are known to be vile people who chew tobacco and swear—the kind pointed out on the street by mothers to their children. "You see?" they say. "You see?"

At the time I heard Billy Sunday, I was working for a newspaper, which shall be nameless, as an indentured apprentice reporter and researcher for 35¢ an hour—barely enough to keep me in drink, but enough to keep my mind on things other than Heaven and hell. I was in thrall, as they say, to the Demon Rum and his Master, the Devil—or at the very least I hoped my colleagues on the paper saw me in such a light, for they were all professional newspaper men, and it is enough to make one shudder at the peril I faced.

Billy Sunday was known to be a reformed drunk, or so he said. I *am* a recovering drunk, and during the reformation, so to speak, I thought a lot about Heaven and hell and life and death, and if you've the time, these are some of the things I think about Heaven. I do not believe in hell in the traditional sense, although I have been there a few times, and I *do* believe in both natural and unnatural disasters, some of which lead to death and therefore to Heaven. The *unnatural* disasters all result from Man messing around with the natural world, and those disasters are monstrous and grotesque. As applied to the sins of humankind, there is a subtle distinction between monstrous and grotesque, monstrous meaning of huge proportions, and grotesque meaning repulsive, unthinkable, ugly beyond enduring. Volcanoes, plagues, tornadoes—these are all unnatural phenomena, for nature, in essence, is calm, friendly, giving, and dependable. Only when humankind gets out of hand does she, Nature, throw some kind of disastrous curve, most likely simply to call our attention to our own transgressions.

Hell has been disposed of by simply denying its existence in the context of cosmic probability. Heaven, on the other hand, is a horse of an extramundane sort.

I believe in Heaven for animals, for they are more nearly God's creatures than we are, and may have been, in fact, created in His many images: dogs, cats, sheep, cows, horses—certainly rabbits and chipmunks, ground-squirrels, regular squirrels, birds of the air and fish of the seas, and lakes and streams; the raptors, the killers, who do what they must to survive, or what they have been taught to do by minds more devious and spiteful than their own, most likely in violation of their own finer instincts. My dog rushes at the chipmunk who lives in the rocks under my bridge, thinking to save me from the awful consequences of a chipmunk attack. He knows he'll never catch him—doesn't want to, in fact. And the same with the field mice who made a nest in some leftover insulation stored in the shed. I worry about fiberglass in their little lungs. And surely there is a heaven for the Monarch, that fragile and lovely butterfly who gives us such joy in the summer and then, in the fall, migrates to Honduras to fill the trees in such profusion that the natives refer to them as the trees which burn but are not consumed.

I have lived on the shores of this little lake in southeast Iowa for thirty-one years. I remember it when there was no water in it at all, during those times when they were raising the dam so as to prevent the flood-control waters from mixing with and thereby contaminating the recreational waters—you've got to be careful about things like that. I've stayed and enjoyed this place for so long because of those notions developed watching tumblebugs, pollywogs, trap-door spiders, and because I remember Billy Sunday's reckless threats of a hell in which I do not believe.

I have seen a huge oak on the south shore of the lake so filled, as evening falls, with snowy egrets that it looked like a huge popcorn ball on a stick. Surely there is a Heaven for them, and for the blue herons, the stylish little red foxes, the wolf who stood me off in the road last fall and knew he was in charge. That was the first wolf I had seen in these parts since one near Hillsboro in about 1938. There is no mistaking a wolf—the coyote (I hear them sometimes at night, for they can't make a living in their old neighborhoods since humankind has taken them over) is far more feline in shape and does not carry himself with as much pride as the wolf.

And the deer—there has to be a place for them, and for the quail and pheasants, for the juncos, and the sparrows—the street-people of birdland. Their strut is as important and busy as the jay's or the cardinal's. The sparrows are the ones with chutzpah, among all birds. Surely these, and the busy, exemplary ant, should have a place, safe from harm, someday. And the Canada geese, who have brains about the size of a walnut but sense enough to mate for life and to go south for the winter.

I see a big old snapping turtle sunning himself on a log, and I think: what man has a better life, deserves more the long-term care of The Man? Frogs, toads, snakes, lizards—all bits of wonder, specks of delight in their own special ways. Their instincts guide them rightly, and I am at a sorry loss to know just exactly what instincts humans are cursed with to make them act so irresponsibly. In us, all of us, instinct becomes involved with reason, and you have an apples and oranges problem, the two having nothing in common other than the juices which give them life, and even those fluids differ. In the miraculous moment of conception is the simultaneous sentence to death. I am an old man; I think of these things.

Many years ago a bearded old man went up into the mountains and came back down with a couple of slabs of stone, and he told the people that these were the *Laws*.

The people responded by saying, "Wow! Look at all these good things we are not allowed to do! Now we can do them and enjoy doing them, because they are sinful, and being sinful is fun. What a blast!" And they went out and killed in the name of religious belief everyone who didn't believe as they did, and they have been killing ever since the time of Cain, more often than not without a sound reason of any kind. I do not know of a war which settled, once and for all, *anything*.

Not only do men kill each other with improbable relish, they spend hour upon hour of time and ton upon ton of money devising increasingly horrible ways of doing it. Of course, being the highest of all life forms gives them unquestioned license to do these awful things to each other.

Years ago Don Marquis dashed off a little story called "The Revolt of the Oyster," set in archeological time at that point where the two superior species then on earth (man and oyster) fought each other for supremacy. Sadly, I think, the oyster lost. It would have been a better contest, indeed, if the struggle had involved the cockroach instead of the oyster, for the despised roach has managed to exist, without major evolutionary change, for hundreds of thousands of years. Can man outdo the roach? Man has changed, to be sure, but no one can claim for the better, while the cockroach was worse to begin with and isn't the least bit apologetic about it.

So here we are with no hell, a Heaven for animals and all living things (where they can be safe from Man), and none for man himself. I offer you the thought that if there is a Heaven for man, it should be one well apart from Animal Heaven. Those creatures should not be made to consort with the likes of us in the afterlife—it's hard enough for them in the present.

Rose

CARMEN KRAEMER CLARK
1989

Time stands still in Tete Des Morts township, Jackson County, along Iowa's Mississippi shore.

A French explorer, Father Hennepin, gave the region its name (translated "heads of the dead"), but that morbid label never over-shadowed the land's natural beauty, or disturbed legendary spirits sleeping and dancing in her forested hills.

To countless generations of Indians, Tete Des Morts was hallowed ground. They returned to the hills every spring to draw spiritual strength for another year, to make peace and hold council. It was there among the wooded slopes they mounded the dead with red earth and clay.

Today the huge council bluffs and gentle finger ridges are home to white descendants of sturdy Luxembourgers and Germans who rooted their dreams in American soil. It took raw strength and single-minded determination to wrestle a living from Tete Des

Morts's rocky ground and to wrest and haul native limestone from hillside quarries to construct the barns and two-story farm dwellings which pepper many hillsides to this day.

As one hand washes another, those calloused settlers struggling to soften the rocky land were themselves smoothed by Tete Des Morts's beauty and isolation.

A tale from this region, where eagles nest and fur trapping is still a human tradition, must be a mixture of past and present. For in Tete Des Morts, earth and spirit meet.

E VERYONE SAID THERE WAS something unusual about the vacant old farmhouse my husband and I hoped to rent through the winter of 1978 until we could start building our own place a ridge or two away in rural Tete Des Morts township.

Even Walt Blitgen, who owned it, said we'd have to do a lot of painting when he agreed to let us move in. I was prepared for something strange when I first went to look the house over, but pleased with what I found.

Exotic, symmetrical, multicolored designs, first penciled, then painted in every imaginable color scheme on almost every wall and floor bore out old Rose Duesing's reputation as both a character and an artist. Even a wooden chair against one intricately patterned wall was part of the design.

Old Miss Rose had lived her entire 88 years on the place, alone for as long as most neighbors could remember. She occupied herself (probably in winter) painting those colorful, primitive designs absolutely everywhere in the ranging eight-room farmhouse. She put off-white chickens sitting on clutches of broad-brushed eggs in neat gridwork on grey-green oilcloth in the old country kitchen. She had turquoise and brown and black almost Navajo-looking vertical open patterns in the 20-foot stairwell and the long upstairs hallway. (I wondered how the old lady managed that one.) She even painted a leaded-glass pattern on the attic windows.

Yet, Rose liked living the old-fashioned way, close to the earth, close to nature, and close to God, according to those who knew her. She was old-German, a daughter of original German settlers to the area. She spoke German to her dog, and regularly walked four miles to St. John's Lutheran church, carrying her old (probably German) Bible.

Rose dug her own huge garden with a spade, hoeing with a time- and labor-worn lopsided blade. She stored her vegetables and larded-down barrels of cooked pork in the house's cool stone cellar. Old age may have slowed Rose down a little, but she never seemed to break stride.

The house's old stone section was typical nineteenth-century Tete Des Morts: thick-walled two-story limestone with hardwood beams above each portal. Prosperity had brought a much larger wood-frame wing to the house, but by 1978 standards, Rose's house was uninhabitable.

The house had a refrigerator, a single switch-controlled light in the main room, one all-purpose electric outlet underneath it, and no indoor plumbing. Miss Rose had lived without any electricity (or refrigeration) at all until immediately before her death.

People were amused by my enthusiasm for living in Rose's house. I didn't mind. I thought the place was cozy, and I didn't mind lighting with kerosene lamps. We plugged our modern conveniences—vacuum cleaner, TV, blow dryer—into that outlet, one at a time, for the year we stayed.

We had come to the area from Kansas City a few months earlier. In the city, being neighbors meant little more than sleeping on the same block; sharing a culture meant little or nothing. Here, people lived by tradition, by unwritten code, a far-flung but knitted community with few loose ends. Rose held a key to understanding our new life. Her painting and her lifestyle told us something about the area and its people that our neighbors could not. The simplicity and solitude of her home cushioned our culture shock with natural beauty, time, and space to reflect.

I fell in love with the hundreds of giant blue iris blooming in Rose's yard in the spring. I liked the tall rangy cedar near the kitchen. In that tree lived a raucous screech owl.

Inside the house I grew to admire the raspberry, pink, and red-purple lines of a bowtie quilt pattern in the southeast downstairs room. The "bowtie room" was a lovely, bright, and breezy spot where I felt close to Rose. It faced her old apple tree, outhouse, barn, and the distant Illinois bluffs.

I grew very fond of Rose. Alone with my three children on long winter days, Rose was a wonderful fantasy. I felt she still lived in the house. I imagined her between the lines, peeking out, darting from room to room—spry as ever—watching. If Rose objected to our intrusion, I never sensed it. Strange as my ways must have been to Rose, I think I was a companion to her. She was certainly a companion to me in the magnificent isolation of Tete Des Morts.

Rose was unique. I fed on her energy and perseverance in the painted designs, most of which I left alone and enjoyed. But the story of her untimely death gnawed at me, always.

Its irony and tragedy pressed as urgently as her spirit in the designs. Rose was run over and killed by a car, five years before, as she crossed Highway 52 to check her mailbox. It happened shortly after she returned from a trip, one of the few times she had ever left home for more than an afternoon.

Walt said she probably wasn't watching for cars. She had been excited—unnerved—about the electricity he ran into the house while she was away. It was a surprise, a convenience to her in her old age. Rose thought there was a demon in the wire filament of that bare bulb, Walt's grandson said. She thought it was unnatural to tamper with darkness.

The tragedy was an abrupt end to Rose's madness of solitude, painting away—from attic to kitchen—going over designs she didn't like anymore and covering her favorite floor designs with protective layers of newspaper.

I still chuckle about that old lady climbing ladders to bring her wildest symmetrical dreams to even the farthest reaches of the house. Walt often brought her leftover paint from construction projects where he worked. He said nothing made her happier; she almost cried.

I couldn't help wondering what Rose thought of the Clarks, this unknown family who moved into her house fresh from the city and painted the chickens off the walls.

Rose knew how to handle the hard country life; we did not. Bruce and I did some pretty dumb things that bitterly cold winter, fumbling in the country. We read books when we should have been stockpiling firewood, as we ran out of fuel in January. I took the cloudy plastic storm windows off her west windows in fall to improve my view; this nearly froze us, as the winter wind found its way through cracks around the sashes. I couldn't decide if she would be horrified or amused.

I was a terrible housekeeper, and I'm sure in her early years Rose was not. Lost without a dishwasher and washing machine, I let my children run around the house naked. Dirty laundry and dishes piled up everywhere.

I would have shocked Rose, or at least set her tongue clicking, but

I also imagined her an earthy character. Rose doted on Walt's grand-children, handing them sacks full of homemade cookies whenever they stopped by with him. She lived alone, self-sufficient, bashful perhaps, but not a recluse. We were different from each other, Rose and I, but I knew we shared many joys in that house.

Even so, five people living in that house without modern conveniences had serious drawbacks. Washing dishes, a chore I detested particularly, meant heating water on the stove to fill my sink, which drained directly into a 10-gallon bucket below. I'd wait until we were out of dishes, then laboriously heat a large, thin aluminum pot of water, fill the dishpan, and use the remaining water in the pot to rinse dishes and then clean sticky cooking spatters from the tiny gas range nearby. It took nearly an hour to boil enough frigid well water for dishwashing, and I often forgot I was heating the second pot by the time it started to bubble.

There were old curtains on a west window next to the small gas-burn-ing kitchen stove. The walls in that tiny room were fiberboard. I consid-ered the arrangement a fire hazard, but couldn't bring myself to remove the curtains from that dark kitchen lean-to.

One winter evening in 20 degree below zero weather, I remembered in a flash as I drove home from a full day's shopping and errands in Dubuque, 18 miles away, that I had left a pan of water heating on the stove nine hours before. I had ten more miles to drive in the darkness before I could learn the awful truth, but I know what had to have happened.

The pot held no more than two gallons of water. It was on high flame when I left, and probably half an hour from boiling. It would take about three hours to boil away that much water on high, but when it boiled out, the pan's bottom would heat to white-hot from the flame, it would begin to cave in, and that molten aluminum under a steady fire for several hours would take those curtains to the flash point.

Fire! The kitchen would go first, then the flames would spread to the newer section of the house, consuming everything two generations of Duesings tried to accomplish on Tete Des Morts ridge. Miss Rose would be driven from the house forever, leaving only the 18-inch walls of the original stone structure standing.

My cheeks stung with the shame of my carelessness. I felt my heart-beats quicken. I struggled to take slow, steady breaths, my knuckles white against the steering wheel. There was nothing I could do now. Whatever happened had already happened and was done.

I chatted with the children a time or two in the car, but the lump in my throat grew too large for words. My eyes strained to see smoke ahead from the top of every hill the car climbed.

There was no way out. A week before we had connected a new liquid propane tank which fueled the stove. The burner was definitely turned on "high." I remembered it clearly.

Turning the last curves toward home, I was fighting tears. Were the Bellevue volunteer firemen's cars still lined up along the winding lane? What a miserable, cold night for a fire!

I imagined the firemen's tired, smudged faces behind icicles hanging from their red helmets, as their boots crunched through the charred remains of our meager belongings. Behind them, Rose's designs would be ghostly shadows on a few sooty stone walls. I was nauseated.

Finally, our ridge appeared in the distance. I stepped on the gas. The car moved as if in slow motion. I couldn't see smoke.

I turned into the lane—no cars there, no evidence of traffic. Had they all gone home? The car crept up the half-mile winding lane. The house was there. It was dark, but the walls were all standing. I looked for jagged circles of glass broken out of the front windows and a black kitchen wall. Nothing.

I stopped the car and we rushed inside. I was incredulous. The stillness was overwhelming, but there was not even a hint of smoke. Had I imagined the pan and the burner? Impossible. I knew the stove was on when I left.

I stepped into the kitchen and fumbled for matches to light a kerosene lamp. As its glow crept along the floor and up the walls, the scene was unmistakable. My pan was on its burner, but half full of water. The knob was turned, just as I remembered, on "high," but there was no flame. The fire had simply gone out—but there was no gas smell. I turned the control off and then on again to see if the line was clogged. Flames shot up, instantly, licking the bottom of the pan as brightly as ever.

I stood there in the glow of my kerosene lamp while my heart's pumping stabilized. I began to realize the room was cold, and I was shivering. I took a long, deep breath.

There was really no explanation for why the fire went out. I used that stove constantly for five months before that night, and I kept using it for another eight months before we moved out. Never again did a burner die. A draft strong enough to blow the fire out was impossible.

If Walt had come into the house and seen the burner on, he obviously would not have blown out the flame, but turned it off. Yet the control was wide open. There was no smell of gas, no clog in the line.

This is a true story, but I don't talk about it much. I'm not at all superstitious, but I sincerely believe Rose put the burner out—I just don't know how.

That night I could sense Rose more strongly than ever. It was as if she was telling me, haltingly, urgently, from the top of the room where the shadows flickered between yellow and brown painted stripes. Earnestly, abruptly, she communicated.

It wasn't to save the designs. She did it for us. The painting projects had served their purpose, occupying a lonely, creative old woman. But stopping the flame wasn't necessarily an act of approval or friendship, either.

I think it had to do with old-timers like Rose not wanting to waste anything. It also had to do with the children and even me, a modern-day oddball, turning the house into a home. I think Rose saw a future for that old house on Tete Des Morts ridge, and we were part of it.

But mainly, I realized as the shadows flickered in the old kitchen, Rose knew it was the only neighborly thing to do.

The Letter from New York

BY MICHAEL CAREY

1990

When Iowa wasn't Iowa
but Missouri, a young man
got word he'd gotten a letter.
So that day he planted watermelon.

Daily, when his chores were done
he weeded his garden. Then,
one September morning, he picked
a wagonload and headed south.

No one here had anything
but coonskin caps and wolf scalps.
But that wouldn't do for the government.
No one in Savannah had money either
and by now there were two letters:
25 cents apiece. Couldn't
stamp a letter with a watermelon.

So, he waited by the back door
and when the postman went home
he sold him his whole season.

One hundred and fifty years ago
on this very spot, Amos Johnson
opened those letters. She said,
yes, she would. She said, "Yes," and
all his meager harvest was worth it.

Greener Than Green

BY DAVID MANNING

1992

LATELY I'VE BEEN taken with the idea that the Greens should take root in rural Iowa. Yes, I mean the same Greens who, largely invisible in the states, have been spicing up European political life and thought for the last decade. No, I don't necessarily mean The Green Party USA, which was formed in 1991 as the political arm of the movement here. Whether or when a social movement should take on the burdens of being a party in a system hostile to new parties is a separate question. Until the movement has flourished, that question is moot. But it has seemed to me that local folks for whom ecology is primary should gather under a Greens banner.

A recent experience erased all doubt. I spent an afternoon at the Miles Thresher Days, a smaller version of the more famous Old Threshers Reunion. The demonstrations of domestic crafts, from basketmaking to horse- and steam-powered grain threshing, were celebrating, through re-enactment, the ingenuity (and stamina) of former generations responding to the challenges of their time in this place. These activities were, for the most part, refreshingly quiet. But every few minutes, regardless of where we were on the grounds, the smooth whirrs and hisses were overcome by the sound of a single internal combustion engine, only slightly muffled, revved to the red line. It was the mud run where, off in a corner, the Pepsi generation was celebrating its ingenuity (and buying power) by driving various sorts of cars and trucks into custom-made mud until they could no longer inch forward. It was home-made entertainment, with familiar faces at the wheel. The most successful contestants drove machines modified for the occasion, with bodies perched above over-sized wheels, well suited for little else.

I must admit it was exciting, in a small-town kind of way: the mud flying, the lurch, wallow, and indignant roar of man and machine against the earthy element, especially when someone would actually emerge at the far end, unrecognizable and victorious. But I can't stop pondering that scene. For the generations who threshed with horses, then with steam tractors, mud was a real obstacle. The team or machine that could make it through was getting the cream to towns like Miles, and bringing back the flour. But the wealth generated by our ancestors' craft has long ago rocked or paved the road. Now, despite the real challenges of our time and place, the new crop of settlers in this land spins its wheels.

Why are we still disengaged? We know about overpopulation, species extinction, ozone depletion, and global warming. We know about mushrooming poverty, the national debt, and government out of control. How can this year's parade look so much like last year's, only with larger combines? Well, I suppose the youngers are taking their cue from the elders. The elders learned early that people are important, stuff is not, and progress is our most important product. No wonder, then, that they're having a hard time coming to grips with a world that's progressing toward oblivion. So here we are, an excursion bus on cultural cruise control, no one at the wheel, headed for Dead Man's Curve. A few passengers don't know what is happening. Most, however, can see it but won't let themselves believe it because they can't imagine traveling any other way. If you're ready to bail out, I'm here to argue that we should both be local participants in a global Greens movement.

But why join anything at all? Why not just continue to inch your way into the Establishment without frightening your neighbors, and then, when they least expect it, strike your blow? Obviously some people can make that work, and green programs are showing up in some very brown places. Iowa's REAP program and groundwater legislation come to mind. But most of us aren't secret-agent types and don't function well behind enemy lines. We need the nurturance that comes only from sharing and planning with those who share our vision. We may be surprised to see the strength and number of our allies, once we're all out of the closet. Besides, there is a certain power that comes with candidness.

But why not join one of the dozens of organizations already working for a greener world? Is there really a niche for another? I'm sure there is, at least for us rural folks. Perhaps you, like me, maintain memberships in several groups, each out there saving its slice of the world. We mail off checks and get back magazines or newsletters about places we've never seen and people we've never met. Local chapters, when they exist, meet so far away that the trip feels ecologically unsound. And for every group and its cause I support, there are dozens of others I must deny. Meanwhile, none of this has visible impact on my neighborhood or my social life. It leaves a big itch unscratched, and I can't be the only one who feels it.

What's missing is a vehicle to take us to a sustainable human society, built on the chassis of ecological values. It must be radically inclusive, since we're all needed. It must be intensely local, because home is where we live. But it must also be as global as the atmosphere, as specific and insistent as the latest NOT IN MY BACK YARD campaign. But the slogan must broaden to include everyone's back yard. After all, in the immortal words of Pogo, "We have met the enemy, and he is us."

Now we could conjure up such a buggy from scratch, but why not join the Greens? It is just this mix of local emphasis, fraternity/sorority, and earth-consciousness that is the backbone of the Greens's program. Our bus is waiting at the curb.

But how can a leftover liberal like me travel with decentralists? Sure, we could do without big business, but hasn't it been big government that has extended our civil rights, defended endangered species, air, and water, and promoted the general welfare? Let's look into that a bit. From a Greens point of view, the syndicate in power, from Miles to Miami, is a symbiotic arrangement between the Fortune 500 and their addicted consumers. For generations, folks have been willing to compromise basic human needs like self-sufficiency, community, and harmony with "nature" in order to obtain and consume more goods and services. The process began in earnest with the industrial revolution and has picked up steam ever since. Consumption beyond need, however, doesn't satisfy like the needs which are sacrificed, and the resulting hunger calls for increased consumption. In terms of the bus metaphor, it's powered by a treadmill: we tread ever faster, we're fed ever more, and we leave the driving to them. The role of government, primarily, is to keep the system working. As of late it's been slowing down, so chief cheerleader Bush has chided us to eat more. There are widespread doubts that this strange greyhound can be kept running, but the man in the White House in 1993 will have convinced a majority of voters that he can do just that. Ignore the talk about change. Each major party is running on the same promise: WE WILL KEEP THIS RIG ROLLING.

Greens, on the other hand, would make an entirely different promise: we will help you off the treadmill, help you break your addiction, and share the driver's seat. They would not promise to make your life easier; on the whole, life around here is never apt to get any easier. But they will help you make it better. Moving economic and political decisions closer to home is not an arbitrary plank in their platform, but one of its girders.

My daughter Elizabeth reminds me of why this is so. Now six months old, she is learning to eat so-called solid food from a spoon. Being normal and healthy, she has made it clear that she would rather grab the spoon herself, though the meal takes longer and more food is left outside than makes it inside. In her stubborn struggle to guide that spoon lies a primary Greens premise: that there is more gut-level joy to be found in grabbing the spoons in our lives than in being spoon-fed with great finesse.

Those of us who have lived both in Iowa's cities and in its villages have seen first-hand how active participation in community life nurtures vital people. Paton, about the size of Miles, needed me and every other kid for the team, and for the band, and for the class play. The school couldn't afford a competent math teacher, but it sent Loren Shriver into space with the brightest and best.

Greens theorists, of course, can give us a long list of reasons why political power must be reclaimed at the community level and our economies must be based on supplying local needs with local renewable resources. But I suspect that the most important reason is the nature of the human animal. We won't, and can't, nurture the world by remote control. So I'll just have to let go of some habitual attitudes and trust that grassroots empowerment will do it better in the long run.

Now don't get me wrong—I don't expect the Greens or anybody else to get us around Dead Man's Curve intact. We're all in the same bus, but we're not all going to make it. We're not all making it now. So do we despair, or do we grab the wheel, like the spoon, in hope? Lately, every time I close my eyes in despair I see Elizabeth's face, screwed in concentration, oatmeal ear to ear, trying one more time, and I know I'd better get on with it.

The Would-Be Caesars of Millard

BY RAYMOND M. TINNIAN

1992

> At an early day in this section, while yet could be heard the frightful
> howl of the timber wolf, the idiotic clack of the prairie chicken and the
> vulgar bleat of the buffalo, there was a more noisome creature whose
> braying shamed the jackass and drowned out the suffocating din of all
> other animals combined. We are speaking here of the county seat par-
> tisan. In those days it was an article of faith that God had divided the
> waters from the firmament so lawyers might have some place to stand
> and make speeches. Humanity was created and breathed into life for
> the express purpose of coming to bear on one side or the other in the
> county seat question. The babe is exhaled, suckled, and nurtured into
> maturity in order that he may sign some petition.
>
> —"The History of Fillmore County, Iowa," *Acme and Putnam*, 1880

T HE FIRST SEAT of justice in Fillmore County was located in the
town of Dupont, an edifice founded and occupied solely by a grizzled
old trader of that name. This fellow had gone to Burlington, scrounged
up a petition on some forgotten initiative, put his name at the head of
the page, and got some territorial judge to declare his wasp-filled cabin
the seat of Fillmore County justice. This state of affairs was brief, not

because the town itself was no more than a lean-to and a salt lick, but because once the actual boundaries of Fillmore County were drawn up they did not include the town of Dupont. In keeping with the spirit of the county seat wars, Monsieur Dupont immediately died upon learning that his claim was irrelevant.

Meanwhile, settlers were pouring into Fillmore County proper. In 1856 the population of the county was 1,280. At this time the town of Millard became a growing concern. It boasted two gristmills, two doctors, two stores, three lawyers, and a land shark. Its nearest competitor, Fort Raccoon, had only a sawmill and a post office. At the time the county was organized, Millard was the obvious and unopposed choice for county seat, even though it was situated in the westernmost tier of townships. A small frame courthouse was built, and business was conducted peaceably at Millard-on-the-Wapsi for about a year and a half.

By early 1858, the population of the county had more than doubled to 2,909. Official business was brisk enough to warrant the purchase of a large iron safe for the county records and receipts. It was brought up the river from Davenport in a keelboat. In 1858 people from the northern and eastern townships, exasperated at having to travel so far overland to enter land titles, began to agitate for a more centrally located county seat. By this time Fort Raccoon had come into its own. Even though it was half the size of Millard, it was located almost exactly in the center of Fillmore County. Rumors were got about involving the imminent formation of the "Chicago, Dubuque and Fort Raccoon Railroad Company." Millard boiled into a state of panic.

The vote was held and seemed sure to go with Fort Raccoon, until the county board of canvassers declared the votes of Calhoun, a northeastern township, "irregular, inadmissible, null, and void" on a mere technicality. Without these votes the result was 206 for Millard, 206 for Fort Raccoon. The eastern half of Fillmore County began to smolder with outrage. Although there were only ten voters in Calhoun Township, it was assumed they would have tipped the balance in favor of Fort Raccoon. Fort Raccoon lawyers filed writs of mandamus, certiorari, and habeas corpus. They made passionate speeches. One was delivered by the Honorable Hiram C. Gillette on the banks of the East Wapsi to a crowd of about one thousand:

"Honest citizens of Fillmore County, I hold in my hands a simple wooden box. No jewels encrust its lid, no bands of silver or gold adorn it, yet it is more precious than any ark of fabled treasure. It is a ballot box, the symbol of a free nation. It was for this rude box that the first Americans threw off the yoke of a foreign king, for this box that the blood of patriots colored our flag red, and for this box that General Scott marched into the halls of Montezuma. It is the marble pillar upon which the hopes of all free men rest. It is the fundamental plank of liberty. But now the day of our freedom has passed. A tiny junto of plutocrats from Millard has overthrown this basic principle and perverted the will of the people to their own venal ends. Here we stand, independent citizens no more, our votes nullified, our will meaningless. Now we have the rights of slaves: to work and to die; this and no more! Was ever so vile and cruel an outrage perpetrated upon a freedom-loving people? Has ever a pharaoh, a pope, or a tsar so boldly assumed the mantle of dictatorship as the would-be Caesars of Millard?

"Our choices are thus: we act now, with firmness and resolve, or we can groan forever beneath the iron shackles of a brutal autocracy. In the words of Patrick Henry: 'shall we gain strength by inaction and irresolution? Shall we lay supinely upon our backs, and hug the delusive phantom of hope until our enemies have bound us hand and foot?'"

Apparently they would not, for his audience poured into Millard that night and took the courthouse apart, board by board. There were a few bumps and bruises, but the Millarders were too surprised to do much but run for the woods. Fort Raccooners loaded the county office furniture onto wagons, at the same time two cooler-headed lawyers had successfully petitioned a district judge in Dubuque to overrule the county board and admit the votes of Calhoun Township. The seat of Fillmore County was now both legally and illegally in Fort Raccoon, in a heap on Main Street. The people of Millard recovered from their initial shock and were stirred to irrational schemes of retribution. A dignified and civil solution to the matter was now impossible. Partisans of Millard journeyed to the state capitol in Des Moines and successfully attached a supplementary paragraph to the legislation organizing Fillmore County. The paragraph began: "The boundaries of said county shall be amended as follows—beginning at the northwest corner of the first section of township ninety north and range eighth west of the fifth principal meridian and proceeding thence to the northeast corner of the sixth section of township ninety north and range seventh west. . . ."

No one at the statehouse took a second look at the bill before voting it into law. They did not imagine that a small delegation from Fillmore was intending to detach eight townships from the east half of their own county, which was none too large to begin with. By this seemingly straightforward piece of legislation they made Fayette County eight townships larger and reduced the size of Fillmore County by half, thus putting Millard squarely in its center, and Fort Raccoon into the next county over.

The people of Fort Raccoon could do nothing but stand dazed and helpless while a peacefully smug delegation of West Fillmorians retrieved the county office furniture and the heavy iron safe. Later, when the quietly victorious party of Millard partisans bedded down for the night, the men working the ox team said they were not yet tired and wanted to make the halfway point between Fort Raccoon and Millard before stopping to sleep. Everyone knew that these fellows were from the town of New Pittsburgh, ten miles north of Millard, but no one knew that the men of New Pittsburgh had decided among themselves that they were as close to the center of the new Fillmore County as Millard, and they had as much claim to the county seat. Not that they intended to steal the safe. They merely intended to hide it until the board of canvassers could be forced to take a vote.

The road to New Pittsburgh bore north, proceeding down along the Wapsi bottoms. Whilst the men were trying to make time with the ox team, they crossed a stretch of plank road in the darkness, where the split beams had settled unevenly into the boggy ground. The wagon tipped, dumping the safe into the mud, where it slowly began to sink. In the morning the general party gathered around the scene, half believing that the New Pittsburghers had taken the low road by mistake, as they claimed, and half not. There was no time to pursue recriminations because the safe was barely exposed and sinking fast. Ropes, chains, winches, and even explosives were employed, but the safe continued to descend into the sucking muck at a rate of one inch every twenty-four hours. The following spring, a geologist probing the spot determined that the county records were still sinking at that rate and would likely come to rest on bedrock in about the year of 1870.

Throughout the disturbance, the people of Fillmore had continued to file land claims and lawsuits in the office of a pettifogger in Apex, a town which had emerged from Dupont's original claim. New Pittsburgh and Millard proceeded to steal the diminishing effects of county government from each other until nothing remained and no farmer felt secure in reposing legal documents with either. All official business moved to Apex, just across the line in Lincoln County. Today, the smallest county in Iowa has a courthouse outside of its own boundaries, because of the county seat wars.

Editor's note: Have you ever heard of Fillmore County, Iowa? Good, because we haven't either! This story is loosely based on the histories of Polk, Chickasaw, and Palo Alto Counties.

Diamonds Are Not Forever

The Changing Role of Baseball in Small-Town Iowa

BY ROBERT NEYMEYER

1994

They occasionally can be seen even yet on the edge of small towns—the rough outline of a baseball diamond along with the remnants of a snow fence that served as the outfield wall. This is all that remains of activities that dominated the summers and autumns of hundreds of communities across the state and helped fashion the social fabric of society. But today those memories are nearly as faded as the foul lines that defined the game.

BASEBALL WAS an integral part of small-town Iowa for nearly a century. In the years after the Civil War, diamonds suddenly appeared in pastures and abandoned lots as young boys and middle-aged men tried to attain glory or recapture youth. The popularity of amateur baseball persisted, despite the advent of high school baseball and other sports, until the early 1960s. These town teams were loosely organized, played an irregular schedule, rarely practiced, and usually displayed mediocre skills. Yet for years they provided the town with an identity, an image, and the basis for social order. It was far more than amusement; it was a structure around which community life could revolve.

Baseball was introduced to the state in 1859 in Davenport when a cricket squad decided to experiment with the popular New York game of baseball. Started by clubs as a gentleman's sport in the 1840s, it soon acquired the status of the national game. Illustrated stories in Beadle's dime novels and the newspapers spread knowledge of the game across the nation. The Civil War helped promote baseball. Soldiers played the game to relieve the boredom of the camps and even organized prison teams. On their return, veterans brought this experience to their hometowns where already there was an interest. This combination led to the dramatic expansion of the game, described by one newspaper editor as a "prairiefire" sweeping across eastern Iowa. In 1866–67 nearly every small town in eastern and central Iowa fielded a team, and by the 1880s the sport had spread to northwest Iowa. It was the only regular recreational activity for most communities.

Entertainment was not the only appeal of baseball. There were other factors which contributed to the success and longevity of the game. It gave the emerging economic and political leadership an opportunity to establish a stable and structured environment in which the community could grow and prosper. At the core of this movement was the Main Street merchant whose cash register required a regular flow of customers. Baseball became an important tool for these local boosters.

As part of their effort to establish themselves as the most influential segment of the community, merchants were active in forming and supporting baseball. In cooperation with the newspaper editor, and often the local land speculator, this group used baseball to promote the town's progress. Official rules were sent for, an official-sized baseball purchased and bats fashioned, a field was designated, and a local nine selected. After a practice or two, the editor issued a challenge to a neighboring town for a friendly match. The uniforms were sewn, a captain elected, and the diamond laid out. Game day, either Wednesday evening or Saturday afternoon, found the town full of excitement. A band led the team to the field and fans seated themselves along the foul lines. The game was played under the stern direction of an umpire, usually the local constable. The players, in brightly colored uniforms, performed as both athletes and teachers, showing how the game was to be played. Once finished, the visitors were treated to a merchant-sponsored banquet and innumerable toasts before tumbling into a wagon for the ride home. Baseball was a glorious event for a small town and for the businessmen who aspired to personal and financial gain.

As the small towns of eastern and central Iowa took shape in the years following the Civil War, merchants were seeking business, stability, and identity. It was important for them to define themselves as leaders, and baseball provided that opportunity. The first teams were established as clubs with merchant support and leadership. But it was on the field that merchants, and many other men, established their reputation. The cult of manliness attracted them to the diamond. At a time when frontier exploits of bravery could no longer be realized, many men were looking for ways to revitalize their virility, prowess, and image. Brawling in the alley behind the tavern no longer was an acceptable way to express masculinity. The baseball field provided an alternative. Here a well-hit ball or a nice fielding play gave these men the hero status they sought. Here their distinctive uniforms made them the center of attention. Here they carried the hopes and dreams of all men and boys in town. This new interpretation of masculinity not only increased the importance of the merchant-player, but it enhanced the status of middle-class males in the community and reinforced the dominance of all men. Baseball provided a nonaggressive means by which a new group of men was able to assume leadership in their community.

Baseball also taught discipline and brought stability to the streets. The rough-and-tumble years of early settlement had been full of drinking, fighting, and considerable lawlessness. While the vigilante movement had done much to rid the countryside of horse thieves, the battle for Main Street had not yet been won. Loudmouthed loafers, rowdy young men, and gangs of teenage boys could create a negative image and frighten away customers. Baseball was one way to teach discipline and discourage antisocial behavior. It was a game of rules with an umpire to interpret and enforce them. Accepting the rules on the diamond was the first step to accepting the values of society off the field. The good players practiced sportsmanship and self-control. They did not argue umpire decisions, fight when they lost, or swear or drink in front of women and children. These were lessons for all men, but especially those who wanted to succeed within the community. The national game taught respect and order which served the merchants and town leadership well. A stable Main Street was a prosperous one.

Merchants used baseball as a mechanism to compete with neighboring towns. These communities vied with each other for retail business, new commercial ventures, railroads, and settlers. A winning baseball team attracted rural people to town and the stores. This, in turn, could be used to bring new businesses to Main Street. A growing business community would have the financial leverage to entice a railroad to build through their community which, in turn, would attract more people and business. While baseball was an important part of this formula, the value was usually limited to the early years of a town's growth. But baseball also established identity and recognition. A county championship enhanced a town's regional reputation. To defeat a traditional rival on the baseball field was to gain bragging rights for the winter. To have a local player move into professional baseball gave credibility to the entire community. Few other activities could define and enhance a small town's image as successfully as a good baseball team.

Over the years town teams continued to reflect the personality of the community. Despite the scandals and the unsavory image of the national game, baseball in rural Iowa retained much of its original character. While the crisis of masculinity had passed by the 1920s, the search for hero status had not. Both men and boys wanted to be "just like the Babe," dreaming of doffing their cap as they trotted around the bases after hitting one over the fence.

Merchants remained active sponsors of the game but their support became more conspicuous. Uniforms were emblazoned with the names of car dealerships or hardware stores to better direct the fans. Social restraint was still present and sportsmanship important as Sunday baseball became generally accepted. The lesson of temperance, now the national policy, validated the worth of small-town lifestyles. The competitive spirit was intensified as second and third generations faced each other on the field. Those rivalries became the heritage of high school sports, allowing them to be continued until the towns no longer existed.

Baseball was able to survive the Depression and World War II, but was unable to withstand the onslaught of slow pitch softball, golf, and television. By the late 1950s most town teams were on their last legs. Manliness was now a function of physical durability. The search for fame within the community was reduced to fathers trying to impress their immediate families, who made up most of the crowd. Oft-mended uniforms, with embarrassing holes in back pockets worn thin by tobacco tins, advertised businesses long closed, though some dignity was maintained as T-shirts with beer ads were prohibited. Sportsmanship was a necessity as players had to double as umpires. Community identity and glory were now entrusted to the school football and basketball teams. The influence of baseball was disappearing rapidly.

A century of baseball ended for most small towns in the 1960s. Diamonds were converted into senior housing. Record books were lost in attics or sold at estate auctions. The names of players on team photographs were forgotten and trophies were discarded by the local historical societies. The old dominant values were eroded as the population became more transient. New residents could not understand the barriers that divided communities existing only a few miles apart. Convenience store chains were no longer interested in sponsoring local activities and the Main Street business district was almost nonexistent. The glory of the game was remembered only in nursing homes and in centennial histories. Baseball's contribution to the lifestyle of rural Iowa was over.

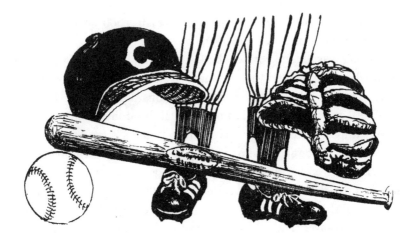

Local Ghosts

BY DAN BRAWNER
1996

THEY FRIGHTEN US. They fascinate us. They shake our faith in science. But, I am convinced, the most startling attribute of ghosts is that they are everywhere. After having had a close encounter with a ghost two years ago, I began asking some of my friends and neighbors in the Mount Vernon/Lisbon area if they ever had seen one. I was astonished at what they told me.

When I casually remarked to Dennis Herrick, publisher of *The Sun* newspaper in Mount Vernon, that I was writing a story on ghosts, he admitted this was not an unfamiliar topic at his home.

"Like most sensible, rational people, I don't believe in ghosts," Herrick began. "But there is one in our house."

As a career newspaper man, Herrick is not overly excitable. He has covered his share of spirited city council meetings, howling Iowa snowstorms, and the mass-possession of otherwise respectable citizens during Lisbon wrestling tournaments.

Since 1876, when *The Sun*'s newspaper editor, W. T. Baker, apparently was murdered in his office for an ill-chosen remark about city hall, publishers of *The Sun* have been thoughtful folks.

So when Herrick and his wife, Beatrice, first heard footsteps in their living room as they sat in the basement family room, they were not inclined to panic.

Herrick said, "A couple of times we looked at each other and went upstairs, expecting to find one of the kids or a burglar and found nothing. It happens regularly."

A veteran reporter, Herrick admits he is at a loss to explain the disembodied footsteps.

"I presume ghosts don't have any weight," he reasoned. "But you can hear the boards creak and you can hear the footsteps."

The Herrick house is only about 20 years old and, as far as anybody knows, not the site of any unspeakable horror that would provide an attractive campground for wandering spirits. But the Herricks have chosen to be hospitable to their uninvited guest.

"We mind our business and the ghost minds its business," said Herrick. He added, "I should point out to anybody who might want to buy my house someday, this is apparently a benevolent ghost."

Herrick never saw his ghost. But Frederic Will, a former comparative literature professor and fellow Mount Vernon resident, has seen one.

"It was a year and a half ago," Will said. "It was a humid, late summer evening. I was sitting at the computer in the second-floor study, all alone in the house except for Biscuits, our dog. I was feeling lonely. Usually, I don't. I like to be alone in the house. I looked up because I felt something over my left shoulder. I looked toward the corner and there I saw something like a flickering, filtering shadow of a person, translucent, but with an outline of what seemed like a young girl, about the age of my daughter Carson, who's now 11."

According to Will, the ghost looked somewhat like a photographic negative. She was dressed in a filmy Victorian gown and seemed to take no notice of him as if intent upon her own business.

"I was a little startled, or frightened, and I ran out of the house across the street where I saw my neighbor who was, as always, washing and polishing his old white car. When told of this, he, a born-again Christian who lives in a world of miracles and phantasms, thought it of no interest at all and dismissed it as some demonic aberration.

"That chastened me and I went back into the house and sat down at the computer, this time with no fear. I felt warm, relaxed and very good, as if the house now belonged to me entirely and as though I'd had a widening and spiritual experience. Now, a year and a half later, I think back on it with no doubt that it was a real experience and with some feeling that it was a disclosure leading somewhere."

Since then, Will's seven-year-old daughter, Kyle, has seen the ghost, and he has seen it a second time.

"Kyle was quite relaxed about it," Will said. "She wanted an explanation, but she was not afraid and we talked about it quite calmly."

Will said he looks upon the appearance of the ghost as a kind of sign.

He observed, "I felt it was saying to me, 'Keep your ears and eyes open. There are mysteries out there.'"

Not long after the spirit first appeared in his home, Will decided he was ready for a new direction. He is remarried to a woman from sub-Saharan Africa and is helping to found a liberal arts college.

Pat Charboneau of Mount Vernon hasn't seen a ghost since she was 12, visiting her grandparents' farm in Greenwood, Wisconsin. A frank, no-nonsense person, Charboneau could say a spaceship just landed on Main Street and I'd grab a camera, because I know the place would be full of little green men. She took advantage of a lull at her kitchen shop, Le Sous Sol, to tell me about the girl in the window.

Charboneau and her cousin, who was about the same age, were visiting her grandparents' farm. The house, a big, four-square, federal-style building, was erected on the stone foundation of a house built in the 1850s that had burned to the ground when a field hand set fire to it. Everybody had made it out safely, except for a young daughter.

"I woke up just before dawn," Charboneau said. "I was thirsty. They had this big open staircase. I went through the living room into the dining room and I saw a figure sitting at the window seat of Grandma's beautiful bay window.

"All I could see was the outline because it was early morning. I said, 'Oh, hi!' because I thought it was my cousin. But she never looked at me. The girl had long wavy hair and she was sitting there in a kind of pinafore dress. I could see her feet. Because of the light, she looked ephemeral. Because I was tired, it didn't seem odd to me that she was wearing clothes instead of a night dress. I went to the kitchen, got my drink, and came back around through the dining room. But she wasn't there. I thought she had gone back up to bed."

The next morning, Charboneau asked her cousin what she was doing up so early sitting in the window seat, but she didn't know what Charboneau was talking about. She never mentioned the incident to anybody for many years. Then one day, she told her mother about the little girl.

"Her face just got white," Charboneau recalled. "She admitted she had seen her many times when she was a young girl. She stopped seeing her after she reached puberty."

Charboneau remembers the girl in the window was not a threatening presence. But recently, when she asked whatever happened to the farm house after it had been sold, her mother said it had sat abandoned until it had once again burned to the ground.

When Vicky Pospisil of Mount Vernon was four years old, her father was helping put up a CB radio antenna at his office building in Kansas City. A gust of wind caught the antenna. Instinctively, her father caught it and was electrocuted.

Vicky's mother had two young children and no income. She was devastated by her husband's death.

"I think she kind of 'checked out' for a while," Vicky said. "I remember being at my grandparents' once, because I was spending a lot of time there during this period. A little girl and I were sitting on bikes. She said, 'What happened to your mom?' I said, 'I don't think she loves me anymore.'"

Pospisil said it was soon after this that her father's spirit came to her. She recalls that she was in bed and was feeling sad.

She said, "It was his biggest concern, not that I understood his death, but that I understand that my mother loved me and she'd get over the loss."

Two years ago last summer, Pospisil's daughter, then four-year-old Hillary, began having trouble sleeping.

She said, "Hillary always had been such a sound sleeper. She started yelling at me in the night that there was somebody in her room."

Because of her own spiritual experiences as a child, Pospisil would not tell Hillary that the presence was just her imagination. So, two or three nights a week throughout most of the summer, Hillary would wake up in the middle of the night, saying somebody was disturbing her.

"What I began to notice," Pospisil said, "was that I would awaken to the sound of a child's voice coming through the truck CB radio outside and from the base station downstairs. It was very unsettling. I didn't recognize the voice and couldn't make out the words. I just heard the talk and within seconds, Hillary would wake up and say, 'Mom!'"

Pospisil said she couldn't understand how the voice could come from the truck and the base station at the same time, unless somebody was speaking on their band from within the truck. If the radio's receiver had simply been left off the hook, they would have heard everybody within range. But aside from the child's voice, the radio was perfectly quiet.

Pospisil recalls that one night she woke to the sound of the voice on the radio. She looked up to see Hillary standing beside her bed. Hillary said, "I saw it."

"I got out of bed immediately. Hillary turned and walked into the bathroom. She sat down and said, 'I saw it.' It was almost as if she was asleep. I said, 'Hillary, you saw what?' She looked up at me to tell me. Just then, the smoke alarm in our hallway went off. You could have peeled me off the ceiling."

Although there was no fire, everybody's nerves were jangled, so Pospisil put Hillary back to bed and did not ask her again what she had seen. But that night, she realized they had a real problem. She contacted Marcia Brandt, her friend and a spiritual healer. Brandt gave her an ancient prayer of protection to create a protective dome over their home. The voice on the CB never came back after that and Hillary was able to sleep peacefully.

Weeks later, Pospisil and her family attended Sauerkraut Days in Lisbon, where she ran into a friend whose daughter is about Hillary's age. They all spent time together, but Pospisil did not mention Hillary's experience.

Two weeks after that, Pospisil's friend called to say that her daughter was having trouble sleeping and complaining that there was somebody in her room.

Pospisil passed on to her friend what Brandt had given her. She speculates that whatever was bothering Hillary seemed to be traveling from child to child. Although her friend's daughter has not been disturbed since by the presence, Pospisil said with some irony, "Woe to the child who got on the bus with her that day!"

Six years ago, Marcia Brandt moved to Mount Vernon where she practices massage therapy. Though raised a Presbyterian, Brandt started reading on spirituality in the 1970s. Although she says she rarely attends church, spirituality is never far from her thoughts. "Wherever you walk outside," Brandt said, "there's God."

Brandt says that part of her work involves spiritual healing. She is quick to point out, "All healing is from God. If the person is ready and open to receive it, you can assist them to do that. It's like you're an extra battery. You jump-start them."

Besides helping Vicky Pospisil's daughter, Brandt often assists her customers in spiritual matters. She casually comments that she has spiritual encounters on a daily basis. Sometimes she says she hears a spirit's thoughts. A former music teacher, Brandt sometimes receives messages through songs.

Brandt said recently when a customer was in her shop, they could sense a presence, but were not clear who it was.

She said, "The song that went through my head was, 'These Boots Are Made for Walking,' by Nancy Sinatra. The gal at the table knew it was her cousin because it was a song they had sung when they were kids. They'd dress up like Nancy Sinatra. She said, 'That's Lisa!'"

Although she says she never has seen a ghost, she has felt their presence. "Sometimes the room will look fuzzy or misty," Brandt explains. "Sometimes you feel pushed. I've felt that."

Two years ago, the owner of a local business who preferred to remain anonymous reported strange incidents, such as voices that came through a broken intercom and Christmas lights in the basement that burned out at the same place on the strand each time they were replaced. Brandt consulted with a friend who claims to communicate with spirits. The spirit reportedly told her it would continue to burn out the lights because it was interfering with his energy.

"To me, that is not an evolved spirit," Brandt said. "Ghosts are just confused. They're stuck. Some don't want to go on to the next level. They don't understand they have died."

Can ordinary folks feel the presence of ghosts?

"Have you ever walked into an antique store and felt funny?" Brandt asked. "There are people who still are attached to their furniture."

According to local legend, there once was an attic ghost in the house currently occupied by Mr. and Mrs. Don Stine of Mount Vernon. And, apparently, she liked the windows left open. When the house belonged to Cornell College theater professor Joseph Svec, the family was witness to disembodied footsteps, attic windows mysteriously opening on their own, and once an autoharp that actually lived up to its name and played itself.

It is said that around the turn of the century, a nurse was left in charge of the original owners' little girl. The girl fell down the steps and died. During the girl's funeral, the nurse hanged herself in the attic. It took the Svecs two seances to get rid of the nurse's ghost.

Harry Phelps of Lisbon never claimed to have seen a ghost. But around 1957, just after he moved into his house near Sutliff, he got a scare just the same. One morning, after Phelps and his brother had returned from running their trap lines, he heard a thunderous rattle, as if he had been standing next to the old plank Sutliff Bridge as a car drove over it. He ran outside and heard the car approaching and the boards rattling. The sound faded away as he stood there. The Sutliff Bridge was over a mile from his home.

The house was built around 1840 on stone dug from the Sutliff quarry, and Phelps wonders if the builder had carried something of the old ghost town with him when he laid the foundation. What was the logical explanation? Phelps reckons it had something to do with the atmospheric conditions. "It still happens every once in a while," he said.

My Lisbon house was built in 1870 and looks as if it should be haunted. When I first moved in, I did find a secret passageway behind a boarded-up doorway which led down stone steps into a basement, all reference to which is suspiciously absent from the abstract. Once I reached the bottom of the stairs, I could see why. The wiring was a nightmare. The floor joists were a horror. Judging from the catacombs in the dirt floor, the entire place was possessed with mice. The ghost came later.

Two years ago in late December, I woke from a sound sleep with the feeling somebody was in the room. The alarm clock indicated it was just after 5 a.m. I raised quietly up on one elbow so I could hear better if my prowler moved. Previously when I lived in Phoenix, I had awakened once to discover somebody in my kitchen. I was not anxious, this time, to surprise a frightened thief.

I lay perfectly still for about ten minutes. The house was so absolutely black that I could not see even three feet to the bedroom door. Then, without warning, I felt something sit on the edge of the bed. The bedsprings compressed—not as much as if an adult had sat down. Maybe half that much.

My mind was racing. I couldn't see or hear anything. Although I was thoroughly awake, I was trying to rationalize how this could—or could not—be happening. Then, the bedsprings decompressed without a rustle and whatever it was, was gone.

I felt oddly pleased with the whole experience, even cozy, as if some maternal spirit had stopped by to tuck me in. To my knowledge, the ghost (if that's what it was) never returned. I'd like to think there is a spirit watching over me, someone kind, someone peaceful, and someone who wouldn't mind making the bed once in a while.

Welcome to Engle Country

A Review and an Appreciation

BY WINSTON BARCLAY

1996

THE *Wapsipinicon Almanac* is published in the heart of what has been known for decades as "Grant Wood Country." The luminous, stylized images in Wood's paintings have made the rolling, hump-backed countryside around Anamosa and Stone City familiar territory the world over. Having known Paul Engle, who once lived in the now-ruined Green mansion near Stone City, I'm certain that he knew exactly what he was doing when he christened an overlapping piece of Iowa "Engle Country." As much a citizen of the world as Wood, Engle was also a seasoned contractor in the construction of his own legend and an expert practitioner of gilt by association.

His posthumous memoir, *A Lucky American Childhood*, published by the University of Iowa Press as part of its series "Singular Lives: The Iowa Series in North American Autobiography," is another chapter in the Engle legend, and a welcome one. The volume bustles with all the qualities and complexities that made Paul so charming and so exasperating—the indefatigable vitality, the shameless self-satisfaction, the love of a good story, the keen powers of observation, the feistiness yet gentleness of spirit, the hearty sense of humor, the unalloyed bullshit. Paul was always stimulating company, even when he made you cringe a bit, and in *A Lucky American Childhood*, he still is. Those who knew

Paul will hear him speak every line, complete with winks, guffaws, and dramatic whispers of feigned confidence.

Of particular interest to many readers in this area will be the book's keen evocation of life in Cedar Rapids during the teens, 20s, and 30s—the sights, the sounds, the smells, and the characters that Engle recalls with unabashed nostalgia. It was an age when English was still the second language of much of the immigrant population, and the Old Country's ways of living and thinking were still much in evidence. "Some of the new arrivals chopped the English language as if it were a side of beef," Paul writes, "but we communicated."

He revels in the sheer sensuality of that earlier time, regardless of its pains and privations, and he openly laments the way that modern, comfortable, hygienic life has distanced us from the earth, animals, and the primal processes of life. He judges today's children disadvantaged for never learning the subtle communication of rider and horse through sensitivity to bit and reins. As his introduction puts it, in exclamatory style, "Kids don't hold the ends of reins any more. Deprived!"

The time that Engle paints in loving detail was also an era whose values now seem antique, or even alien. He describes his profane, tough, and temperamental father, Tom, who was frugal with all emotions except anger, and whose children both respected his seven-day-a-week, 15-hour-a-day sacrifice and feared his hairtrigger violence. Bedridden, raging against the constraints of age and injury, Tom instructs his son, "There's people who work and there's bums." Paul virtually weeps for his long-suffering mother, Eva, who was socialized to tolerate every struggle and slight without complaint.

And, ever the parochial Iowan, he clucks his tongue at his misguided uncle who gave up a few fertile acres north of Cedar Rapids for fighting wolves on a large spread of poor soil and pine-tree swamp in northern Minnesota.

The darkest and most polemical section of the book recounts Paul's experiences in Germany during a summer of his Rhodes Scholarship tenure. Set against memories of his Jewish friends and benefactors in Iowa, and reflected in a visit many years later to Auschwitz, he describes the darkening clouds of Nazi persecutions. In exchange for a set of Rilke's poems, a Jewish bookseller in Berlin pleads with Paul to help his young daughter escape. When a month after his return to England, Paul locates sources who have the connections to accomplish the feat, his letters to the family are returned with the terse notation, "Disappeared." "Do not be patient with the frightfulness of the human race," he wails. "Howl, howl. From your dark cave, howl."

But even in that section, roiling with grief, anger, and guilt, Paul builds his central thesis: that he was lucky to have had these experiences—to be born and raised when and where he was, to face those challenges, to interact with those personalities in all their diversity—and lucky, certainly, to have a boss at the drugstore who was so proud of his young clerk's poetic interests that he stocked literary magazines he never expected to sell, knowing that Paul would devour them in the back room.

For an old man still in love with language, falling through the ice of the Cedar River on his paper route more than a half-century before was not just a dramatic near-death experience, it is a memory he is lucky to have, a story he is lucky to tell.

So, who was this Paul Engle, anyway, that we should care about his recollections? The fact that this question must now be asked, only a few years after his death, is testimony to the short attention span of cybersociety.

Fading social memory was certainly on the mind of Hualing Nieh Engle, the Chinese-Iowan novelist who shared the last 25 years of Paul's life, when she left me phone messages and wrote me a letter shortly after the volume's release. She remembered that I referred repeatedly and favorably to Paul in an article I wrote several years ago for *The Des Moines Register*.

"Have you seen Paul's new memoir?" she asked. I said I knew of it, but I had not yet seen a copy. She promised to send me one (which she did, immediately—it was on my desk the next day) and said, "I know from what you wrote that you cared about Paul. I feel so sad for Paul. I think he is being forgotten. Maybe you could write something about the book?" I suspect she is feeling forgotten, too, still living up on Dubuque Street in their spacious house overlooking the Iowa River, with the echoes of the hundreds of writers with whom they shared drinks, and laughs, and stories, and the love of language.

I took her concern seriously and I hope she will accept what follows as I intend it, despite its reservations, criticisms, and judgments—as an appreciation. After all, aren't you suspicious of saintly portraits?

The idea that Paul Engle could be forgotten is an odd concept, even for one who acknowledges the transience of all things. Paul was one of those people who often was described as a "force of nature"—seemingly invincible and immortal. For most of his life, he was an Iowa celebrity, achieving a notoriety and authority usually inaccessible to poets.

And being a celebrity suited his bigger-than-life persona. He was one of those people the spotlight followed—or perhaps he brought his own spotlight with him. Big, raw-boned, and perpetually animated, he commanded and expected attention wherever he went. You always knew when Paul was present because, even if you hadn't felt him arrive, you soon heard his unmistakable voice, and the roar of his unrestrained laughter would rise above every other conversation.

Paul was genuine, not in the sense of being without guile, but in the sense of being a vivid, uncompromising, unrelenting presence—passionately engaged in every moment, voracious in his appetite for life. He was the kind of person for whom there was no such thing as a waste of time (perhaps heeding the instruction of his severe, dogged father). He was, in that sense, the embodiment of Walt Whitman's poetic ideal, a free individual exulting in his existence, luxuriating in its sensual and intellectual joys, and shouting the wonder of his life.

But the rough-hewn poetry that was Paul's original claim to fame from the 1930s into the 1950s has not proved enduring. I am unaware of a single major anthology that contains his work. And the University of Iowa institutions for which he was responsible—the Writers' Workshop, which he led to prominence, and the unique International Writing Program, which he and Hualing created—have somehow managed to thrive without him, proving that they were more than extensions of his personality. And, unfortunately, he alienated so many of his natural allies in the last years that they were disinclined to rally remembrance.

Paul always had unqualified admirers, other than himself, and I'm sure he still does. He was a pivotal character in the lives of so many writers that it could not be otherwise.

Take the case of Bharati Mukherjee and Clark Blaise. Mukherjee was the sheltered daughter of a prominent Calcutta Brahmin family when she first heard of Paul Engle from a visiting academic. Inspired by the factually flawed stories she heard about the Writers' Workshop, she dispatched a package of handwritten short stories addressed to Paul Engle, Ames,

Iowa. Paul's celebrity was such, at that point, that the package found its way to Iowa City and he invited her to the workshop. She arrived totally unprepared for the Iowa winter and survived by borrowing the cast-off clothes of Paul's daughters.

In the midst of that bitter winter, a young French-Canadian-American writer, Clark Blaise (now director of the IWP), lacking even bus fare, hitchhiked across the country from Boston to join the workshop. On his first night in Iowa, in Paul Engle's living room, he met Bharati. Their lives as accomplished writers, and as partners in life, cannot be conceived without the timely intersection of Paul Engle. To log the consequences of all the convergences Paul catalyzed, by design or chance, would be as daunting as sequencing DNA.

I have talked to writers who will proclaim without reservation, "He made my career as a writer," or "Without Paul Engle, I never could have been a writer. I owe my whole career to him." He had a nose for talent and a crusader's determination to nurture and promote it. He built the Writers' Workshop to a stature where it became perfectly natural for America's finest young writers to study there, and for the most famous and accomplished writers of the day to teach there. The other creative writing programs that now thrive at university campuses everywhere are copies of what Paul constructed in Iowa, and many are, in fact, led by Iowa graduates. Not bad for the sticks!

Admiration and devotion were particularly common among the IWP writers because for many the Iowa sojourn was a peak experience of their lives. For writers who had lived under repressive regimes, the International Writing Program offered their first opportunity to live, converse, and write in freedom. Paul loved to tell about the East European writer who burst into his office to proclaim, "This is the most wonderful day of my life." Paul assumed that the man's work had just been accepted for publication or that he had learned of a major literary award, but the truth was more elemental. "Today for the first time," the writer confided, "I walked down the street without looking behind to see if I was being followed."

The passport of one Chinese writer was revoked shortly before his anticipated travel to Iowa and he was placed under house arrest. But during the years of his incarceration, Paul remained quietly steadfast, keeping up a steady stream of correspondence, providing encouragement and support for his distant brother writer.

When one of the I W P's many Polish writers learned of Paul's death in 1991, he immediately published the news under a headline that translates, "Our Paul Engle Is Dead." Such was the impact of this horse-breaking, shit-on-his-boots poet from rural America that he was claimed as the personal, treasured possession of writers half a world away.

In his last years, Paul was honored with the Award for Distinguished Service to the Arts of the American Academy and Institute of Arts and Letters, becoming, in the process, the first artist west of the Mississippi to be so honored by that high-toned eastern institution. Paul was nominated by another writer who gave the Writers' Workshop credit for his career—Kurt Vonnegut, who was on the verge of abandoning his literary ambitions and the financial scraping they entailed when the offer of a teaching job at the UI renewed his hope and paid his bills. To this day the literarily inclined will point out the Iowa City house where Vonnegut wrote *Slaughterhouse Five* during that tenure.

But in America, for the most part, Paul virtually disappeared into retirement. It was in other countries in all parts of the world that his legend prospered (do the words "A prophet is not without honor" come to mind?). Whenever his health permitted, he and Hualing were off on some literary safari speaking at conferences and ceremonies, basking in testimonials, and returning with trophies. In fact, they were enroute to accept yet another award when he collapsed in Chicago's O'Hare airport in 1991. And at his memorial service, writers from East and West credited the IWP's role in the democracy movements on both sides of the planet.

So Paul was not wanting for glory. But most who knew him, even some of the writers whose careers depended on him, view him with a sometimes troubled ambivalence. In a nagging paradox, some feel simultaneously blessed and damaged by their association with him. For example, I've heard stories from once-starving artists about how he wielded scholarship checks like imperial pardons—the needy recipients were never left in doubt about to whom it was they were beholden. You hear about the tyranny of his literary taste, the ruthlessness of his machinations.

And many felt that Paul was—sometimes destructively—never able to distinguish between himself and the programs he directed. Paul was often, as the vernacular puts it, "difficult." Taking up his legacy was not an easy task.

It may seem to many people that to give him too much praise now would appear to be a concession to his over-exercised ego. When one of Paul's former students expressed her puzzlement and anger that his memorial service was not better attended, I could only speculate that perhaps some people felt that there was nothing they could add—that whatever adoring remarks needed to be said, Paul had already said, repeatedly, about himself.

I certainly remember the ambivalence I felt the first time I met Paul Engle. When I was an editor at the *Daily Iowan*, the University of Iowa's campus newspaper, one of my writers suggested that we collaborate on an extensive feature about the International Writing Program, which Paul and Hualing had founded a decade before. I knew that Paul Engle was the famous "father" of the Iowa Writers' Workshop, but I began with little in-depth knowledge of the International Writing Program.

The Engles welcomed us with extravagant hospitality to their home, which, we soon learned, was the unofficial headquarters of the IWP. The writers were housed right next door in the Mayflower Residence Hall, and the Engles's door was always open. As was wholly appropriate, the IWP was more of a social experience with fraternal rituals of food and drink than an academic pursuit, and the Engles were the hosts supreme.

Paul was in his most charming and expansive and solicitous and quotable mode, dramatically recounting his favorite stories that illustrated the worldwide importance of the IWP. We heard, of course, about the Nobel Peace Prize nomination that Paul and Hualing received in 1976 and how much it would have meant to the program if they had won; about the Romanian writer whose body was discovered in the rubble of the Bucharest earthquake clutching what Paul assumed was "the most valuable thing" he could grab as the building collapsed—the manuscript of his story about Iowa; about the Iron Curtain guards who viewed with suspicion the returning writers' large badges with the strange inscription, "Homecoming 1969. Go Hawks!"; about the Israeli concentration-camp survivor and the German writer who surmounted the horrors of history to become fast friends.

I came away from that meeting with my head spinning—disoriented and befuddled. To some extent, my dumbstruck mental state reflected my immediate realization of the genius—the miracle, even—of the IWP, the authentic and almost ineffable importance of this international summit of creativity and the human spirit in the heart of Iowa.

But to a greater extent it reflected my shell-shocked response to Paul. You don't often meet a midwesterner—and even more rarely a small-town midwesterner—so willing and anxious to boast. A typical Iowan would let the facts speak for themselves and frame the presentation with qualifications, apologies, and self-effacing mumblings. Paul's bravado was the antithesis of midwestern humility—the self-deprecating character that Garrison Keillor portrays so accurately and so hilariously in his stories and monologues. As a born and bred midwesterner, I didn't know quite what to do with someone who proclaims himself a Son of the Soil as if he were proclaiming himself the Son of God.

What particularly upset my equilibrium was that never before had I met anyone who was so self-aggrandizing and yet whose high self-opinion seemed completely justified. What Paul demonstrated was not vainglory. I felt then, and I continue to feel, that what Paul and Hualing accomplished was every bit as important as they pronounced it to be. Perhaps they were even modest in their assessment.

As much as I enjoyed his company, I never quite got used to Paul's style. He could come on so strong, with his boundless capacity for self-appreciation, that it was often embarrassing. Equivocation was not among his skills. And in the last years I know that many other people were increasingly embarrassed, and simply fed up. He would show up at an event, have a little too much to drink, and ramble on sentimentally long after the audience was rustling and coughing nervously.

Figuring out what I really felt and thought about Paul, and his capacity to simultaneously attract and repel, took a number of years. Part of the slipperiness of assessing Paul Engle—and the reason that I am emboldened now to write about him so candidly—is that he was not a hypocrite. He recognized, accepted, and even celebrated his faults and foibles. He acknowledged his internal battle between generosity and belligerence. These were not things to be ashamed of, in his Whitmanesque view—they merely made him a more robust character. The quaintly rhyming poem that serves as an introduction to *A Lucky American Childhood*—and imagine the nerve of conceiving of such a poem—begins with the lines:

> The name Paul Engle trembles on his tongue.
> Should it be bellowed, sneered, whined, bleated, sung?

and later takes up the theme:

> He likes his liquor, but his hands don't shake.
> He talks too much, merely for talking's sake.
> He seldom bores you, but he makes you mad.
> He's not really evil, only bad, and again;
> Some think him worse, now, than he really is.
> Some think him better than he really is, or:
> Watch his slick hands whenever he will deal.
> Some find him gentle, glad to share a meal,
> Others, abrasive as an emery wheel,
> Generous with his time, a tender heel.
> His nature contradicts his contradictions.
> He sinks his teeth into the neck of his convictions
> And hangs on while the jealous kick his ass,
> Knowing such bitter pettiness will pass.
> What he believes, he shouts with too much breath.
> He'll cry "Imagination" at his death.
> Some meeting him think at once, how horrible,
> But some (how wise!) think him adorable.

He would acknowledge, without hesitation, that he possessed an enormous ego and he would plead no contest to charges of self-promoting manipulation. In *A Lucky American Childhood* he at one point describes how as a young man his ego "grew like corn in August." In fact, he would enlighten you that only someone with his self-assurance, stubbornness, persistence, ruthlessness, conviction, and chutzpah could have accomplished what he accomplished.

With a sly trickster's grin, he explained how he convinced UI administrators to endorse Hualing's crazy International Writing Program proposal. By then they knew him well enough, by personal experience or reputation, to realize that you didn't just say "no" to Paul Engle. He was the sort of fellow who, once he got a notion in his head, would make a charming nuisance of himself until he got his way. And if necessary, he would dispense with the charm. So they said, fine, as long as you raise all the money, go ahead. Paul's assumption was that they were so certain of his inevitable failure that they felt there was no danger in granting their imprimatur.

Who wouldn't have predicted failure? It was Paul himself who, according to one of his most oft-repeated stories, screamed at Hualing that it was the craziest idea he had ever heard. When she proposed the idea out by Lake Macbride, his outburst was so explosive (so Paul claimed) that a great blue heron was spooked from the shallows where it had been fishing and took flight with muscular flappings that seemed to echo, "Crazy! Crazy! Crazy!" All the objections he immediately raised were legitimate ones: Where would they get the money? How would they house the writers? How would they even find the writers off in every corner of the globe?

I'm certain that the assumptions of certain failure made Paul even more resolute in his pursuit of success, at an age when most men of accomplishment are content to rest on their laurels. For years Paul and Hualing virtually put aside their own writing—a gut sacrifice for both of them—to raise funds, form international alliances, set up correspondence with writers, and sweet-talk and arm-twist within the university. I realize now that some of the aggressive self-promotion of our first meeting was a variation on the standard, well-honed line that Paul had learned to wield in fund-raising, a hard-ball realm where humility and soft-selling are the tools of failure.

One of the most revealing and explanatory things that I learned about Paul over the years was that he regarded writing as a sacrament—a divine calling, the most important thing a person could be. Once when I called him on the phone, he cautioned (with all the expected drama) that he would have to speak very softly because I had happened to call at a very significant moment—in the next room Hualing was writing the final page of her novel. What he meant was not that loud conversation might distract her, but that the completion of a literary work of art was a sacred moment that demanded hushed reverence.

Paul's conviction was that a writer is the conscience of society, the one who makes comprehensible what was otherwise confusing or hazy, the provocateur who pokes the ribs of complacency, the challenger of injustice, the guardian of freedom. So in being both a writer and a mentor and facilitator of writers, Paul realized the things that he valued the most. The success of all his students became his success. The peace and understanding he promoted by bringing the world's writers together were personal triumphs, the private exorcism of his nightmare of Nazi censorship and persecution he witnessed and the futility of his youthful opposition to it. He became what, in his opinion, most qualified an individual for admiration and respect.

Hearing Paul's voice, as I do, speaking the lines of *A Lucky American Childhood*, I experience the memoir on two levels. On the superficial level, it is an affecting, romantic remembrance of another time in this place, a story of Iowa youth in a lost time. But on another level I detect Paul's urgent assumption that these incidents take on special, monumental power because the young Paul Engle is destined to become THE Paul Engle, who, in his own immodest but accurate assessment, "has helped, with money and sympathy, more young American and foreign writers than anyone else in this country." That is why his narrative can unselfconsciously intermingle passages of radiant insight and observation with descriptions of the trivial and mundane ("we always called him 'Dad' . . ."). And why at one moment he can be a soaring intellect, and at another can stoop to leering, dirty-old-man stuff with a nudge and a wink that make you squirm.

Finally, recently, I arrived at a conception of Paul—a hypothesis or heuristic device, I suppose, or perhaps a rationalization—that for me resolves a good deal of the dissonance: I realized that Paul Engle was not primarily a poet, or an arts entrepreneur, or any of the other roles he filled with such verve. He was a conceptual artist, and his lifelong project was the creation of this bigger-than-life character, the Whitmanesque individual, Paul Engle—who was invented by him, and was him, simultaneously. Paul Engle was a part he loved to play, and he was a virtuoso at the whole Engle schtick, right down to those feigned confidences I mentioned earlier, the dependable moment where he would lean in and lower his voice to a whisper, as if he was letting you in on some sensitive, privileged information never before revealed.

So, here's my plea, advocated with all the subtlety of Paul Engle: Let's forgive him his excesses and trespasses. For our own benefit rather than his, we should regard him now without judgment, just as he generously viewed the assorted customers of the Cedar Rapids drugstore so many decades ago—the minister who enjoyed a forbidden "seegar" in the back room, the anti-tobacco crusader hooked on candy ("She was the first fanatic of my life," Paul writes, "and I was delighted with our relationship"), the grandmother who outwitted Prohibition with an open-ended prescription for the appropriate "elixir," the construction worker to whom Paul served a double shot of Bromo Seltzer as a hangover remedy after "a real barn burner."

Paul Engle deserves a chapter in every Iowa book of history. The University of Iowa should name a building after him at the very least, and not because his ego expected it, but because his accomplishments and contributions deserved it. (If there's no afterlife, then no concession is granted, and if there is, well, he'll roar an uninhibited, approving laugh.) Good, constructive, positive work is so valuable a commodity that we dare not demand sainthood as well.

We must remember Paul Engle, and the little sentimental slice of him in *A Lucky American Childhood*, for no other reason than that they are memories worth keeping—here in Engle Country.

A Lucky American Childhood, by Paul Engle. University of Iowa Press, Iowa City, 1996. 190 pp., $24.95, hardback.

Interstate

BY GARY ELLER

1998

THEY'D JUST OPENED the interstate stretching across North Dakota and with my new driver's license I had to see how it felt driving a four-lane highway in a Chevy V-8. The nice flat surface so unlike the clunky pavement around home and the cloverleafs straight out of *Popular Science* magazine simply commanded me to step harder on the gas.

So I shouldn't have been surprised when the patrolman thumbed me over. But the ticket he wrote upset me so much that I backed into a U-Haul at the rest stop near Mandan and smashed the right rear taillight of our brand new four-door Chevrolet. As it got dark I sat there, scared and hungry, with three silver dollars that would buy just enough gas to get home if I dared go. I watched the truckers with their heavy walks go in and out of the lavatory, and I could almost hear my dad's voice from that morning: "Do Not. Take the car. *Out of town.*"

A man with a farmer's tan sat eating a banana at the picnic table. A woman walked a dog. I thought how happily I'd trade lives with either of them when a man with a long chain dangling from a leather pouch in his back pocket stopped beside my window. "I see by your dealer tag you're from Rolla," he said.

I brightened slightly at the mention of my beloved home town.

"Going past Dickinson?"

I shook my head.

"See my rig, Swift Premium?" He gestured with his elbow. "I got to get my niece to Dickinson for college. But I'm not supposed to take on riders and the weigh station's coming up."

The contradictory directives I'd been raised with—never talk to strangers, always mind your manners—tugged at me. "I go north at the Hebron exit," I said.

"That's fine. You can drop her at Norm's. It's right there. She's from around Rolla, my niece is," he said. "I hate putting her in with just any-body. Tell you what, talk to her. All right?"

He climbed into his rig and a girl in a pink mini-skirt and white T-shirt climbed down. I was unsure, but the man *had* pronounced Rolla correctly, instead of *Raleigh* like strangers did.

"You're Jim," the girl said.

"Who?"

"That figures. That s.o.b. What next." She whirled around toward the rig which was rolling away under a cloud of black exhaust. "Swift Premium, my fanny," she said. "Would you mind opening the door? I can't do it with these nails."

Inside the car she hardly glanced at me, but took a minute to open and close the glove compartment and feel under the seat.

"I hear you're from Rolla," I said.

"Raleigh?" she said. "Where's that?" She hammered a cigarette out of a fresh pack and punched in the car lighter. "So," she said, "I suppose you want to . . ." and she used the F word. "You better pull over there where it's darker. I'm not putting on a show, too."

My first thought was one of astonishment. *Women could use that word?* My next notion was that this was going to make a lot of firsts for one day.

I turned on the ignition. The gauges came to life. My palms felt moist. In the light she looked older. Not as old as my mother, but older than college. I started the car, but killed it letting the clutch out. I turned the key again and this time flooded the engine.

"Well. What are you waiting for?" she said.

I sniffled. My hands trembled on the wheel. I turned aside so she wouldn't see the emerging tears. "I wasn't supposed to even leave town and when my parents find out about you I'll be in trouble for *that*, too."

"Wait a minute. How old are you?"

"Eighteen," I said, sniffling again, figuring a lie now wouldn't hurt.

She clicked her tongue and lit another cigarette.

"So what'd you do," she said. "Get your little girl friend in trouble? I know you didn't rob a bank, not with that baby face."

I took out my awful, dirty used hankie and wiped my eyes. Then I told her everything—the ticket, the taillight, the silver dollars snatched from the chest-of-drawers, how I'd never get to use the car again. I spared telling her it was sure to get worse when my dad smelled her cigarette smoke on the upholstery.

She stared at the highway where the ribbon stream of traffic had slowed for the evening. "I need the john," she said. "Don't go anywhere."

I waited, as told, listening to the crickets beating their fearsome sound in the dry heat of the evening. I was convinced she wouldn't come back.

"Here's what you do," she said, when she returned, and she handed me six quarters. "Use the phone in there to call your mother. Tell her you're okay and you'll explain everything when you get there. You got that?"

I nodded and blew my nose.

"Tell her what time they can expect you," she said.

I nodded again.

"Say that you'll be careful and while you're at it," she said, "tell her you love her."

Mother answered on the first ring. While I poured out everything, a man in Bermuda shorts stood stretching beside his blue station wagon and the woman leaned out to say something to him. The man looked around and said something back to her. She got in his car and they pulled away.

I washed my face before getting behind the wheel to hit the interstate, which was filling with nighttime traffic crossing the continent. As I switched lanes, I came up behind the blue station wagon and spotted the orange glow of my friend's cigarette bobbing in the darkness as she chatted with the man in Bermuda shorts. I followed for a few miles until the Hebron exit where I eased off to the north while the blue station wagon rolled west and disappeared from my life forever.

Wadena!

BY STEVE MARAVETZ

1998

Here we present an insider's account of the notorious 1970 Wadena, Iowa, rock festival that roiled the waters of Lake Iowa for many years. Never had anything so weird, wild, anarchical, and BIG happened in this peaceful state. Memories of "Wadena" still were vivid in 1995 when a young promoter staged a 25-year "reunion" festival near the original site. County officials slapped a slough of rules, regulations, and restrictions on the reunion festival; most observers judged the "redo" event something of a well-intentioned but unsuccessful attempt to re-create an event from a wild era, long gone.

Cracking the Defenses

It was late July 1970. We were circling the perimeter looking for a crack in the defenses. The sun had just set and we could hear the choppers circling above us, their spotlights stabbing the canopy of trees. We dove headlong into the underbrush several times when the harsh white glare of 75,000-foot candles threatened to expose us.

We didn't talk much. Willie's shadow was on my right flank and I could barely see him gesture toward the light of a distant campfire. Then I saw what he was warning me of—a mounted sentinel circling the edge of the woods. A radio crackled. I knew he was talking with the pilot upstairs. I figured we were cooked.

We swung left, which I think was south. We moved slowly in the darkness. A downed tree blocked our path. I crept along its length. Suddenly my feet gave way and I was tumbling into a pit. Nothing was broken, but my elbows were scraped, my face had been clawed by branches, and I was filthy. Sweaty from fear and the humidity, I scrambled out and rolled onto the grass, eyes closed. When I opened them, Willie's face was inches above me. I was beaten.

"We have no clue where we are and no idea where we're going," I said. "Let's just give ourselves up."

"It's gotta be that way," he whispered, pointing to light coming through the trees. "We've gotta be close. Listen!"

I held my breath and listened. The warbling of Buffy St. Marie wafted through the thicket. But I knew her voice was being amplified by a three-story wall of speakers driven by a kabillion watts of power. The stage could be miles away. My arm was bleeding and the mosquitoes had descended to feast.

"Look, let's just find one of the security guys and offer him ten bucks. Shit, I just wanna clean up," I said.

"Okay," Willie agreed. "The next person we see, we give ourselves up."

He helped me to my feet and we edged toward the nearest campfire. Not wanting to risk any sudden movement, we eased out of the shadows and into the firelight. A man looked up. He was large, very large, bald with a gray ponytail. He wore a tie-dyed T-shirt, a fringed leather vest, and a beaded headband. He peered at us and waited for us to speak.

"We're just trying to get to the Wadena Rock Festival," I said. "We've been wandering in these woods for a couple of hours."

"Well, man," he said, taking a long pull on a joint and offering it to me as he exhaled a cloud of fragrant blue smoke. "You're in."

I was 17. Rock festivals were popping up everywhere. Woodstock had happened a year earlier, and it seemed there were a hundred attempts to re-create that event. For each one that succeeded there were dozens that died on the drawing board because of court fights, injunctions, local opposition, and most frequently, lack of capital. What became Wadena was originally planned for Galena, Illinois, but local authorities nipped that in the bud. The organizers, Sound Storm, Inc., shifted the site to northeast Iowa. The event became Galena at Wadena and finally, Wadena.

I went to Wadena to see naked women swim in the river and to smoke dope. Maybe sex. Two out of three ain't bad.

I hadn't planned to go until Greg Wilson, a buddy of mine, called me at work Friday afternoon and said we could ride with his older sister. He painted such visions of wet pink nymphets and ass-kicking pot that I could hardly refuse. I was at an age when my body throbbed with testosterone, and I'd heard about the looseness of those hippie chicks. So of course I said yes.

The traffic was horrendous. The festival was held in a pasture bordered by the Volga River about two miles outside the burg. Cars, vans, and buses lined the gravel roads for three or four miles in all directions. By Friday an estimated 10,000 people had arrived, even before a district judge lifted an injunction and allowed the festival to get underway.

Throughout the weekend, thousands of young people decked out in all manner of outrageous dress carrying coolers, backpacks, and sleeping bags streamed toward the site. Outside the entrance gate hung out a couple hundred forlorn-looking kids who were unable to scrounge up the $15 admission. An impromptu marketplace developed as they tried to peddle whatever they had for the entrance fee.

On Saturday, they reduced the admission price to whatever one could come up with. By Sunday, it was a free festival. Before it was over, estimates ranging from 8,000 to 40,000 were made. The most common number was between 25,000 and 30,000. How many were there really? Who knows? It was a bunch.

The Music

There was a lot of music at Wadena. A LOT. Music from Friday afternoon until dawn on Monday. Presented was an incredible hodge-podge of rock 'n' roll, blues, folk, rhythm and blues, and stuff that really couldn't be categorized.

Despite the fact that the music was ostensibly the reason for the festival, the media ignored any mention of the acts. If you read the newspaper accounts of the festival, there is almost no mention of any bands that appeared. My memory is fuzzy at best. I know Poco was there, along with Little Richard, Mason Proffit, Albert King, and Illinois Speed Press. I think a local hard rock band called Enoch Smoky was there but maybe I'm wrong. I never liked Enoch Smoky.

Only two acts really stick in my mind. The first was Buffy St. Marie, a Native American folksinger with the most annoying voice on the planet, with the possible exception of Tiny Tim. Her trademark sound was a caterwauling tremolo, a noise reminiscent of someone gargling stickpins. She was singing as we were sneaking in and continued for what seemed like hours, careening from song to song, each one addressing an ever-more-maudlin subject. I still despise her music.

The other was the Chambers Brothers, a black band that got its start in Mississippi as a gospel group, went on to record such soul and R&B numbers as Curtis Mayfield's "People Get Ready," and had transmogrified into a psychedelic rock band. They flat kicked ass.

After moving to Boston, the Chambers Brothers traded in their satin shirts and suede shoes for Nehru jackets, love beads, and granny glasses. Some might say they'd sold out to the commercial prospect of crossing over to the white youth audience, but racial lines in the music world were more blurred back then. Along with Jimi Hendrix, Sly and the Family Stone, and Richie Havens, the Chambers Brothers had become a black psychedelic act.

I remember four tunes vividly. The first, "Time Has Come Today," got some airplay on what were known then as underground radio stations (Clyde Clifford's program, *Bleecker Street*, on KAAY in Little Rock was one example) but the live version was unbelievable. Backed by a sixty-foot screen on which a light show direct from the Fillmore West was projected, the Brothers took the crowd on a 45-minute trip into the weird. The recorded version (still available on the band's reissued greatest hits CD) only hints at the flights of vocal and instrumental surrealism in their live performances. Anchored by the tick-tocking of a cowbell, the group screamed like banshees and laughed like ghouls during the lengthy instrumental. They carried me away to a place I'd never imagined. Like, I felt I was in Frisco, man.

At Wadena, they showed they could still boogie during a smoking version of the Otis Redding classic "I Can't Turn You Loose," replete with grunts and good God, y'alls! that would have made James Brown proud. And of course, they did "People Get Ready."

Their encore was "Love, Peace and Happiness," a title which wouldn't have a chance of being taken seriously today. But in 1970, all things seemed possible to a 17-year-old hippie wannabe. The song, which recalled their gospel roots, filled with sweet harmonies and soaring vocal solos. It, too, went on for what seemed like a dreamy hour. By the time their set was over, they had the crowd around their little fingers and had made me a lifelong fan.

Press Coverage or "The Death of One Thousand Quotation Marks"

The media had no clue how to cover Wadena. The majority of the people there had relatively short hair and relatively mainstream dress. But the hippies garnered the ink. Most of the reporters from the larger towns had seen small groups of Hawkeye hippies tossing frisbees or hanging out, but many of those who came to Wadena were far more exotic, far more hardcore, far more "out there" than their counterparts from Ames, Des Moines, Mason City, or even Iowa City.

And if the reporters were baffled by the kids, they were totally befuddled by the lifestyle, especially the drugs and the jargon. Proof of this is evidenced by the thousand, maybe hundred thousand quotation marks newspapers used to inform their naive and credulous readers about what the "hippies" (or "heads" or "freaks") were up to.

The "freaks" went into the "shopping area" to buy a "hit" or "tab" of their favorite "acid" or a "lid" or "joint" of "pot." If you were "into" "speed" you might score a "cap" you could "snort." Some of them, having been "ripped-off" by "pushers," "bummed out" and had to be taken to the "trip tent" where they "came down" or "crashed" from their "bad trips." Others, having a more "groovy trip," went on to do their own "thing," which was "cool" and everyone could "dig it."

Overall, it was hard for the average Iowan, a "straight," to understand. It just wasn't their "bag."

Some of the problem was that the reporters couldn't sort out the truth from the bullshit. And there was lots of bullshit. When reporters talked to festival goers, the attendees loved nothing more than to jerk the chains of the scribes, whom they viewed as members of the establishment.

One newspaper account quoted a worker at the trip tent as saying at least 10 people had come in claiming to be God. Another claimed one youth was so hopped up it took eight men to hold him down and sedate him. There are NFL players who would kill for dope that good.

Some of it was just plain bad reporting. A wire service story claimed that area hospitals were being overrun by youths overdosed on various drugs. That turned out to be flat untrue. Another newspaper account said that "many of the youths appeared to be underfed and malnourished."

But even worse than the bewildered reporters were those who made themselves out to be hipsters. A *Cedar Rapids Gazette* reporter wrote, "One girl came up to this reporter just after I bought a sno-cone. She handed me her bottle of wine, tipped it to my mouth, then took a bite from my sno-cone. Then she left. No words were said. None were needed."

What the hell does that mean?

A Million Ways to Get High

The media coverage of Wadena was mighty prurient, with most of the stories focusing on the drugs and the nudity. There *were* a lot of drugs, just about every drug imaginable: marijuana (AKA grass, pot, boo, tea, weed, MJ, reefer, gage, Panama Red, Mary Jane), of course, along with hashish (blonde, brown, black, temple ball, red Lebanese, and opiated), 250 kinds of acid (windowpane, orange sunshine, blotter, Black Cadillacs, LSD-25, and Owsley, to name a few), mescaline, psilocybin, MDA, speed (snorted, swallowed, and shot), opium, angel dust, cocaine, heroin, and probably a dozen others. A postmortem by state officials claimed as much as $250,000 worth of drugs had changed hands. As with the attendance, pick a figure, any figure.

One thing for sure, there were ten thousand ways of ingesting that dope. During those three days at Wadena, I saw more ways of taking drugs than in all the years since. One of the simplest and most effective was the Big Top.

Someone—no one knew who—had gone to the trouble of dragging a 20' × 20' tarp to the festival site. From the time I arrived until the time I left, the unfolded tarp was home to a serious pot party. It didn't matter if you possessed any reefer. You simply crawled beneath the tarp and hung out until you copped your buzz. There were always a dozen joints being passed around and the tarp kept the smoke from escaping. To breathe was to get high. The Big Top was a constant source of entertainment for the onlookers. It was major fun to watch the glassy-eyed crawl from beneath the tarp and stagger off to seek their next amusement. I visited it often.

While selling drugs was a lucrative proposition, you didn't have to deal drugs to make money off the counter-culture. You could always sell paraphernalia.

This will probably make me sound like a curmudgeon, but I'm pretty sure the craftsmanship of paraphernalia was much higher back then.

Today you see so much junk on the market, like the roach clips made from cheap alligator clips with the tacky painted feathers that the carnies give for prizes at Solon Beef Days. It seems no one takes pride in their work anymore.

At Wadena it was different. There were artists in bone and brass, beads and leather. There were blankets on which the artists displayed their wares and on which they worked, carefully hewing and stitching and carving and stringing. It was a matter of pride to own a fine-carved bone pipe or an heirloom piece of leatherwork—probably a lot like the feelings an NRA member has for his $5,000 shotgun.

Like many novices to the drug culture, I was infatuated by the array of pipes. Hookahs that would make a pasha proud, water pipes, stash pipes (with a chamber that held a small amount of marijuana through which the smoke was drawn, thereby enhancing its potency), pipes made from metal tubes, lengths of garden hose, glass, plastic, antler, bone, corn cobs, clay, rosewood, soapstone, and just about every other substance in which a hole could be drilled.

As I was to learn at Wadena, no self-respecting hippie would be seen without a stash bag. Stash bags usually were made of leather or beaded fabric, designed to fit on the belt or over the shoulder with a strap. The stash bag held all the tools of the alternative life-style. In it were rolling papers, roach clips, small vials for cocaine and patchouli oil, hash pipe, matches, extra screens for the pipe, a single-edge razor for chopping drugs to a fine consistency, a small mirror for snorting ground or crushed drugs, a short piece of straw for the same purpose, and a cokespoon. (For years, the best cokespoons available outside of headshops were plastic coffee stirrers from McDonalds. When this became widely known, the company switched to wooden sticks for obvious PR reasons.) Sometimes the stash bag also would hold an aluminum gram scale for avoiding "rip-offs." And, of course, Marlboros. Always Marlboros. If the owner was really lucky, the bag might also hold some crumbs of marijuana or a couple of hits of acid.

Despite the counter-culture's stated ideal of a communal existence, everyone was not equal. There were a thousand ways in which the alpha freaks were identified—length of hair, number of patches on the bell-bottoms, the type of headband, number of Dead concerts attended, the physical attractiveness of the "old lady." It never hurt one to resemble

Jerry Garcia, or at least to look vaguely guruish. One way in which the experienced were separated from the amateurs was by rolling papers.

Zig Zags were easy to come by but aficionados preferred more exotic brands like Blanco y Negro or Bambu. Using flavored rolling papers, like chocolate or strawberry, branded one as the rankest of novices. I probably had strawberry/chocolate/banana papers when I went to Wadena. True "potheads" used ungummed papers. For the first 10 years of my drug use, I always looked for the papers with the heaviest gummed edge. Even after many tries, my friends still laughed at my "joints."

Down by the River

Since I'd arrived at Wadena after dark, I had to wait until the next day to check out the scene. I peeled my face from my sleeping bag at dawn and surveyed the landscape in daylight for the first time. It was a sea of lumps under blankets and curled up in sleeping bags. Some people just lay sprawled on the ground where they'd collapsed the night before.

Smoke from near-dead campfires drifted skyward in the humid morning air. Wine bottles, plastic garbage sacks, paper, and other detritus were scattered everywhere. Lines already were forming at the porta-potties. I got up and walked toward the fringe of the festival site. Somehow by unspoken agreement, paths had been kept free between the tents, blankets, and sleeping bags. There were a few main avenues into which fed smaller arterial paths. Just like a city.

A variety of flags rippled in the breeze. There were American flags, Canadian flags, Confederate flags, state flags, North Vietnamese flags, the ubiquitous peace flags, along with colorful handmade and homemade banners of all types. Each flag served as a landmark for people trying to return to their own space. Go toward the upside-down American flag, turn left at the blue bus, down the path until you get to the black-and-yellow checkered banner, then look off to your right for the rest of your group. There they were . . . between the orange pup tent and the striped lean-to.

One of the main reasons I had come to Wadena was to check out the naked chicks swimming in the Volga River. I asked someone how to get there and headed off on my vision quest.

I worked my way down the path toward the river. It was a muddy path, slick with the footprints of a couple thousand people. When I got to the river, which is really more like a creek, I was disappointed. Even at 9 a.m. the midsummer heat already was beginning to build and there were a dozen or so people trying to cool off or clean up. But no naked chicks.

By mid-morning, air traffic over the site was starting to get heavy. During the course of the festival, more planes flew over Wadena than had over London during the blitz. Curious private pilots and their passengers made the trip from everywhere within fuel tank range. It's a miracle there weren't any mid-air collisions what with all the pilots craning their necks to get a peek at the weirdos below.

I made numerous periodic trips to the river during the course of the morning. Each time the outcome was the same: no naked chicks. I stood in line for 45 minutes to pay two bucks (an outrageous sum at the time) for a paper container of chop suey. Another buck got me a warm little bottle of Ripple wine (the unofficial beverage of Wadena—you had your choice of red or white). My fast broken, I made my fifth trip of the morning down the muddy path. Eureka! Between the leafy branches of the cottonwoods, I saw . . . bare breasts! I quickened my pace and skidded to a stop on a sandbar. There were naked chicks at last! Not attractive ones, but bare-ass all the same! It was only a matter of time before the wet pink nymphets Willie had promised would arrive to bathe and preen themselves for me. I sat on the bank and fired up a reefer. This was what a rock festival was all about!

Then I caught some movement out of the corner of my eye. I turned and saw three men dressed in overalls. They were creeping behind a large bush at the water's edge. They hadn't seen me, so I scooted back until a tree hid me from their view.

They were obviously farmers, and it was equally obvious what they were up to. They were sneaking down to peep at the naked hippie women bathing in the Volga. I tracked their movements by the seed corn hats that floated above the top of the brush along the river. Then I saw something even more amazing. Following behind the men were three women in house dresses. Their wives had accompanied them on their gawking expedition. It wasn't the reefer that made this seem like a very weird situation.

What's even more extraordinary was that this was by no means an isolated incident. During the course of the festival, hundreds of people, many of them, shall we say, engaged in agribusiness (more than a few of them women), sneaked down to look at the bathers. You have to wonder what kind of process led to the decision to brave the hassles to get there.

"Jake, this is Dewey. The wife says she wants to go bowling. I'd kinda like ta check out them hippies over on the Schmitt place. What's that? That's what I told her. Hell, we can always go bowling. Pick ya' up at five!"

I can honestly say the Wadena Rock Festival is the only time in my life I felt like I was on display. It became a free event on Sunday and hundreds of tourists poured in to wonder at the levels to which the youth of America had sunk. The young people were the attraction, like monkeys in the zoo. It was not uncommon for a man in a banlon shirt and Sans-a-Belt slacks to walk up to a festival goer, whip out his camera, stick it right in your face, click the shutter, and head off to find the next side show.

Alas, the nubile nymphets never materialized. There were a few naked chicks but none in which I had any interest. If the youths of Wadena were emaciated, that certainly was not the case with the naked women. But throughout the festival, I'd head down to the river every hour or so to make sure I didn't miss anything.

Groovy Pigs and a Groovy Governor

If the media had no clue about how to cover Wadena, members of the law enforcement community were equally in the dark about how to police it. Wadena had a single cop, and during the festival he was, shall we say, overwhelmed trying to keep up with the traffic coming through town. The festival site was outside his jurisdiction. That problem fell into the lap of the Fayette County sheriff and the Iowa Highway Patrol. The uniformed cops stayed outside the gates for the most part, wisely choosing not to antagonize the crowd. Sound Storm had hired its own security force. They were the ones Willie and I had eluded when we sneaked in Friday night.

Inside the festival, a host of narcs circulated. State narcotics agents and their counterparts from the Bureau of Criminal Investigation wandered around, taking pictures but making no arrests. While some politicians and newspaper columnists fumed about lack of action by the cops in light of the flagrant drug use, it didn't take a genius to see the officers were pursuing the only sane course. The head of the highway patrol was asked if they intended to crack down on the drugs. He replied, "You have to wink your eye at a few things out here."

At one point, the Fayette County attorney admitted the drugs "were flowing like popcorn," adding, "anybody who wants to make a citizen's arrest is welcome to be our guest. However, anyone who goes into that compound and comes out alive would be lucky."

So the cops were reduced to standing by helplessly, their duties consisting mainly of doing what they could to assist with injuries and illness and trying their best to bring some semblance of order to the traffic situation. Their efforts did not go unnoticed.

"The pigs in Iowa are really groovy," said one of the stagehands.

Then the governor showed up. Robert D. Ray, a Republican, had been elected two years before. It was at some political risk that he came to Wadena, supposedly to check out the "situation." Apparently, he didn't think it likely the festival would threaten the future of the free world and told the attendees to "have a good time." A firestorm of outrage followed. Editorial writers and politicians from Ray's own party went ballistic at the thought that the governor himself would not only visit such a place, but would actually encourage drug use and promiscuity.

Ray Walton, at the time a candidate for Iowa attorney general, said, "Wadena witnessed the biggest sex orgy in the history of Iowa over the weekend." Virgil Borchert, a former Fayette mayor, called Ray's actions "political suicide." But perhaps the greatest lambasting of the governor came from *Waterloo Courier* columnist Bill Severin, well-known as a denizen of the far right.

Severin, who wrote the column "The Iron Duke," could never seem to bring himself to refer to the festival without using the words "orgy" or "drugfest." The Duke, who styled himself an astute political observer, wrote, "Governor Robert D. Ray's off-the-cuff comments at the Wadena Rock Festival may prove to be the political faux pas of the year."

He was close. Ray went on to serve 12 more years as governor and left office as the most popular state chief executive officer ever. Had he wanted, he'd probably still be governor today.

Aftermath

I left Wadena just after dawn on Monday. I had long since lost Willie. I'd run into a group from Waterloo and we'd partied together since Saturday afternoon. The music ran all night Sunday and into Monday morning. The dew still was heavy as I picked up my sopping wet sleeping bag and began the long trek to the car with the group, who had promised me a ride home. I was totally, absolutely, completely fried.

The crowd had thinned considerably by Sunday night. Still, hundreds of people, most of them looking at least as bad as I felt, streamed like refugees down the gravel road. Wadena was history, at least for me.

For our hosts from Sound Storm, there still was a great deal to be done. They would spend many of the next few months being chased by creditors and warrant servers. For all I know, they might still be in court. It's no wonder that anyone who ever produced a rock festival never did a second one.

If you didn't live through the time, it's hard to imagine the level of antagonism between generations. Letters poured into newspapers decrying the youth who had become so wanton as to give their lives over to sex and drugs. The *Waterloo Courier* ran this comment from a mail carrier:

"You just can't imagine the human race could sink that low. Get them all together out there just like they were in a concentration camp and let the government haul them to California in cattle cars and ship them to Viet Nam."

The Iron Duke, always the guardian of society's values, penned, "I hold that too much permissiveness in homes, the schools and the courts is largely responsible for the kind of conduct exhibited by many of the young people who participated in the Wadena orgy."

(Three weeks earlier, Severin had covered the Butler County beauty pageant, at which time he asked an 18-year-old contestant for her measurements. There you go.)

In the end, Wadena was the tiniest blip on the radar screen. No one got hurt, there was no violence, a few cattle lost some sleep, some farmers and their wives got an eyeful, some drugs were ingested, some music played, some cops got some overtime, the Viet Nam War continued. Within two years, rock festivals were pretty much a thing of the past.

It's hard—no, it's impossible—to imagine an event like that happening again, although the Lollapaloozas sort of try. Even if it did, I'd avoid it like the plague. Once you reach your 40s, you have little desire to live on the ground, eat bad chop suey, drink warm wine, listen to music played way too loud. And the only chick I'm interested in these days, naked or otherwise, is my wife. But I'm glad I went. I had fun. And that's the only reason any of us were there.

My Two Years in a Box

BY MELVIN CORSON
2000

I HAD BEEN STANDING around on that small-town northeast Iowa depot platform and at least thought I was getting in nobody's way. Curiosity always has been part of my makeup, along with a wonder at first visualizing exotic items of merchandise. When I first saw something new, my interest would be aroused, and I suppose I subjected the adults within range to a barrage of questions.

The depot platform was about the best place for this to happen, and frequently I was there at train time. Farm implements from Minneapolis and Moline. Food items from Battle Creek, Cedar Rapids, Dubuque, Timbuktu, Milwaukee, and a multitude of other places that a kid of seven years could wonder and ask questions about. Charlie the conductor was quite friendly and I'm sure told me about many of the places he had been. The others may have been just as friendly, but they had to unload the freight and didn't have time to bother with persistent and probably dumb questions from that nuisance kid.

Vinegar barrels had to be slid down a skid to the depot platform; crates of chickens, crates of eggs, and other items of produce had to be loaded. The brakeman usually was busy shuttling the larger shipments of coal, lumber, portland cement, empty butter tubs etc. in their freight cars to their proper place on the siding as these items took a day or so to unload.

Some incoming food items were shipped in containers which had to be returned to the shipper. Among these items were the large, wax-paper-lined bread boxes from bakeries in Dubuque and McGregor. These boxes, having been used over and over for years, were permeated with the smell of fresh bakery products. It was one of the pleasures of my childhood to lift one of those box lids ever so slightly (so as not to let all the vapors escape), insert my nose into the space, and savor that delicious aroma. The boxes were about 36" by 30" by 30", and I got the idea that if I were inside I could enjoy that fragrance much more completely.

Not thinking that the men, though however busy, had observed my action, I was totally unprepared for what happened. Someone, I'll never know who, closed the latch on the box and I was put into the baggage car as if the box were empty. The train was on the downriver run, back to the terminal at Turkey River Junction. The next town downstream was Garber, near the confluence of the Volga and Turkey Rivers. My grandfather and uncle lived on a farm about a mile out of town. The depot agent obviously had telegraphed ahead for them to come to the station to ransom me.

I am sure that my father must have been in on the plot, too, as they would not have dared do this to me without his knowledge. It may seem like a cruel thing to do to a seven-year-old, but things were different in those days. I'm sure that a stunt like that now would meet with all kinds of legal and media repercussions.

Not being aware of where the train went after leaving Littleport and feeling the swaying motion of the baggage car, I was terrified. The thoughts running through my mind were varied: would I end up pulling an oar on a slave ship or be sold as fresh pork to some cannibal tribe in Pango-Pango?

To pay for my ransom I had to sleep on a horsehide rug at Grandpa's, work snaring gophers for my uncle, and sit at the table for three meals every day to gobble that terribly good food that my Aunt Mary prepared in abundance. At the end of this incarceration I was returned to my parents in time to begin school that fall.

My title "two years" seems a big exaggeration, but the nine-mile train ride (about a half hour), to a kid who didn't know he would be unloaded at the next station, seemed interminable.

The Iowa Sky

BY MIKE KILEN

2003

I DROVE BACK to Iowa four years ago in a beat-up van that I didn't want but got in the divorce.

The sun was setting as I crossed the border, and I couldn't help feeling there was a beginning or an ending here somewhere on the horizon. I was alone.

The sun's glow painted the thin, high clouds pink and purple, splotched against light blue sky that grew darker to the east. The place felt like a huge colored dome, plopped over the top of my van. The world suddenly was bigger and yet familiar again.

I grew up in northwest Iowa where the wind blows across flat fields every day and you dream of doing nothing else but leaving. I married, had children, and worked several years to do just that: to leave.

When I moved the family to Nashville, I asked why the sky was hazy in summer and was told the city sits in a big hole over which sits the moist air. Hills and trees surround you, even on city streets.

People there write songs and stories about strange folks, simple neighbors, cheatin' partners, and the hills and hollers. But I never heard any songs about the sky.

In Iowa, I began to remember as I drove, we look to the sky and write about how in the world we can connect with each other, even know each other, on this vast, open landscape. We feel smaller here.

"Once you cross a land like that you own your face more," wrote William Stafford, a favorite poet that I remembered while I drove. I met Stafford in 1993. I looked into his welcoming blue eyes one day at Mount Mercy College in Cedar Rapids, where he was appearing for a reading to college students. It was not long before he died, and he told me a story about when he left Iowa for good.

He had just finished a stint at the Writers' Workshop in Iowa City back in the 60s and he was strapping the last of the family gear to the top of an old car.

"It was hard to leave our friends," he told me. It was especially hard for his little son, who had a special neighbor friend named Donna.

"As we pulled away our son asked, 'Will our sky be fastened onto Donna's sky?'"

Years later Stafford finished his book *Writing the Australian Crawl* with this line: "Our sky is still fastened onto the Iowa sky."

As I drove I wondered if this was my sky.

My soon-to-be former wife wanted to move back to Iowa. I did not. Surrounded by the Tennessee hills and trees, I felt new, awakened to a freshness and wonder and creativity. Under this canopy of trees, I felt an openness of spirit. But my children would live under this Iowa sky and so I had to follow. I wanted to follow.

So many asked me why I returned. I met a poet from Tennessee who now lives in Ames, and he told me he missed his landscape. Neal Bowers had written of the country he now lived in, the corn and soybeans swerving around country graveyards, and lamented: "Those of us not born into this feeling must / stop the car on country roads, / walk into tall fields among starched leaves, / lose direction, wait."

Because I was from here, I didn't have to wait. Coming back is actually easy; it's the staying that is hard. Covered by sky but whipped by winds, again I heard the whispers of dissent from the young. They are leaving Iowa. The governor was traveling on recruiting trips to other states begging people to return. The saga of dying small towns had been uncovered, repeated a million times, and finally accepted as inevitable.

They were seeing bland nothingness across this flat land. Perhaps the governor should have handed out brochures about the sky. It is our sea. The clouds are our dimension, like mountains in the distance. It is our history. Farmers pray to this sky at night, for sanity or rain. After the glaciers flattened this land, the farmers cleared the view to the horizon. Trees were chopped down and tall grasses mowed, leaving a vast horizontal.

Out in the open now, as one year passed to two, I felt a loneliness in rural Iowa. The openness that had given generations comfort had isolated many. While the sky is a welcome light blue in spring and brilliantly dark blue and warm in fall, the winter can be gunmetal gray.

After a while, when the traumas of your life fade and things become familiar to your skin again—love and promise and daily routine and minor disappointments—the sky becomes a white ceiling and you must figure out if you are content or bored.

"No country leads so softly to nowhere / as those slow shoulders that curtain the horizon," wrote Iowa poet James Hearst. Is that a comfortable nowhere?

Ask Iowa folk singer Greg Brown. He recently wrote a song called "Summer Evening": "But on a summer evenin' when the corn's head high, / And there's more lightnin' bugs than stars in the sky. / Ah, you get the feelin' things may be alright, / On a summer evenin' before the dark of night."

I have settled into my house long enough to know all the dirt is mine. I have washed the windows to look out to see what the sky is doing. I have sat in rain to watch my children play ball and found new love under stars. I have tried to resist the cliché that sunny is happy and gray days are depression, billowing pillow clouds are contentment, and a storm is anger. But you feel it. Nearly every movie shot in Iowa features the sky and the emotions it creates. Iowa becomes a cow-tossing danger zone in *Twister* and the rain falls with sadness at the closing of *Bridges of Madison County* and aging men feel the recognition of our smallness on the vast horizon in *The Straight Story*.

So I return to Stafford. He wrote a poem called "Sky": "I like you with nothing. Are you what I was? What I will be? / I look out there by the hour, so clear, so sure. I could smile, or frown—still nothing. . . ."

As I enter my fourth year back in Iowa, the sky was welcomed, ignored, and remembered again, like a lover's attentions. It doesn't always take a writer to remind you. I talked to a farmer recently who fell to his back next to his machinery in the field one day, a massive stroke leaving him still. All he could do was look up at the sky, wondering whether he would live or die. There was a quietness in the moment. He was but a dot below this blue dome. But in the horizontal, he was connected. Recovered now, less closed in his Iowa manner, he told me one thing that sounds so simple. "We need to stop and look up."

Driving across Iowa

BY ANNIE GRIESHOP

2003

I AM DRIVING across Iowa. My pup Orson is in the back of the truck, and we are heading west.

Back there, under the topper, Orson travels in his own little self-contained universe: bed, food, water, toys, and best of all, plenty of windows so he can watch for trucks and bridges. Orson has a special fervor for big trucks and bridge abutments, both of which cause him to spin in circles and yip. We will spend most of this trip watching, waiting, spinning, and barking joyously. Since he weighs 50 pounds, I am thankful that he is content to ride in back.

Orson spins in order to see things better. I turn at apparently random cross-roads for the same reason. I plan my journeys with at least a vague route in mind, but I seem to be constitutionally incapable of sticking to it. Give me a likely-looking road headed in the right direction and I'll turn the corner. On this particular trip, I need to go west about twice as much as south, and I'll get where I'm going.

I have a great aversion to freeways. Mostly they're just plain boring. Everybody drives too fast and too close, and I am easily hypnotized by the perpetual sameness of the environment—concrete and steel, concrete and fiberglass.

But I'm a very fast driver when turned loose on a county highway. I tell folks that I take the back roads because when I do see a deputy, he's already on his way somewhere else and doesn't have time to pull me over. That's just an alibi, however. I drive the back roads because they're interesting.

Driving a county highway is like walking up to somebody's back door rather than entering the front of the house. Having been raised in a small midwestern town, I am very uncomfortable about using front doors. I invariably head around back no matter whose house it is.

When you go in the back door, you see the kids' toys and the stuff on the porch: rows of work boots and the dirty towels waiting to go in the wash. You walk through the kitchen—or maybe you don't go any farther than the kitchen since that's where everything happens anyway. But when you go in the back door, you know you're home (even if it's not your home).

The back roads are like that, too. Driving on the county roads, I get to see where folks live and what they do. I have the time and opportunity to really look at where I am. We all wave in passing. There is a sense of being "at home," even when I'm not specifically sure where I am.

As long as I pay attention to the road numbers, I can wander pretty freely and still keep moving in the right direction at a pretty good clip. A–J are east-west roads, K–Z run north-south. The A-prefix roads are nearest Minnesota, while the Z roads are closest to the Mississippi River. I am traveling from the D–X region to the land of G–L.

I am driving across Iowa. It is early April, and I am headed from Hopkinton, a tiny town just uphill from the Maquoketa River, to Omaha, a much larger settlement on the far side of the Big Muddy. My journey is being shaped by water—old, long-gone water under my wheels, and newer water all around me. In the course of this trip, I will travel through the Wapsipinicon, Cedar, Iowa, Skunk, Des Moines, Raccoon, and Boyer River watersheds. All but the Boyer eventually end up in the Mississippi.

Water has shaped this land in so many ways: ancient shallow seas that left behind memorials of sandstone and limestone, glaciers that crushed and scraped their way south and, in their retreat, created the rivers that cut and tumbled what the seas and glaciers left behind. The slow seep of acidified ground water formed caves by eating away at the limestone, dissolving the tiny, crushed, and compacted shells that form so much of the bedrock in this state.

Rivers meander, cutting new channels, trading a load of sand for the precious topsoil they carry away, creating ponds and lush meadows in the oxbows they abandon. Water moves over, around, under, and through everything on and below the ground. Freezing and thawing, it pries loose whole bluffs of rock and sends them sliding into rivers. We are riding on land in motion, swept along by water—a process easier to understand than the theories of continental drift or plate tectonics.

Human intervention speeds up the process—blasting away hillsides to build roads, channeling the rivers to control flooding. I love driving through those rock-walled road cuts knowing that I am inside the old sea bed, zipping along over the bones and shells of the dead. Channeled rivers, however, look sad and defeated. They remind me of old zoos where animals were kept in artificial environments, endlessly pacing, waiting numbly for escape.

Because it is early April in Iowa, I have to expect the unexpected. First, a sleet storm as I cross the Cedar. Then the spring blizzard in the Iowa River valley, where the road is so slick that I have to back up and take a second run to get up a hill. And finally—after driving out from under the storms—the stupendous, breathtaking beauty of the cloud banks across the Boyer River valley, north of Denison, with a cyclone of large birds rising down the river.

They're too far away for me to tell whether they're eagles or early buzzards, but my guess is buzzards, given their location and number. I always feel sorry for buzzards in this weather when it's too cold and overcast to provide much thermal lift. They are so big that they need all the help they can get taking off. They are so ungainly on the launch and so lovely when soaring. As with many things related to death and disintegration, they look better from a distance.

Everything moves; everything changes. Beyond the human time-frame, nothing remains for long. It's hard not to wax philosophical in this environment. A friend once told me that it helps to be a minimalist to live on the prairies. I don't see anything minimal about this landscape, however. Slow, perhaps, but not insignificant.

I am driving across Iowa. It is early April, and I am headed to Omaha for a shape note singing. There I will be part of a group singing hymns in a way that went out of fashion in this area more than a century ago.

My thoughts circle around time, tradition, and environment. I have been thinking recently about the native prairies—about how this land really looked when nearly all of it was covered in tall grass. Now is a perfect time to try to envision that past. Because it is early spring, I can see the contours, the bare bones of the land in most places. But those bones are wrapped in fences and roads now, clotted with farms and small towns in various stages of growth or decline, the contours disrupted by human endeavor. I have trouble seeing the profile of the original prairies, imagining a horizon with nothing taller than trees.

Although I have wandered through several restored prairies in Iowa, I am quite sure I don't really have any true understanding of that vast sea of grass and what it meant to those who lived in it. What I have experienced was a small patch set aside amid the farmland, explored during one season or another. What the settlers entered, however, was a year-round immersion in an environment unlike anything they had known before.

It didn't take them long to destroy that environment, but what was it during the short time before they subdued it? What was it like to watch the prairie grow, to be buried slowly in tall grass? In the spring, you could see forever... see your neighbors' lives, watch them break the sod, hear them drive their teams as they made a small dent in the prairie. As the season progressed, however, the growth of the tall grass inexorably cut each off from the other, sequestering every homestead. The horizon shrank with the season. Loneliness was as real as the wind.

And so was beauty. In settlers' memoirs, I read descriptions of the prairie's beauty, of its wonders and their amazement at being set down in this land of plenty, their appreciation of its riches. They recognized all that, and yet they single-mindedly worked to bring it under human domination, thereby destroying it. Men wrote later about hearing the prairie cry, about watching it run red as with blood from the wild strawberries when their fathers plowed it under. They understood at least part of what they were losing, even as they worked so hard to ensure its destruction.

Because of their labor, I have the leisure to drive across the land and think idly about their lives and experiences. It is easy for me to criticize their decisions, their priorities, their methods—but it is impossible for me to truly understand who they were or the shapes of their lives. I can empathize with them from a distance, but I cannot experience the environment, interior or exterior, in which they lived. They were in the constant presence of loneliness and death, just as they were in a wash of beauty and bounty. Sometimes I wonder if they didn't need to destroy one or the other, simply to settle the paradox inside themselves.

I am going to Omaha to sing old hymns. The folks who tamed the wilderness sang many of the same hymns in the same way we do, but their experience was so different from ours that I have to wonder what the words meant to them. We will sing about death in many guises and from many perspectives, just as they sang about it and lived with it. And we will sing about hope and faith, about grace and salvation just as they did.

Our place and time are so far removed from theirs in many ways, and yet I feel as though we are holding hands across the years, as though their ghosts sit in the hollow square with us and sing along. All facing the center, we sit in four groups to make a square. Tenors and altos form opposite sides of the square; basses and trebles sit on the other two sides.

When we sing, we turn our faces toward each other and our backs on the world. We sing "this world is not my home." We sing "death shall soon disrobe us all of what we here possess." We sing "let this feeble body fail and let it fade or die; my soul shall leave this earthly vale and soar to worlds on high." Singing about death in this way, it is hard not to feel joyful about the prospect.

These are the songs, this is the theology of people who went off into the wilderness and carved out a new society from the raw materials they found there. They had slashed and burned the eastern woodlands into submission, and now they were going to beat the prairies as well. With hymns like these, how could they fail?

My people were not particularly adventuresome. They came from Ireland and Germany, got off the boat, settled in western Ohio, and never moved again. They chose America because the famine and wars they faced at home were worse than the unknowns across the sea. They came to a land that was crisscrossed by canals and railroads, the forests already cut and tamed. They finished the construction, built the good roads and houses and mills, put the final touches on civilization. They sang European hymns.

They would not have liked the hymns we sing. Strict Catholics, they would have been repelled by the fundamentalism of these hymns, the very idea of being washed in the blood. Their experience was of Latin chants, of towering brick churches like cornerposts in the countryside, of priests who controlled the community and acted as gatekeepers for God. These hymns, and the theology they represent, would have sounded like chaos to my ancestors. So I certainly am not "born-to" when it comes to this musical tradition or this theology, but I am surely "convinced"…at least as far as the singing goes.

Geological time is equally important to me. I love the vision of Iowa under warm, shallow seas populated by trilobites—of giant beaver and woolly mammoths slogging through the runoff from the retreating gla-ciers, hunted in the larch and spruce forests by the first humans who arrived on the scene. For many of the folks with whom I sing, my vision of that is impossible, because their biblical world is not that old. Happily we gather to sing, not to debate dogma, and I know that they love me despite our differences.

I move through an exterior environment of highways, rivers, land, and time, carrying with me an interior environment shaped by time and family, by tradition and personal experience. Orson spins his way across the landscape, probably less dizzy than I am, as I contemplate time and place, seeing their interplay at every potential turn. The land and I have been shaped by time, by the seasons, by the beliefs and choices of others.

I am driving across Iowa, and it will be good to get home.

Lucy's Scarf

BY BETTY MOFFETT
2003

I T'S LATE AT NIGHT in late December, and the plane from Heathrow is overdue.

That's the scenario I made up. The reality was much less glamorous. It was about 9:30 p.m. (pretty late for me). My husband and I, retired teachers who have taken up small-scale farming, were waiting to meet his sister Lucy; the airport was in Des Moines and the plane was right on time. Any glamour would have to be provided by Lucy, formerly a New Yorker, now an expatriate living in England just outside of Cambridge where her late husband was a venerated teacher of literature at the university. Lucy accompanies bel canto singers on the piano, volunteers at the elegant Fitzwilliam Museum, and holds soirees in her back garden. She visits us twice a year, and I dread every visit.

Again, reality is less dramatic. Lucy and I are friends. When she visits the Midwest, I look forward to long walks and talks with this perfectly nice woman. But every time we pick her up in the Des Moines International Airport, she commits the same sin: she makes me feel dowdy.

This time, however, I thought I was well prepared. Before leaving our farmhouse in the dead center of Iowa, I'd put on my newest polar tech pants and my beaver earmuffs. I had changed the boots I use for barn work. I had fluffed up my down jacket and refreshed my ChapStick. As an accessory, I had brought a thick biography of Iris Murdoch instead of the mystery I was really reading.

Then Lucy appeared, smiling, in a soft black sweater and trousers (not pants) and a taupe (not tan) coat. Her hair curled softly and obediently;

eight hours on the plane had not flattened a tendril. Her black pumps had just the right amount of shine, just the right amount of heel. I hugged her; she was delicately fragrant.

Her presence transformed me. Moments before, I'd felt pretty good. I'd been surrounded by pleasant, practical people dressed intelligently in lined jeans and long, thick scarves, and I had blended comfortably into the environment. Lucy's appearance changed us all—me especially—into country mice. I resented the transformation.

Since everything I wanted to say began with "Damn it, Lucy," instead I said, "What a beautiful scarf." It was an inane statement but a true one, and better than the alternatives. Indeed Lucy, like so many of us, was wearing a piece of fabric around her throat, but it was draped, not wrapped, and it was a William Morris print silk, not navy wool or fleece. The blues, greens, and creams of it rippled as she walked. Ridiculously, I decided that scarf made the difference between Lucy's appearance and mine, between Lucy's LIFE and mine, and I told her again how much I admired it

"I like it, too," she said. "It was a gift from my friend Patricia—you remember, the publisher who has the little place in Ireland. She's so generous, sometimes it's embarrassing." I did remember meeting Lucy's rather famous and flamboyant friend; the memory did not improve my mood.

We loaded Lucy's slender bags in the car, and I insisted on riding in the back seat. I wanted to deal with my petty thoughts and to give brother and sister a chance to talk. Typically, Lucy asked about our news: did we miss our long association with the small, intense college where we'd taught for decades? Was our little string band still performing in the coffee shop? And then they settled in to discuss Dad. Though Sandy and I certainly are one reason for Lucy's trips to the Midwest, she visits most of all to see their 97-year-old father, who lives gracefully in a retirement home near us. An hour on Interstate 80 through Iowa's dark winter fields brought us to the guest room Lucy always occupies. We walked together to Dad's apartment where we left the two to a happy reunion.

I spent part of the next morning wrestling with envy and covetousness, sins much more deadly than any Lucy had committed. By the time I called her at noon, I'd had what seemed like a little victory. Lucy's visits, I reasoned, were just infrequent enough to let me forget how different, how foreign she seemed to me. Not foreign in the sense of English; I knew people in England who could pass, though unwillingly, for midwesterners. This was not true of Lucy: each time she arrived, she seemed to have come from a land where perfection was possible, where no one watched sports on TV or read bad novels or ate candy bars, to name a few of my minor transgressions. This impression always lessened in the days she spent with us, but it did not disappear.

My insulated mittens seemed bulky, so I put on my leather gloves for the quick drive from our farm to Dad's place. Tapping on the door, I walked in to find father and daughter lingering over a late breakfast. Dad was handsome as always in a soft blue shirt and a tie. Lucy was as close as she can get to dishabille. In her dressing gown (not a bathrobe) and without makeup, she looked a little tired. But still . . . arranged, collected, composed. I decided she was incapable of sloppiness, that she simply could not wear the knits and Nikes I relied on. Nevertheless, we had a pleasant visit. Dad lovingly pointed out the parallels between Lucy's life and mine: college connections, music, and even volunteer work since I'd recently joined the board of our local museum. I was certain my gentle father-in-law was unaware of the irony in the comparisons, starting with Cambridge University and tiny Grinnell College.

Lucy, as always, had come bearing gifts. Mine was a package of beautiful note cards from the Fitzwilliam. Months ago I'd mentioned how much I admired hers, and she never forgets such a hint. Then she and Dad proudly revealed their projects for the three weeks of Lucy's stay: they were going to read aloud all of James's *Portrait of a Lady*. When Dad left the room, Lucy told me that Dad already was concerned about poor Isabelle Archer, beguiled by a way of life that didn't exist. Always tender toward her father, she hoped he wouldn't worry too much about Isabelle's illusions. I left for a tennis game, hoping my long-time opponent would feel tender toward me.

The few weeks of Lucy's visit passed quickly. The four of us had congenial gatherings—take-out Chinese at Dad's apartment, a leisurely afternoon at our farmhouse where we sang old hymns and took Dad to see our small herd of longhorns. Lucy and I mapped out a two-mile route through what she called the pretty part of town, and we walked together as often as she could bear to leave her father. On our first outing, she asked about our two grandchildren, and said SOMEDAY she hoped to have some. Her son, who still lives in Manhattan, has had liaisons with several gorgeous women, none of them permanent. I told her we were going to keep the children while their parents spent a night out to celebrate their anniversary. She told me she was taking her son to Paris on the Eurostar for his birthday. I wondered again about irony.

On another walk, when I asked her about the latest soiree, she laughed and said, "Isn't that funny? We use that word as a joke. We just do some readings—Shakespeare or a poem someone's working on—and I play and Eleanor sings Verdi or Puccini." And later she volunteered that Patricia's place in Ireland was "just a small house really, nothing like an estate."

Somehow this genteel modesty and self-effacement only made Lucy's world seem more attractive. At home that night, I had to remind myself of some important truths: I have an excellent husband, some very good friends, two good dogs, a few good acres of land, and a pretty good horse. My grandchildren live nearby. I would trade my good and steady life with no one.

Besides, I'd be uncomfortable in Lucy's world of music and travel and poetry. I'd be conspicuous, awkward, a hayseed.

One day I suggested varying our usual route: we'd go to our place and take Hyde and Sheik, our two big Labs, through the paths Sandy has made in the prairie we're restoring. Lucy was game, and did her best to dress for a slog through the concoction of mud and snow that is Iowa's winter specialty. But her best was way too good—thin leather boots and the taupe coat she'd arrived in. I insisted on outfitting her, and soon she was bundled in insulation and Gore-Tex—and she looked absurd. We both laughed while Lucy slipped out of her clumsy cocoon and back into her own attire. When we finished our trek, she was cold and Hyde had left a muddy swoosh on the front of her coat, but she was still, and definitely, Lucy. Then she said something that startled me: "I envy you for knowing where your home is. I'm not sure how long I'll stay in Cambridge. Maybe I'll move back to New York. Maybe," she said, smiling, "I'll come here to retire."

In the last week of Lucy's stay, the two of us were invited to lunch by my friend Wendy. A lawyer by profession and a musician by avocation, Wendy had attended a singing class in Cambridge the previous summer. At my suggestion, she had called Lucy and they'd gone together to

Evensong at King's Chapel. We three arranged to meet at our little town's one good restaurant, and I looked forward to the event.

I finished cleaning horse stalls and dog pens in plenty of time to shower and dress. Though it was cold and I was tempted to don my usual layers, I decided to aim for a sleeker look. I could hear my mother saying, "One good piece can make an outfit," so I pinned her gold reciter's medal to my dark red sweater. Looking in the mirror, I could again hear my mother's voice: "You look very nice."

Lucy arrived at the restaurant a few minutes after Wendy and I did. We exchanged cordial greetings, decided it was an occasion and ordered wine, then began the easy, pleasant talk of women who like each other. It was chilly in the restaurant and Lucy kept on her coat; I could still see the shadow of her brush with Hyde. Wendy and Lucy talked about a chamber ensemble they both admired and the acoustics in King's Chapel. When they asked me about our band's next performance, I was amused, not irritated, by the contrast. We all laughed at the possibility of including Hank Williams and Vaughan Williams in the same program.

Just before our salads arrived, Lucy slipped off her coat. She was wearing the William Morris scarf. It still looked nice. She looked lovely.

We lingered over salmon; we had another glass of wine. I felt like a character in a one-act play, a supporting character. Finally Wendy said, "I hate to break up this party, but I have to get back to the real world of work." Lucy excused herself—to pick up the check, I knew—and Wendy asked, "What does she think of us here? We must seem like a bunch of clods to her."

"Oh no," I said, and had no idea if that was true.

The museum board was meeting on the morning Lucy had to catch her plane back to England, so she and Sandy made the trip to Des Moines alone. I was glad not to witness the brave, sad parting between Lucy and her father. And I was sorry that her visit was over. Sandy had described her as an "easy keeper," and we'd laughed at the implied comparison between Lucy and livestock.

At supper that night, Sandy reported that Lucy had cried only a little when she left and that she planned to return in the spring.

"And she sent you this," he said, handing me a small plastic bag with "Caviar House" printed on it.

I opened it and the scarf poured out on the table.

"I am really embarrassed," I said. "I practically begged your sister for this scarf." And, terrified that a fold would dip in the chili, I put it quickly back into its bag.

The next day I got it out, intending to wear it. Then I reviewed my agenda: put up flyers downtown for the weaving demonstration at the museum; attend the class I was auditing at the college where the dress code is jeans and flannel; and play another fierce game of tennis. The scarf didn't fit the schedule. It didn't fit ME—as Lucy's life didn't fit me—or mine hers. I thought of sending it back to her, but decided I would keep Lucy's generous gift as a talisman against envy. And because it was beautiful.

Houses on the Hills

BY LARRY STONE

2004

T HERE GOES the neighborhood.

When I saw yet another new driveway being bulldozed along the ridge road, with the prospect of yet another house and yet another security light to come, I couldn't help but resent the intrusion. After all, I'd come to northeast Iowa for solitude. Who did those intruders think they were? How dare they enter my hideaway?

All over the Driftless Area—northeastern Iowa, northwestern Illinois, southwestern Wisconsin, southeastern Minnesota—the trend is accelerating. People have discovered the wonders of this paradise and many want to move here to live, or to buy their own piece of this unique landscape. Whether they're retirees escaping from urban centers, families trying to get back to their rural roots, or back-to-the-landers hoping to live more sustainably, people like the "rural charm" of this scenic corner of the Upper Midwest.

There's a catch, however.

"You can only sell rural charm once," mused a friend.

In other words, by moving into the country and building houses overlooking the scenic hills and valleys, we're in danger of spoiling what we came to find. The rolling, unspoiled vistas are becoming dotted with homes and metal storage sheds. Cell phone towers sprout from ridges—in part to give us urban escapees umbilical cords to keep us in touch with the metropolises from which we're fleeing.

Admittedly I'm a bit of an expert on the subject. After all, my wife and I also came to northeast Iowa, lured by the scenery, solitude, wildness, and wildlife. We moved from Des Moines in 1974, settled for several years in the picturesque community of St. Olaf, then finally built our dream home on an old farm along the Turkey River.

So I tried to rationalize: *I'm* not really an intruder because I've lived here 30 years, and I didn't bulldoze any trees to build my house. I seeded down the cornfields that were too steep to farm. *My* house and restored-prairie yard actually *improved* the land. But these johnny-come-latelys surely don't have all those high ideals in mind; they just want to horn in on my space.

Or so my logic goes.

But I wonder what *my* neighbors thought a couple of decades ago, when *I* was the one horning in on *their* space?

So let's take another approach. My house in the country is O.K. because it sits on 100 acres of land near some 70-year-old farm buildings. It's not like I destroyed a natural area to build a ticky-tacky housing development. . . .

But what about the small farmer who used to grow corn and hay on my hills? Didn't I displace him by taking the land out of crop production? Or consider the local deer hunters and mushroom pickers who once roamed the land at will. Now I insist that first they must come and ask my permission. I've taken away a bit of their freedom.

The people who once dumped their trash alongside the road through my woods probably resent my arrival, too. Now they must haul their garbage to the dumpster at the county seat—and hope they arrive during the scheduled drop-off hours. Ah, the hassles of civilization.

Sightseers notice a difference, too. Instead of the deserted road with overhanging trees and few signs of humans, they encounter my mailbox and driveway and house. A ride in the country isn't quite the wilderness adventure they once experienced. (If they get stuck in the snow or mud, however, they now have the convenience of my phone to call for help, or my tractor to pull them out!)

What about the wildlife? Well, we may have had less impact on the critters than on people. Deer literally sleep in our yard, eat from our garden, drink from our bird bath, dally in our driveway. Turkeys and pheasants sometimes strut within yards of the house. Rabbits and chipmunks nibble the flowers. Coyotes howl so near that they may wake us at night. After dark, our trees may reverberate with the calls of tree frogs and whip-poor-wills and katydids. Bald eagles roost on our bluff in the winter. Turkey vultures sun themselves on the barn roof. Raccoons raid the bird feeders.

Perhaps we've corrupted those animals. Deer didn't evolve to eat green beans, zucchini, and tulips. Raccoons are supposed to eat berries and crawdads—not black oil sunflower seeds. What did turkey vultures do before the era of road kill for lunch and a barn roof for early morning sunbathing?

But let's face it: our rural landscape is changing. Or more precisely, we are altering the face of the Driftless Area, and of other parts of Iowa and nearby states. Dozens—hundreds, thousands—of other people are building houses in the country, planting trees, seeding prairie. Instead of a farmhouse with a few outbuildings and small crop fields, you're likely to see an acreage with a newly built log home, a patch of prairie flowers, and a pasture for several saddle horses.

The transition has meant a business boom for Myra Voss, a real estate agent in Elkader, Iowa. She regularly sells property—often for more than $2,000 per acre—that she and other agents once dismissed as "billy goat land." When she started in the real estate business in 1990, the same land might have sold for $500 or less. People nowadays are buying rough land for recreation, solitude, scenery, or homesites, Voss said. Some just want land with trees.

Crop land prices have increased, but not nearly as rapidly, according to Voss. She explained that agricultural buyers must prove to their bankers that the land will "cash flow," or earn enough income to pay off the mortgage. But the new breed of recreational land customers don't hope for profit—only enjoyment. And they frequently pay cash.

Some buyers are nostalgic retirees who moved away from their rural homes for careers in urban centers, but now feel the urge to return to their roots. Others are hunters or fishermen who live and work in bigger cities, but want to buy weekend retreats to assure that they'll have access to land and water to enjoy their sports.

Sometimes young families are seeking what they hope will be a quieter, safer life in a rural community with good schools and friendly neighbors, Voss said. And with access to the internet, it's becoming easier to work from home—wherever that home may be.

Typically people looking for land are Iowans and have at least some rural background, Voss observed. It would be unusual to have a big city customer who decided suddenly to move to the boondocks.

It remains to be seen whether buyers of recreational land will keep the property as long as previous owners, Voss noted, since many Clayton County farms have been in the same family for decades. People who buy weekend homes or recreational acreages may use the property only until they develop other interests, she said.

Mary Bahlke, a realtor associate with McCoy Real Estate in Galena, Ill., attributed at least part of the demand for rural land to the events of September 11, 2001. "People want to get out of the cities," she explained.

Acreages or recreational property sell quickly, Bahlke remarked. She cited a 25-acre tract with a Victorian farmhouse that brought $375,000 after only eight days on the market. A 140-acre hill farm, with distant views of three states and the Mississippi River, sold for $3,800 per acre. Occasionally farms are subdivided into homesites, with one- to four-acre lots selling for $18,000 to $50,000. People are ready to pay handsomely to live in a rural setting.

For many customers who lived in suburbs, the hills of the Driftless Area are "a whole nother world," Bahlke said.

Bahlke thinks low interest rates have added to the appeal of owning land. Buyers age 38 to 50 have decided to purchase retirement property now, rather than wait. They're looking for river views, proximity to golf courses, or places to ride their dirt bikes. In some cases, young families are seeking land to enjoy for camping or hiking with their children, with dreams of eventually building a home for their retirement years.

Most buyers are from Illinois—both from the Chicago area and southern parts of the state, Bahlke said. A few come from Iowa and Wisconsin, and some Californians have come to the Midwest to escape the fear of earthquakes, she adds with a laugh.

* * *

Smugly I realize that others are catching on to what I've known all along. But I still wonder whether I *want* to share the secret of the Driftless Area.

In one way, I welcome the "back-to-nature" interest. Doesn't it prove that people really are getting reacquainted with the land? That they're more concerned about the environment? Shouldn't we be able to recruit these folks in the battle to protect the earth from would-be despoilers?

Well, not necessarily. By choosing to live in a rural area, we've by default made the decision that we'll drive our polluting vehicles more. We consume more petroleum, spend more money on gasoline, contribute to global climate change, fan the flames of instability in the Mideast, and increase pressure to search for oil in the Arctic and on other fragile lands.

Our houses in the country may require more utility lines, improved roads, school bus stops, mail delivery, fire protection, and other services. We're probably costing other taxpayers more than if we lived in a house in town.

Our country lifestyles also may cost us more. In addition to the essential automobile and fuel, we've got to maintain our own wells and septic systems, erect satellite dishes to receive our favorite news, sports, and reality TV programs, and pay extra for the internet hook-up that allows us to surf the World Wide Web.

But there's another side of rural development that's beginning to catch the attention of economists. An Iowa State University study noted the potential for recreation to boost the economy of rural areas. For example, housing developments near lakes lure people who have money to spend. In a region that's struggling financially, a few new houses costing $200–$300,000 can be a significant boost to the tax base.

Could rural development turn out to be the salvation for counties that have been struggling economically? With the decline in the number of family farms, shrinking enrollments in many school districts, and the loss of small businesses in rural communities, most counties welcome people who are willing to build homes or other structures that will increase the property tax base.

In Clayton County officials sought money from a Vision Iowa grant to help build a golf course, resort hotel, water park, housing development, and trail near McGregor. But the project bogged down after a series of questions about the legal problems of the developer, environmental impacts of the project, and the procedures followed by county officials in approving the plan. The Vision Iowa board finally withdrew its support—but county supervisors still hope the development can move ahead with private funding. Local opponents have vowed to continue their fight, however.

So for whom should we root in this dispute? County supervisors insist that we should protect family farms and farmland—yet they welcome developers who are likely to crowd out the farmers who've worked the land for decades.

County economic development officials tout our beauty, solitude, and natural resources for attracting new business and residents. Ironically, if their sales pitch is successful, that "rural charm" could disappear with an influx of people all wanting to "get away from it all," to live again as pioneers, to experience their own bit of wildness.

Half a century ago, writing in *A Sand County Almanac*, Iowa native Aldo Leopold recognized the folly of that quest.

"Man always kills the thing he loves, and so we the pioneers have killed our wilderness," Leopold mused. "Be that as it may, I am glad that I shall never be young without wild country to be young in. Of what avail are forty freedoms without a blank spot on the map?"

Is This Heaven?
Then It's Not Iowa

BY VERL LEKWA

2005

IOWA LOOKS like hell. And in deep summer, it feels like it, too. I know what Iowa looks like because I'm an expert. (Expert: anyone 25 miles from home.) I've seen every nook and cranny, and I don't even know what a cranny is. But I've seen it. Because I've been in every one of Iowa's cities and towns.

In 2003 when I completed visiting and rating every town on the official Iowa DOT map, my mind went back over 50 years to the first time I went beyond a state bordering Iowa. I loved history and platted a trip that took my family to Kentucky, Tennessee, and Arkansas. (Abe Lincoln, Andrew Jackson, and Nashville's Parthenon were the major magnets.)

We saw poverty, big time. Broken-down houses, rusty cars in yards, unpainted sheds, weeds right up to the porch (which often had an old washing machine in a prominent place). A real eye opener for a boy from a small, generally neat Iowa town. But when I took a critical look at Iowa a half-century later, I saw way too much of that same disorderliness and ugliness. The South had moved north.

From childhood my interest was history, and I carried that from a small-town eastern Iowa upbringing to the University of Iowa and into 34 years of teaching, mainly in high schools. The military took me to post-war Korea; to visit relatives I have been to Scandinavia twice. I also have lived on the west and east coasts and in the Rocky Mountains. So to view Iowa cities I had the advantage of having lived in various places in this nation and abroad, with the added benefit of viewing differing urban areas.

My trips started innocently enough one October day on my way home from visiting a cousin. I often travel county roads and with each small town I visited, I remarked at the beauty of the season and considered how much of Iowa I hadn't seen. Maybe I should keep a map and cross out each town as I visit it, I thought. And a later thought: why not try to visit them all? And yet later, why not try to rate them for attractiveness. So when I pulled into my driveway, I had a plan. A man, a plan, Iowa (not Panama).

Why would anyone want to view all the cities of Iowa? I am prepared for the question because my wife has asked the same thing. The answer is, of course, that I don't know. I do know that my mind seems to like organizing and classifying (insecurity?). And I know that viewing one's state up close seems no more foolish to me than viewing gardens, art works, ball games. And a whole lot less foolish than watching television. I was now retired, I loved Iowa, I had a few dollars to waste (not being a drinker, smoker, or gambler), the open road beckoned, and I took off.

From that trip in 1998 until 2003 I visited towns, generally while on the way to something else. When all of eastern and most of southern Iowa was done, I began a series of three-day trips with tight schedules, outlining which roads to take and where to stay the night. Thirty to thirty-five towns a day and eventually all 1,181 towns have been visited.

In each city I looked at the topography before entering the town, looked at the entryway, visited all downtowns, swung out through residential areas and looked down side streets, viewed parks and water bodies, noted the effects on the city of industrial areas, and then came up with two scores: one for all natural features (topography, lakes, rivers, trees) and one for man-made things (businesses, houses, streets, layout of the city, parks, etc.). Using a complicated mathematical formula hidden away in the bowels of my desk (to keep it from those who might use it without paying a fee), I came up with a single number for each day. Scientific? Not in the least. But I challenge anyone to come up with a truly scientific measure for attractiveness, and to make such an assessment as mine without a huge cost. Tell me what makes an attractive woman and I'll tell you what makes an attractive city.

After putting these numbers in my computer I began to categorize. The cities I thought were most attractive I cut off at a low score of 250. The highest scores were just over 300. This included 98 cities. Those above average were next, a total of 141; those average were 360 in number; those below average 267 (scores here were from 180 down to 155), and those which were at the bottom were 150 or lower and numbered 314. So my calculations showed over 26 percent of Iowa towns (or in many cases unincorporated areas which were on the map) were really visually offensive.

My ideal town?

Well, the ideal has some gently rolling hills and a flat section. A river meanders along one edge, with much public access, and a lake has many uses. Exposed limestone cliffs are a plus. There is a dam with water trickling over it and a bridge designed with beauty in mind. You never cross the river without your heart being lifted.

The entryways are substantial and welcoming. The town is laid out with order short of boredom. A grid pattern is interrupted by an angling or curving street. There are some small green areas here and there in the street patterns, as well as substantial parks. Trees of a variety of species abound.

Houses must by economic rules vary in size, age, and quality, but all are maintained. Shrubs are plentiful and flowers are common and are found in the downtown area. The downtown has maintained buildings with appropriate signage, good sidewalks, and signs of community involvement. (Signs of community activities are a plus.) Streets are free of potholes and with curbs and gutters. Next to decent buildings, curbs are the single most important thing that aids in a community's attractiveness. Heavier industries in our ideal city show our muscles and need not be hidden. They can be tastefully painted, landscaped, signed, even if they are elevators or warehouses.

As for favorite cities, just a sampling. I like Orange City and other Dutch and German cities in the west, and Shenandoah in the southwest. Des Moines and Cedar Rapids are among my favorite large cities, and Clear Lake and some of those in the Okoboji area gain from their lake settings. And Decorah and Cresco in the northeast. And Pella, maybe the nicest of the lot but needing a bit of interesting topography. (Marry Pella and Decorah and watch the offspring.) Mount Vernon is nice, and Mount Pleasant. And those Catholic cities of Dubuque County! Approaching a small town on a hill with a huge spire, I'm hooked before entering the town.

I found that half of all my top-ranked cities were in six areas: the Iowa Great Lakes area, the predominantly Dutch area of the Sioux County region, the Des Moines–Ames and Cedar Rapids–Iowa City areas, the Amanas, and Dubuque County and the Mississippi River north and south of it from Lansing to Bellevue.

On almost all the miles I drove I was alone. (My wife was with me on some short trips, but after the first few towns her eyes glazed over and she didn't care what Scotch Grove looked like.) Being alone, I had time to think. What is Iowa really like?

It has more variety than most citizens realize. It's definitely not flat. I could imagine the Dakotas in the northwest corner and Kentucky in the southeast. That's a big difference. And there's a big difference in what is seen in large cities and small towns. Generally larger cities look better.

Towns under 3,000 too often look like the hell that I've mentioned. My theory is that officials in larger cities are less close to their people and can order cleanups without fear of losing friendships. In small towns there are those numerous links which make city officials hold back: we'd like to get Jim to clean up those junked cars, but our kids go to school together, we see each other in the store, we don't want him to get mad and move out. Better leave the problem alone.

Larger cities also have greater access to financial resources. They have greater clout applying for grants, they have more able and active financial institutions behind them, they have professionals working on their behalf. And more educated, more driven people tend to move where they find work, which is most often in larger cities. They often use that education and drive for the benefit of their communities.

Those in larger cities may also view their cities as needing to be progressive and attractive to survive. Those in smaller burgs know that all the mowing and painting are not going to bring a factory to town. The larger cities are living rooms, readied for company; the smallest ones are downstairs dens with beer cans under a chair and the sofa frayed.

My ratings were only for cities, but obviously I saw most of rural Iowa in traveling between those cities. The scene in rural Iowa is that after a war. The agricultural revolution—and it's been nothing short of that—has left us with tens of thousands of rotting buildings, overgrown yards and feeding areas, rusting machines and rotting fences.

I had time to think. Yes, and over and over again I thought, what can be done about this? So I jotted down this idea and that, plan A and B. Finally I had a 10-year plan which was sent to the governor. (He asked for it. He wanted ideas for shaping Iowa's future. His return letter thanked me.)

The plan was for rural areas and those cities under 5,000 or so. Above that number there are paid professionals who can tackle appearance problems. If Waterloo looks bad it's the city's own fault, in a sense. If nearby New Hartford has problems, it needs help in making a plan.

The state could be organized into areas with volunteer overseers, then similar county groups organized. Make it volunteer, inexpensive, fun. Get a slogan: "CLEAN: Cleaning the Land, Everybody a Neighbor."

The plan would call first for a survey of those things which should be saved. A windshield survey at the least would determine that an old bank had qualities that were unique, or that a barn should somehow be saved. This done in the first years, the plan would move on to cleaning up and razing the remainder that was obviously an eyesore. One year for wooden things in rural areas (the thousands of chicken coops now rotting away, the leaning wooden fence posts, the unused small sheds, the barns ready to topple). Fire departments could be called on for controlled burns. Clubs would be asked to help on properties where the owners were willing to join the cause, but needed extra muscle. The Lions' Club hauls to the landfill a shed and its junk; an Athletic Boosters Club tears out an unsightly wooden fence. All in the best tradition of Iowa friendliness and help.

After 10 years much of the junk has been removed and thousands of gallons of paint have been applied. Iowa looks better. We are prouder of our state. We have moved out of hell into purgatory, and are ready for another plan.

I love Iowa. My people have been here since 1862. I love four seasons and where can you experience them more than in Iowa? But we have been given a slice of heaven and we are not the stewards we should have been. In too many cases, in too many broken-down towns, in far too many corners of even larger cities, on farm after farm, we do not look like the heavenly place we should. Instead, we look like hell and we must do something about it.

Demolition
The Sixth Season in the City of Five

BY BETH CHACEY DeBOOM

2006

STELLA'S HOUSE HELD the magical aura of a museum, a repository of delicate treasures, collected over a lifetime by a woman who had an eye for the exquisite. At least that's how I remember it. I was a young child and distant memories are fallible that way. But I do remember clearly my mom and me visiting Stella Bachelder, by then an elderly belle, and tiptoeing through an echoing foyer, creaking up the broad set of wooden steps to the second floor, to be greeted at the door by Stella, a petite woman who wound her silver-blond braid around her head.

Stella's splendid apartment was to the left, one of four identical flats in the 4,876-square-foot apartment her contractor dad, John Cail, created for his family somewhere around 1912. A builder for the city's affluent, Cail lavished his craftsmanship on his own home: every apartment had a fireplace, front and rear entrances, built-ins, even laundry chutes. A stately yet unassuming example of Craftsman design, the "four-flat" was perched at the intersection of Fourth Avenue and Seventh Street in Cedar Rapids, its hallmark deep front porches spanning the building's front, upstairs and down.

I like to imagine that it was her dad's trade that instilled Stella's adoration of old buildings. Widowed just a few years into her marriage, she became the city's first female building contractor. Somewhere in those years she also became a preservation activist decades ahead of her time. Somewhere and somehow she crossed paths with another spirited activist, a young mother who wore her 1970s mini skirts to fight city hall's proposed highway that would slice through some of the city's most exquisite old homes, a woman who wrapped her waist-length Titian-colored hair in a bun on top of her head. Her name was Jackie Chacey—my mom.

The city had begun tearing down its historic treasures after urban renewal swept the nation in the 1960s. At some point, in protest, the defiant little Stella armed herself with the only weapon she had: a camera, loaded with black and white film. Stella asked my mom if she'd drive her around town to save, if nothing else, the image of each grand structure that was living on borrowed time. So the kindred spirits hit the streets, rolling from house to house in our family car, a slope-backed 1967 Buick Riviera.

Stella directed my mom to steer through her childhood's near-downtown neighborhood. Click. Click. Click. Then they worked outward to other progress-vulnerable historic streets. Not only did Stella immortalize the exteriors, she found a way to preserve the interiors. On the back of many photos, Stella scribbled notes, things she knew from visiting the houses, or from being the daughter of the man who built many of them. "Ballroom on third floor." "Elevator in this one." "The teacher of the Wright brothers lived here." When they were done, the photos were tucked into envelopes and stowed away.

I was too young to record any of this in my memory. But my mother spoke of it often as I was growing up, always when we would drive past a vacant lot that days before had held a gracious house, a sight that would cause my mom invariably to groan, "There goes another one," followed by, "Stella said that one had a . . ."

Stella had become past tense sometime in the early 80s. In her will she bequeathed those photos to my mom, who lovingly tucked them into our expensive living room end tables, a place of honor right alongside our family photo albums.

Then just 10 years later my mother was gone too, dying unexpectedly one night in my last few weeks of college.

With the rest of my world falling apart, I sent Stella's photos to the city's historic preservation department for safekeeping. Almost all of the houses were gone by then, I noted, shuffling through the piles of photos before handing them over to their new keeper. And so was Stella. And now, too, my mom.

But Stella's house remained.

I passed it often over the next decade.

It cheered me. I could not help but think of them both and me, their pigeon-toed tag-along little girl, as I passed the house on my way to the nearby main post office or downtown. More surrounding houses slowly disappeared, and I watched parking lots take their place and downtown workers park where once families made homes.

But still, still, Stella's house stood.

We were hemorrhaging houses nationwide. I always was drawn to the articles in *The New York Times* or *The Wall Street Journal* describing the demolition of our past. By 2002 the National Trust for Historic Preservation identified 100 communities in 20 states that were experiencing tear down in historic neighborhoods. By May 2006, that number had tripled to more than 300 communities in 33 states.

But, still, somehow, Stella's house seemed destined to survive; in fact, perpetually well kept. For a while I noticed it was an inner city oasis to a green-thumbed tenant who made an upper porch into a lush urban garden. I noticed the house daily now. I had become a downtown worker and parked my station wagon, with its two back-seat booster chairs and family clutter, in a lot right across the street, a lot that once held a church. Each morning I said hello to the house, to Stella, and to my mom.

Then one pristine sparkling spring morning, the house stared at me mournfully. Sheets of plywood had been nailed over Stella's front door.

Clouds converged on my day. And on countless days afterwards as I awaited the wrecking ball to swing. I was grieving. I had grieved enough to know the grip of melancholy. But can you grieve for a house, I wondered? What was I mourning, really? I was mourning the loss of yet another bridge to the past. Every year since my mother's death took me farther away from her. Literally, connecting, physical pieces of her were disappearing. This one was 4,876 square feet of loss.

I skipped anger and went directly to denial, or was it acceptance? Was holding on to the past keeping me from appreciating the present and looking to the future? Are preservationists just bleeding-heart idealists who are stuck in the past? Move on, I told myself. Be a big girl and just move on.

But I'll be damned if the ladies would let me. They were standing on my bridge to the past, waving me down. Long ago they had sown the seeds of activism and historic preservation in a little girl's mind. Now I was a woman: With a cause.

I did some digging. Mercy Medical Center, current owner of Stella's house, wanted that house and every other possible structure in the neighborhood in case they needed the land down the road, someday, for one of their sprawling, land-hogging medical buildings. Or for one of those sprawling buildings' parking lots. Coe College, a near downtown private college, was doing the same thing: Wholesale demolition of nearby houses and neighborhoods and community—just in case they, too, someday wanted to expand the tiny campus, say, eight blocks away.

"We cannot only look back, and we cannot only make new," says Paul Goldberger, a Pulitzer Prize–winning architecture critic for *The New Yorker*.

In my search for meaning, I came across Goldberger's words. I realized what a complex world historic preservation is, with emotions on one end and purely economic decisions on the other.

Mercy made its demolition decision strictly with an eye to someday making something new, old be damned. Penned in by McKinley Middle School and the main post office, the near-downtown hospital needed Stella's land for "potential northward growth." "We can't ever be shortsighted," Bob Olberding, director of plant operations, told me. "Unfortunately," he added, "sometimes you end up tearing down a really good one." I'd like to say this story has a happy ending. But like so many stories of its kind, business thumped the little guy.

Too late in the process to do anything to save it, home builder John Cail's handiwork came crashing down on a sunny and humid Friday. It did not crumble easily. I watched the cranes' claws grip and fight that afternoon, tugging hard to tear down what a craftsman had built to last forever.

I licked my wounds. I wrote a eulogy of sorts to the house for the *Cedar Rapids Gazette*. I'm an editorial writer there. Writing often is my therapy. From there I figured I'd move on.

But Stella's story prompted incensed e-mails and phone calls. Apparently I was not the only one who had cherished this iconic house. An e-mail arrived from a woman in California, who said her mother was Stella's cousin. The woman's daughter had sent the article to her. "I was, in a word, appalled. Again. . . . Unfortunately Cedar Rapids has a miserable track record of treasuring and saving memorable, worthy, and eminently historical buildings . . . I don't think Cedar Rapids has relinquished its crass Business First and Foremost attitude towards life."

Amen, sister. Our city, population 160,000 or so, is criticized widely as the least historically sensitive city in the state. Tear downs are frequent, with no protest and with no required public notice. In our struggling downtown, ornate exteriors long ago were covered with ugly steel facades, their interior ceilings dropped and capped with ugly panels. One of our more painful mistakes happened in the 60s and lives on in the community's collective, elephant-like memory. In the 1960s the city tore down its luxurious Union Station—to put a parking ramp in its place.

The result of all this short-sightedness (and I have to think it's related) is a city that is struggling to keep its young people here, that is losing its cultural offerings, that has a reputation as downright boring, stale, one of the least vibrant cities in our state.

With guilt-fueled retrospection and some temper that is the hallmark of the red hair I inherited from my mom, I began to investigate what could have been done, or what could be done in the future to protect other special places.

I discovered if Stella's house had been in nearby Iowa City, the public would have been given a 10-day notice to salvage, to document, and perhaps to persuade the owner to reconsider. In Cedar Rapids, historian Mark Hunter was pushing for a similar waiting period. Since then, we've urged the City Council to adopt this waiting period and the outlook is good for approval of it. But is it enough? No way. Not even close.

What needs to change is something more intellectual. Businesses like Mercy need to stop thinking only of clear cutting, and find a way to incorporate these still-useful structures that give our communities distinct personalities. They need to stop thoughtless destruction of neighborhoods and the communities these neighborhoods inspire. Please pause, and plan, and be part of the community instead of rolling over us with bulldozers and dollars.

What I want to ask is this: Does anyone here actually believe that the steel structures and parkades that grew skyward in Cedar Rapids during the urban renewal movement will inspire the next Grant Wood to immortalize them on canvas?

These older buildings not only remain useful, they give a sense of place. "There's just a connection with those types of structures that you just can't have with those modern strip malls and big box superstores," says Randy McVey, long-range planning coordinator for the city of Cedar Rapids. Without our distinct landmarks, "You might as well be in Hong Kong," he said.

Amen, brother.

Without our distinct landmarks we *will* be lost.

"Preservation is saving the landmarks so your children can find their way home," said Dr. Michael Kramme, executive director of the Iowa Historic Preservation Alliance, repeating a line he once heard at a conference. "It's kind of corny, I know," he added sheepishly.

But Kramme, without knowing it, put my loss in perspective. What are we if not shaped by the environment, the people, the passionate role models of our childhood? What a tragedy when the bridge between past and present is destroyed.

I live with such loss daily. My children will meet their grandmother through photos and via my stories. But they'll never know what it's like to be cuddled on her lap and embraced by her hearty laugh. Now they'll never meet the house that enchanted us both. I will introduce them instead to the gravel parking lot that sits in its place. And I will growl, more times than they will care to hear, "That's where Stella's house stood until the hospital tore it down."

In our city, I'm hopeful that lessons are being learned so that our mistakes aren't repeated. If the death of Stella's house is a turning point, what a price to be paid, but who better to inspire change than a woman who fought back with a camera and whose legacy thrives 30 years later.

Editor's note: The photo on p. 128 shows the regal Cedar Rapids Union Station being annihilated in 1961.

A Peaceful Jog in the Country

BY MICHAEL ROSMANN

2007

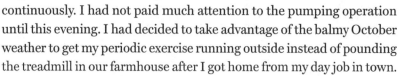

F OR SIX DAYS and nights the tractor powering the pump emptying my neighbor's cattle manure lagoon droned continuously. I had not paid much attention to the pumping operation until this evening. I had decided to take advantage of the balmy October weather to get my periodic exercise running outside instead of pounding the treadmill in our farmhouse after I got home from my day job in town.

As I was jogging in the harvested soybean field south of our farmstead, I noticed foul-smelling brownish water coursing through the ditch leading from the neighbor's field onto my land. "Water doesn't run here unless it is raining really hard . . . and it hasn't rained for ten days. What's going on?"

Numerous rivulets emanated from the bank of a terrace in the neighbor's field and gathered into a two-foot-wide stream as it entered the ditch onto my land. Realizing the liquid was probably toxic and passed through my land and eventually entered the Missouri River, I dashed home to enlist my wife's help. "Our neighbor is emptying his manure lagoon and it's running into the creek."

As my wife and I were completing our inspection of the neighbor's field next to his 4,500-head feedlot, he spotted our truck. Within five minutes the pumping operation stopped. A few minutes later he drove up to our house with one of his three children just as we arrived home.

"I'm sorry," our neighbor stammered. "This won't ever happen again. Please don't turn me in." I surmised he was referring to the Department of Natural Resources, which has responsibility for monitoring Iowa's water supply.

"I'm not saying I will turn you in but I'm also not saying I won't turn you in. That's your responsibility," I rejoined. "But you can't keep doing this. You're jeopardizing our health and your family's health." His daughter coughed.

His wife and their two other preschool-age youngsters joined us on the doorstep along with another neighbor, a woman we had phoned. Thirty minutes of terse discussion ended with a handshake and agreement that he would hold a neighborhood meeting after harvest was complete. No outsiders, just the people in the area affected directly by the dust, smell, truck traffic, and health concerns.

Our neighbor said, "I wish I had never built the feedlot, but now I have this huge investment."

"Let's see what the issues and options are before this goes any further," I commented. Everyone on the doorstep agreed with this strategy.

Four weeks passed. Cement trucks drove past our farmstead on a daily basis. Our neighbor was expanding his feedlot to accommodate 1,500 more cattle.

The meeting was never set, but no one has forgotten. More chapters of this story will follow. I am not signing my name on this report because I promised confidentiality, at least until after the meeting. One more thing . . . I took a sample of the liquid pouring through our land to a chemist. The ammonia concentration was approximately 130 mg/L and the orthophosphate concentration was approximately 6 mg/L. The pH of the water sample was 8.7. Both far exceed legal limits.

Author's note: The feedlot has expanded twice since this article was published in 2007. No community meetings happened. Excessive runoff continued regularly; I notified the Iowa Department of Natural Resources only twice, because the DNR said they couldn't do anything except forward reports to the feedlot owner. I reshaped my waterway and installed two 8-inch tile lines at my own expense to reduce runoff whenever the neighbor discharged wastewater. Currently, my neighbor pumps feedlot discharge onto additional farmland; runoff still occurs onto my land, but less often.

Rest in Peace

BY STEVE HANKEN

2007

T HE WIND CAN BE BRISK in summer or winter, but it's certainly much less appreciated on this January morning as I work the cold galvanized gate latch. Only rabbit tracks mark the way into this prairie remnant of scattered pine trees and weathered stone. These solitary trips to places seldom visited by strangers or friends have become a required stop for me as I tour the graveyards and burying grounds of Iowa. It may seem like morbid curiosity that drives me, but this isn't the case at all. I am looking for the bits of history, the telling tales of those who left little beyond their personalized stone markers or those of their loved ones. I can sense the loss felt so many years before when I see a tiny bed chiseled into the top of a little girl's stone, the covers turned down waiting for the child to return. To see the monument of a vacant tiny chair that continues to collect small children's toys and dolls more than 100 years after the child's passing tells me that modern children, too, find these places fascinating.

My wanderings lead me to concentrate on interesting themes which are repeated on stones in many cemetery lots. Tree stumps, or snags with limbs removed, signify lives cut short or the loss of family members as branches. Popularized by a fraternal organization known as the Woodmen of the World in the late 1880s and a Victorian "rustic" movement, these monuments frequently were copied by stone cutters, each with their particular take on how a tree should be portrayed. Sears and Roebuck provided similar tree-based markers in their catalog—which found much popularity in the Midwest beyond its use for toilet paper! I have seen renditions of trees which appear to be pine in the northeast of Iowa and into Wisconsin. These represent the logs that floated the Wisconsin and Mississippi Rivers and rapidly turned into millions of board feet of lumber. More often you find the stalwart oak. Oaks are well connected to Druid tree worshippers of England, Ireland, and other Northern European areas. Although tree worship fell from favor quite some time ago, the strength of oak continues to be well appreciated. Some of the trees have the look of mechanical speed and efficiency, the bark appearing to be laid out in tight even patterns with the trunk looking as if the square granite block was only rounded enough to take the edge off the hard corners of the original marble block. Some have reference to the Woodmen organization, an axe, splitting wedge, and beetle or the seal of the organization. Many are devoid of any reference to any fraternal organization.

With this tree motif come all sorts of variations on the wood theme: split logs, stacked wood, sculptured wood knees, and bent wood surrounding the regular squared-off stones. I've even seen log cabins complete with a latch string hanging out of the tiny latch hole, signifying eternal friendship to all. The standing trees have variations that are played out according to the wishes of the deceased. In Burlington I came across the usual limbless oak, but this time there was a coat hanging from one limb, a fancy riding hat complete with a feather-decorated hat band hanging from another limb, and yet another held what appeared to be the brass loop of a fox hunting horn. Leaning on the tree was a shortened rifle completing the hunt theme.

Trees with baskets of flowers and fruit are commonly hanging from the limbs. Ropes with anchors sometimes are wrapped about the trunk; this signifies hope in times of trouble. In Anamosa there is the scene of a dead bird lying at the base of a tree with a small bird left in the nest and the father bird watching over the baby bird. Obviously the mother died leaving a small child and husband behind, a significantly moving scene to all even these many years later.

As the chiseled vines climb round about the tree snags, with sprays of calla lily, ferns, and posies of every description cut in bas-relief into the stone, a certain earthliness begins to appear as the marble attracts lichens and moss in softer tones of yellow and green. Depictions of honeycomb (bees and honey production are symbols associated with the work of Christianity and faithfulness) also are found at times interspersed in the flowers and vines. As a sort of cost sharing effect, many have the limestone bark peeled down with many other family members added to the memorial. In one standing tree I witnessed in Missouri, a young girl's straw hat was added, leaning so naturally against the tree with her few years and name etched upon the rim. Surrounding the tree on a second memorial in Springfield, Ill., are a girl's straw hat and her ever-faithful dog standing in wait for her return.

As much as I appreciate finding standout trees, I appreciate even more finding the less obvious markers of the indigent. They're often made of cement or some material available close at hand brought into service for this unusual purpose. The love and care taken by those who add bits of broken colored bottle glass outlining a name in a small slab of cement make it a bit of folk art in its own right. Others have taken even more care in creating memorials from commonplace cement. In a small desolate cemetery along a quiet highway in Louisa County lies a most unusual empty chair constructed completely of cement. On the back splat is a simple heart raised off the surface; crude and rough as the chair may be, the heart says it all. A small rural cemetery in Linn County holds the remains of some poor parents' child; it too is marked lovingly with a small round erratic stone. Scratched upon it is the word "Baby." In pioneer cemeteries that dot the landscape, no time was available to mourn the immediate loss of many beyond the erecting of cairns of stone, unblemished with statements or even the name of the deceased. They stand as a mute testament to a much harder time when life had to go forward and little time was available to mourn the passing of friends and family. Sadly there are many other places where simple plots of land stand vacant and empty, the resting places of cholera victims and others who died quickly in epidemics. Survivors wasted little time on funerals or even coffins. Elsewhere people far from home and prisoners during the Civil War died en route to internment camps and were dumped into these same common burial pits, forgotten by all but those so far away who had no idea where their loved one might be found.

The common laborer, known for his efforts at doing his very best, often is represented by the tools of his trade. In Springville there is a white marble anvil with the silent hammer resting on its face, a memorial to a man known for his ability at the forge and hammer. Shoemakers sometimes have their cobblers' hammer, punch, and awl resting on their stones with a finished single shoe waiting an eternity for its mate. Farmers are no exception; in Cedar County there is a relatively new grave with an arbor over the stone. Entwined in the arbor are cornstalks of iron with tassels spread and ears forming. Some additions have been made; a zip-tied farmer's seed corn cap clings to the frame. Early millers have grindstones for grave markers while modern tradesmen have their business emblazed on their stones like business cards for the hereafter. One wonders if there is a tax write-off in there somewhere. I recall a trip to northern Germany some years ago where I was told a family's gravesite was an indication of the dedication to detail in business. An unkempt stone was a sign of potential neglect in one's business. Maybe this is the connection with today's stones that look more like a stone business card than a marker of eternal rest.

The epitaphs, once translated from their lichen and weathered surfaces, tell stories of immense personal loss. I view memorial stones of brothers lost in the Civil War, so far removed from home, their bodies left where they died. This is a telling story of the over 77,000 who left the fields and farms of Iowa to quell the division of the nation. Many never returned and have no memorial stone to mark their passing. Those who did return home were left scarred both mentally as well as physically. I see no sign or description inscribed for us to know their hardship beyond the military unit numbers. Family markers sometimes give a sobering hint: "died at Andersonville," "died in service of his country," or simply "died at Shiloh" or any one of 100 crossroads, churches, or stream crossings many miles from home.

The Civil War spawned Decoration Day when many set flowers on graves of soldiers. This activity didn't become a legal national holiday honoring all veterans until 1882. The act of decorating Civil War graves had lasted for nearly 20 years without a federal mandate. These soldiers were owed a debt of gratitude by all their communities; these home boys had been wounded and many died and never returned, not even in death.

The family plots filled with children who lived but briefly tell yet another story. In one Keokuk graveyard I found a single family who lost nine children, like clockwork. They were born and they died, ages of a few months to a few years, laid out in a straight and single row. One after another they died until the parents passed away, probably from broken hearts.

Even with all this sobering grief one can find humor and wit. It isn't easy to find and often goes unnoticed, which makes it refreshing when it is noticed.

Sometimes you have to concoct the humor for yourself, like the man whose last name was "Chicken" who was a veteran of the Civil War. I begin to think of comments about this poor fella: "He can't go. Why? He's Chicken!" In Cascade there is the Christmas cookie recipe I found, completely covering the back of a very large stone. It is not some convoluted and difficult recipe, just a simple sugar cookie with all the usual ingredients. My guess is this was the deceased's way of saying life goes on, get over it. I'm not here to bake the cookies, so here's my final gift to you . . . now go, get outta here and bake a batch!

So as the sun sets early on this winter landscape, my review of yet another burying ground is complete for the moment. I return to my galvanized gate of cold steel, replacing the latch as I walk through into the land of the living. One day this trip will be one way for me, but until then I will enjoy the pleasant quiet and solitude, the wind blowing through the pines, the summertime lush green lawns, or the waving patches of prairie. Even in winter, this solitude is comforting in a time of so much hubbub and fast-paced living. The gate latch falls snug in its place as I return to my everyday struggle with the living.

Memo...
from the Director of the
Center for Prairie Studies

BY J. HARLEY MCILRATH
2009

for David Campbell

INTEROFFICE MEMORANDUM

TO: DR. SAMUEL R. GRIEWE, CHAIRPERSON, COMMITTEE
    FOR THE SUPPORT OF FACULTY SCHOLARSHIP
FROM: DR. WILLIAM H. LORTAN, DIRECTOR, CENTER
      FOR PRAIRIE STUDIES
SUBJECT: MEETING OF THE COMMITTEE 5/8/09
DATE: 5/8/09
CC: DR. TAYLOR S. FORD, DEAN OF THE COLLEGE

Sam:

This is to inform you that I will not be attending today's meeting of the committee. Instead, I will be receiving the first in a series of rabies vaccine shots at the Polk County Health Center in Des Moines.

Be heartened, Sam. I would rather receive rabies shots at the Polk County Health Center than attend the meeting of the committee today. This is the silver lining to a dark cloud that might well bring my death— that I must needs be excused from your bloody committee meeting. Praise God! There are injections and let them be painful!

But why the Polk County Health Center, you ask? Why not here in Grinnell? Why not receive the shots at our very own Poweshiek County Health Center? Because they don't know me in Des Moines, and they will ask me no questions. Let me be one more clap-ridden drunk in the waiting room. Let me be one more addict awaiting his methadone. Count me among the squalid and ask me no questions.

But you will ask questions, won't you, Sam? What other purpose has the Committee for the Support of Faculty Scholarship if not to serve as a forum by which you can ask questions? Let me tell you straight up: I was bitten by a monkey while photographing barns in southeast Marshall County.

Two things, Sam, before that infernal bow tie you wear cuts through your throbbing carotid:

1. Yes. I am familiar with the infamous story of the monkey bite Dr. Campbell received in a bordello in Coca, Ecuador. A biologist wasn't he, collecting herbarium specimens from the floor of the rain forest? One finds monkeys in the Amazon, doesn't he? That's what you're thinking, right, Sam? Biologist in the Amazon, yes, but how does the director of the Center for Prairie Studies get bit by a monkey while photographing the vanishing architecture of America's heartland?

2. No. I am not making this up. For all I know, it was the same damned monkey that bit Campbell. Have you looked around the heartland lately? There are Mexicans in Tama, Nicaraguans in Marshalltown, and Salvadorans in Waterloo. You sit in the waiting room of the Polk County Health Center and you might be with Campbell in Coca, Ecuador. The congressman from the Fifth District wants to build a wall on the southern border. Let him build his wall. Too late now, I say. The monkey has bit the professor. The light grows dim. . . .

But you want details, don't you, Sam? "Give us the details, man!" you say. "You speak in generalities! Give me something on which to base a judgment!" Here are the details, Sam. Here you go:

The Center for Prairie Studies is cooperating with the Iowa Barn Foundation on a project to document the existing barns in central Iowa. We lose 1,000 barns a year in Iowa. No one needs them. They are expensive to maintain. The farm economy is depressed, so these buildings are left to rot and collapse. It's a sad thing. Imagine a generation of children grown up with nostalgic memories of their grandfather's pole building. Not even that. The family farm is dead. Did you know? E. B. White writes *Charlotte's Web* today, it takes place in a hog confinement. Imagine Wilbur living in a concentration camp for pigs. Read that story to your grandkids, Sam. Put them to bed with that at night.

But you know all about the project, don't you, Sam? It came before the committee. We talked about the details in minutiae. "How does this serve the college?" you wanted to know. "What benefit do we see for the student in the classroom? Is there architectural merit in these structures beyond simple sentimentality?" Ah, Sam. How I laughed when you lost that vote. The days since that hangover have been a gift.

But I drift astray. Forgive me, Sam. It's the fever. It's the headache and the malaise, I hear you, Sam. "Keep it germane!" you say. "Damn it, man! Speak to the point!"

I was crisscrossing the gravel roads south of Le Grand. I used 146 as my western boundary, took the gravel east for a mile, then turned south a mile and again west back to the highway. Repeat ad infinitum. If a dirt road happened to cut through the middle of a section, I took the dirt road. Wherever I found a barn, I stopped and photographed it. If a person was there, I stopped, said hello, and explained my purpose. Otherwise, I snapped a shot and moved on. There are a lot of barns still out there, but they're not in good shape. If we're lucky, someone's covered the roof in tin to keep out the rain. But Sam, I have to tell you, seven miles south of Le Grand, I found a barn that was a work of beauty. It was like a basilica. It took my breath away. It was a cathedral on the prairie, only humble. It looked to its purpose without ostentation. I didn't take its picture. The thought never crossed my mind. I parked my car in the driveway and got out. The house was gone from the building site. The lawn had been plowed and put to corn. The lot fences were gone. There was an old granary with its doors off—a rusted elevator still ran from the ground to the cupola. The barn itself was massive. The frame held straight and the roof seemed intact. The windows were broken out, but the doors were in place. The shingles were missing in places, and a few boards were gone from the siding. The siding boards were weathered gray without a hint of the red paint that must surely have once coated them. I went inside.

Have you been in the old rural churches of Ireland, Sam? Have you sat in a wooden pew between stone walls in a dim light and felt the dampness of the hymnal in your hand? You can smell the years. They permeate the stone and the wood and the paper. They hang in the air and cling to your clothing. You can feel them on your skin. The years are thick there, they are tangible, and they smell of must. That's how it was in that barn. It was dark and damp and musty. The light fell through the broken window panes. A harness hung from a spike hammered into a pole. There were buckets scattered around—there was an overturned milk canister. I went into a pen and there was still hay in the manger. Christ was born in a barn, Sam. Do you remember? He slept in the hay of a manger. "No room at the inn." Do you remember? You don't want to hear this, Sam, but it's good for you. It's good for us. I fear we have forgotten.

I climbed a ladder into the loft. I climbed a ladder and above me appeared the ceiling of the basilica. Emily Dickinson tells us one knows a good poem when he reads it because it blows the top of his head off. Sam, there was no head left atop my shoulders. What I saw put St. Peter's to shame. Purpose was its architect and time its Michelangelo. All around me giant beams rose through the floor to meet the vast arches of the rafter. They formed crosses. Above me, dozens of crosses formed of roughhewn timber. Where did the timber come from? There are no trees of such size in Iowa. There never were. There was hay still in the loft. Musty old bales held by rotted twine. Where are the men who put it there? Where are the men who baled the hay? In their graves? Worse yet: in nursing homes? I lay back on the hay, and it was damp. It was damp as the paper in the hymnals in Craig's Church in Ireland, and above me rose the crosses. They were no affectation, no mere ornament. They held the weight of the roof, the enormous weight of the roof. Without them, the entire structure would collapse inward upon itself. Think of it. The roof protected the hay from the rain and the snow, but without these crosses it was nothing. Without these crosses it was a house of cards.

And the light. Let me tell you about the light, because it shot through the holes in the roof where the shingles were missing, and it pierced the darkness. All around me, shafts of light shot across the swirling dust particles from roof to floor. Do you remember your childhood, Sam? Do you remember your first Bible? Mine had a picture of the baptism of Jesus. John was raising Him up out of the Jordan and the water was falling from His face and there was a cloud overhead, a big white cloud, and out of it shot rays of yellow sunlight, rays of light like the light that shot through the holes in the roof of the barn, and there was a white dove descending from the heavens. It was the Holy Spirit, the Holy Spirit came as a white dove, and there was the voice of God. You couldn't see the voice of God in the picture, but there was a white dove, and I ask you do you remember because above me, soaring in the darkness through the shafts of light and the roughhewn crosses, were white birds. Not doves, but pigeons. There were dozens of white pigeons soaring above me and swooping down from the rafters through the swirling dust in the light, and my God, the hay was so musty! I could smell the years. I could smell them, and I cried. All alone in that old barn, I cried.

But you don't care, do you, Sam? I am losing you. You don't have time for the nostalgia of childhood lost. I say, "the smell of years," and you wince, don't you, Sam? "Empty words," you say. "A pedestrian stab at poesy." You want me to come to the point, don't you, Sam? You want me to tell you about the monkey. I'm getting there, Sam. Beware the monkey.

You are right, Sam. You know you are. Beauty is fleeting. Epiphany is short-lived before analysis sets in and kills it. When the tears stopped I found myself lying on bales of rotted hay in a dusty barn with holes in its roof. The rafters were streaked white with bird shit. Pigeons. My father called them winged rats.

When the symptoms show themselves, it's too late. Did you know? I am likely a dead man. Either that or I have the stomach flu. It could be either. I am rooting against the flu. If it is the flu, I vomit for 24 hours and then return to the committee. Let me die, Sam. Please, let death take me. I called them on the phone, you see. The Polk County Health Center. I called and I told them the story of the monkey, not in the detail I'm telling you, but I told them the story and they said I must needs get myself in for the injections. I asked for the symptoms. I asked, "What are the symptoms of rabies?" And she said, "Fever, headache, and malaise." And I said, "My God! It's nothing to do with the monkey! It's the committee! These are the symptoms of serving on the committee! We've all been bitten on the ass by Dr. Sam Griewe and the lot of us are rabid!"

She asked for your name and address, Sam, and I gave them to her. She asked if you had been seen by a physician and I said that I thought not. You will know my story is true, Sam, when the State comes knocking at your door. I told her to be sure to address you as DOCTOR Sam Griewe because you would not acknowledge her otherwise. Forgive me, Sam. I know not what I do.

It was a long day photographing barns. I was thirsty and I was hungry, so on the way back through Gilman I stopped at Bob's Tap. Yes, Sam, a farmer bar. It's part of the culture. It's where the people we study congregate, the churches and the bars. It's anthropology, or sociology, whichever, and I was in the field. I was gathering data. Details, I was collecting details with which I could enrich the experience of the student in the classroom: Life on the prairie in the twenty-first century.

Wake up, Sam. You are about to meet the monkey.

Have you been to Gilman, Sam? It's a short drive from Grinnell, but somehow I imagine you have not. There's a grain elevator there, and a filling station. There's a stop sign on a pole stuck in a barrel in the middle of the intersection—and there's Bob's Tap. It's dark in Bob's. There's one window in the front with a beer sign. Pabst Blue Ribbon. When I entered, the bartender was playing cards over the bar with a one-legged woman sitting on a bar stool. She was wearing a dress, but there was only one leg coming out of it, and when I walked into the bar she looked up at me as if I were something she'd never seen before. She looked hard at me the whole time it took me to walk in the door and pull a stool up to the other end of the counter. Once I'd sat at the bar she looked at me hard a while longer, and then she must have seen enough and she went back to her card game. The bartender never gave me a glance. At a table just past the card game sat a fellow with a ponytail. He was wearing a T-shirt with the sleeves cut off and his arms were covered with tattoos. He was staring at a Cardinals game on the television. The monkey was with him.

Sam . . . monkey, monkey . . . Sam.

The bartender was intent on his game and paid me no mind. The wind might have blown the door open and pushed a stool up to the counter for all the attention he paid me. The fellow with the ponytail held his beer glass in his hand and stared at the Cardinals game. Only the monkey acknowledged my existence with indecipherable chatter. The monkey, I would learn, was a flirt.

When the hand was finished, the bartender laid his cards on the bar and looked at me. "What can I do for you?" he said.

"What do you have on tap?" I said.

He didn't say a word. His eyes simply led my gaze to the single tap handle rising above the bar. One, Sam. One forlorn tap handle extended from below the counter like the lone digit on the maimed hand of a drowning man. Blue Ribbon. It's tough in the field. No Guinness. No Bass Ale. A Black and Tan is a dream. The nectar of a foreign land. Forgive me, Sam, I did not ask if they had a nice cabernet. I have let you down. I did not ask the label of the merlot.

"Pabst it is," I said, "and a bag of chips." The bartender pulled a draught and set it in front of me. A dollar and a quarter. A dollar and a quarter for a glass of beer, a bag of chips, and the company of a monkey. The chips were my undoing. But for the chips, I might be sitting across the table from you now watching you eviscerate some poor soul as he attempts to prove his worth to the committee. His life's work rests on the symbolic import of Gabriel's galoshes in Joyce's "The Dead." Without proper understanding of Gabriel's galoshes, *Ulysses* and *Finnegan* remain closed. But the galoshes, Sam! They are a prophylactic! The snow falls generally on the living and the dead, but Gabriel wears galoshes, don't you see. He separates himself from the snow. It is his folly! Surely you see, Sam. Surely the poor soul makes his case. He must, Sam. He must make his case, or his life's work is a ruin! Ah, well. Bring me my chips, Sam. Bring me my monkey and my injections.

She heard the crinkling of the bag as I opened it. She shot across the floor and leapt onto the stool next to me. The monkey, Sam, not the one legged-woman. She crouched on the stool, bounced a bit, and punched my shoulder. She looked from me to the chips, from the chips to me, back and forth, punching my shoulder. I turned to the fellow with the ponytail. He was staring at the Cardinals game. The bartender and the one-legged woman were intent on their card game. I took a chip from the bag and gave it to the monkey. She sat back on the stool and ate it. When she finished it, she asked for another. I gave it to her. When she had finished several chips, I said no and I slid the bag down the counter away from her. She chattered angrily at me and leaned across my body to reach the bag. I put my hand up to hold her back, and on a sudden impulse, I tickled her tummy. She liked it. She chattered noisily but with a different tone, playful rather than angry. Now I laughed, because I'll tell you—I knew a girl in college who was just like that. She was not a pleasant person. Nobody liked her. She was a shrew. A right bitch. But her weakness was having her belly tickled. She had an apartment near mine. We were both taking BIO 120, so I usually stopped by to see if she wanted to walk together. Why, Sam? Tell me why. She usually ran late, and she'd bitch at me about this or that—give me hell for things that had nothing to do with me—and then I'd reach out and tickle her tummy. Strangest thing. She'd be brow-beating me one minute, and the next minute we'd be rolling around collecting the cat hair from her carpet on the sweat of our bodies. I didn't see much of BIO 120, Sam. I see your scowl. You do not approve.

But it was the same story with the monkey. I had her in the palm of my hand. She chirped and wriggled. She grasped my fingers in her paws, sometimes pushing my hand away, sometimes pulling it back for more. I tell you, Sam. I took BIO 120 with this monkey. I turned to the card players. "What's she doing here?" I said. Neither of them looked up. "What's who doing where?" the bartender said. "The monkey," I said. "You don't expect to find a monkey in Iowa."

The bartender and the one-legged woman both looked at me. Then the one-legged woman looked at the bartender. "I seen the monkey before," said the bartender. "I never seen you."

For the second time that day, Sam, my head left my shoulders. The epiphanous moment. I arrived at the place in the forest where the trees came into alignment and my vision reached unobstructed to the horizon. I don't belong here. I am alien to this place. I am the director of the Center for Prairie Studies. I am a scholar. I write books. I publish papers. I don't have the status of a monkey on the prairie. I am a narodnik. My work is gibberish to the people I study. Ask them what life is like on the prairie. They will tell you they wouldn't know. They live on farms. The prairie died with the Indians and the bison—not the bison, the buffalo. It was conquered by Pa and Ma and Half-pint. The prairie has been stuffed and mounted and consigned to a dusty glass case in a forgotten room at the Historical Society. It is infested with mites and losing its hair.

What do I know of these people? What do I know of this place? I spend my life's work hunting out and collecting the seeds of plants near extinction, trying to repopulate them, trying to reclaim the prairie. I dream of the tall grass blowing again in the wind. Weeds. My life's work is to re-establish the weeds that these people have spent generations eradicating. I learned this summer of a place northeast of Grinnell that had been pasture as long as anyone could remember. It was a wet place, good for nothing but grazing cows. Think of it, a piece of prairie that had never seen a plow—a prairie Galápagos! I found it, and do you know what I found there? Corn. Rows of corn. The farmer who owned it had tiled it out that spring and rented it to a neighbor. Do you know why? Because he could rent it for $150 dollars an acre. Economics. It's what killed the prairie in the first place.

Do you think that these people stand in their barns and think how like a basilica they are? No. These people walk into a basilica and their minds automatically calculate how many bales of hay it will hold. They find beauty in things you and I don't see, Sam. They find beauty in a straight row of corn, in a clean field of beans, in a taut fence wire. Who are we to question their aesthetics? Who am I? I spoke to an old farmer, I was working on an oral history project and I spoke to an old farmer, and while we talked, we stood leaning on a fence watching his herd of Black Angus cattle graze in a pasture. I asked him why he had not crossbred with exotics, why he had not introduced Simmental or Limousin or Charolais blood into the herd to increase size and muscle. He watched his black cows on the green grass, and he said, "I wouldn't want a motley herd." Aesthetics! The dollar be damned! Sam, it was the same farmer who plowed under my pristine prairie preserve for $150 an acre!

It was at that moment, as my head left my shoulders and the trees of the forest came into alignment allowing the light to shine on my folly, it was at that moment that the monkey struck. She sank her teeth into the flesh of my right triceps, through my shirt sleeve, clean to the bone. The bar became strangely quiet, except for the sound of the Cardinals game on the television—a swing and a miss, the sound of the ball hitting the catcher's mitt. The monkey sat back on her stool and looked at me. The bartender and the one-legged woman held their cards and watched from the far end of the bar. The tattooed man watched his ball game, and the blood flowed from my arm, soaking my shirt sleeve red and pooling on the bar.

I was calm. I felt no ill will toward the monkey. I asked for the restroom and followed the bartender's gaze to the door. I passed behind the one-legged woman and between the tattooed man and his game on my way. "Shouldn't've give her them chips," the woman said as I passed. Indeed, Sam, I should not have given her them chips.

In the restroom, I flushed the wound with cold water from the tap and staunched the blood flow with paper towels. I will tell you. I do not well tolerate the evidence of my own mortality. Will you think less of me, Sam, when I tell you I am a fainter? The merest glimpse of my own blood is enough to make my knees go weak beneath me. But I held on, I stood in the restroom clutching paper towels to my arm and I fought off the sparkling white light that swirled around me. I steadied myself against the shifting floor. Why? Why did I fight so fiercely against the comfort of the white light? Pride. Pride and fear of the unknown. I had a vision of the tattooed man coming to relieve himself between innings. I envisioned myself lying, bleeding, on the floor as he pushed the door against my body to gain entrance. I saw him step over my prone body, saw him relieve himself at the toilet and step back over me as he left. In my vision, he did not flush. This vision came to me, and I knew that I could not allow myself to lose consciousness in the restroom at Bob's Tap in Gilman, Iowa.

I took a wad of fresh paper towels from the dispenser and tucked them under my arm. I left the restroom and stepped up to the bar. I did not come into the wilderness in a wagon pulled by oxen. I did not survive blizzards in a sod house burning the manure of bison for heat. I did not endure locusts and drought. But this I know. To survive on the prairie, even in the twenty-first century, one must adapt. "Two shots of Jack and some duct tape," I said. The bartender never left the spot on which he stood. He reached beneath the counter and produced two shot glasses and a bottle of Jack Daniels. He stooped a bit to reach the duct tape. The first glass of whiskey I tossed down my throat. The second glass I poured over the wound in my arm. I tell you, for the first time that day they gave me a look of respect.

I replaced the bloodied paper towels with the fresh, and I bound them to my arm with the duct tape. I tore the tape with my teeth. I see you grimace, Sam, but what would you have had me do? Should I have asked for iodine and gauze? Perhaps a glass of the Glenlivet whilst we wait for the ambulance? You will be proud of me though, Sam. You will surely appreciate my gallantry, because whether I was giddy or whether I did it to spite the monkey, I don't know, but I asked for two more shots of whiskey. I took one in the hand of my good arm and with it I slid the other to the one-legged woman. "Cheers," I said, lifting my glass to her. She looked at the whiskey in front of her and gave me half a smile. "Never learn, do you?" she said.

There you have it, Sam. Now you know how the professor came to be bitten by a monkey in Bob's Tap, Gilman, Iowa. But is that a look of perplexity you wear, Sam? Disdain, yes, but perplexity as well? You are wondering why I waited, aren't you, Sam? You are wondering what kept me from driving straight to the hospital. It's as simple as this: it stopped bleeding. I hear you tut-tutting. I see you shaking your head. I ask you:

How would you like to present yourself at the emergency room of the Grinnell Regional Medical Center and announce that you had been bit to the bone by an unfamiliar monkey with whom you had been sharing chips and cheap beer at Bob's Tap in Gilman, Iowa? Precisely. Now settle yourself, and listen. There is more.

The woman at the Polk County Health Center asked me, did I have access to the monkey? That's how she put it, "access to the monkey." I told her I didn't know. I explained that the monkey wasn't actually with me—she was with someone else—but that she had joined me at the bar. I said I thought perhaps the bartender might know how to reach her. I asked why we needed to involve the monkey. Tests. They intended to euthanize her in order to perform tests. Sam, they wanted to cut off her head and look at her brain. I see the gleam in your eye. I see the twitch at the edge of your crazed grin. You're thinking of the committee, aren't you, Sam? You see possibilities. "A splendid presentation, Dr. Matthews, now bear with us while we cut off your head and look at your brain." The trustees won't permit it, Sam. Not a plurality of them.

Now listen, I called Bob's Tap. It's a long distance call to Gilman. Did you know? It's a 12-mile drive, but a long distance telephone call. I called and a man's voice answered. I explained that I was the fellow who had been bitten by the monkey some time ago. I received no response, so I asked whether he knew where I could find the monkey. "Couldn't tell you," he said. I asked did he know the fellow with the ponytail and the tattoos. "That'd be Ted," he said. I asked did he know where I could find Ted. "Prairie View Cemetery," he said. "How's that," I said. "He's dead," the man said. "Don't you read the papers?" Perhaps you saw the story in the *Times*, or in the *Post*? Was there no notice in the *Wall Street Journal*? Was there no obituary of one Ted Osborne, methamphetamine cook, in the *Times of London*? Ah, Sam. You have neglected the paper of record.

I spent an afternoon of my abbreviated life thumbing through back issues of the Marshalltown *Times Republican*. There it was. I found the story—front page news, above the fold, not one week after my visit to Bob's Tap. Ted Osborne, my tattooed man, was killed accidentally while stealing anhydrous ammonia from a tank left overnight in a farmer's field. He was siphoning the anhydrous from the tank into a gas can. He had used duct tape to fasten an inner tube to the gas can and to the tank valve. The inner tube came loose, and he was doused in anhydrous ammonia. He was frozen, burned terribly. The farmer found him lying beside the tank when he returned to the field that morning. The man's pickup was in the field, the driver's side door left ajar. According to the *Times Republican,* Ted Osborne was known to keep a pet monkey, and indeed the corpse of a monkey was found beneath the anhydrous tank. Authorities speculated that the monkey might have had something to do with the loosening of the inner tube from the valve of the anhydrous tank.

I called the Marshall County sheriff's office to enquire after the body of the monkey. I explained my plight and asked could the Polk County Health Center have access to the monkey. He was quiet. For the longest time the sheriff was quiet. What do you think, Sam? They've lost the monkey. No one knows what became of the corpse. The sheriff said there was confusion over what to do with the body. It was evidence, you see, so it had to be saved. But they would not have the body of an animal in the morgue at the hospital, nor would the mortuary take possession of even so near a cousin. He attempted to take the corpse to a local grocer to store in his meat locker, but the grocer wouldn't have the thing in his cooler next to his steaks and sausages. No room at the inn. Do you see? No room for a deceased monkey to rest her weary head. The sheriff was resigned to asking permission of his wife to store the corpse in his own freezer at home, but when he went for the monkey, the body was gone.

The whereabouts of the monkey's corpse did not seem to much concern the Marshall County sheriff. A bit of embarrassment, yes, at his inability to explain the disappearance of the evidence, but no real concern. There would be no inquest. No search for fingerprints, no canvassing for witnesses. What concerned him was my photographing the vanishing barns of Marshall County. "Did I travel alone?" he wanted to know. "Had I noticed anything . . . strange? Smelled anything . . . odd?" He asked could he see the pictures. It seems that people of Ted Osborne's ilk like to locate their methamphetamine kitchens in old barns and forgotten outbuildings. The sheriff's concern—he didn't say this directly but in so many words—his concern was that an over-educated half-wit like me, straying from the shadow of his ivory tower and wandering about the wilderness with his camera snapping photos of quaint rustic scenes, might stumble across the industry of someone like Ted Osborne and come to harm. Ah, Sam. Here are your details. Here is the data from the field with which we will enrich the experience of the student in the classroom. To survive on the prairie in the twenty-first century, one must know how to safely siphon anhydrous ammonia from the tank. One must know to locate his meth kitchen near a hog confinement to mask the stink. Not the stink of the hog confinement, Sam, the stink of the meth kitchen. Did you know that marijuana is the fourth most valuable cash crop grown in Iowa? Did you know? Well behind corn, soybeans, and hay. But more valuable than oats. Oats, Sam. "Amber waves of grain."

Ah, Sam. Fear not. A better day is coming. Do you hear the good news? There is no body. The monkey's tomb is empty. She has gone to prepare a place. Dear Sam, shed no tears for William H. Lortan. I shall follow the monkey to a better place. We shall lie together, the monkey and I, we shall lie together in the moldering hay as the pigeons soar in the dust and light above us. We shall lie in the moldering hay as the walls rot and collapse around us. And on that day, Sam, when the great beams splinter and the roof collapses over us, on that day when the pigeons burst forth and fly free in the blue sky, on that day we shall arise, the monkey and I, we shall arise and emerge from the rubble of the past into a new day, a new world, a new world returned to the old. We shall emerge to the big bluestem and the switch grass. The coneflower and the blazing star. Milkweed and sage. We shall walk hand in hand, the monkey and I, amongst the bison and the elk, hear the song of the goldfinch and the bobolink. The whistle of the meadowlark. Farewell, Sam. And farewell to the committee. Call no hearse. Send no rendering truck to fetch the remains of Bill Lortan. I am at peace, Sam. I am at peace, for the monkey has taken me whole.

Best Regards,
William H. Lortan
Director
Center for Prairie Studies

Rockin' the Corridor

A Music Critic Remembers

BY DEE ANN REXROAT

2010

ONCE UPON A TIME, long before it was known as the Corridor, Cedar Rapids–Iowa City boasted two of the largest, most modern concert venues in the region. Major touring artists such as Sting and AC/DC performed. The venues featured big shows two or three times a month.

A sea of 10,000 bodies could pack into the Five Seasons Center in Cedar Rapids, while the larger Carver-Hawkeye Arena in Iowa City maxed at 15,500. At each concert one of those in the crowd reviewed the show for the Cedar Rapids *Gazette*. For eight years beginning in 1983, I was that one.

I was a classically trained pianist who had discovered an interest in journalism as a music, politics, and philosophy major at Cornell College in Mount Vernon. After completing graduate studies in journalism at Northwestern University, I drove to Cedar Rapids to visit my grandparents. On a whim I visited *The Gazette* and ended up with my dream job as an arts and entertainment reporter.

I wrote some 213 music reviews and was the subject of what felt like as many letters to the editor from angry fans. In reality (I looked it up recently) there were 48 published letters. Twelve were favorable. Fourteen were about New Kids on the Block, a band I had called "masterpieces of marketing."

Like most of my generation, I came of age to a soundtrack of rock 'n' roll. But I had completed an exacting study in classical music that gave me high expectations of performance for music of all genres. I looked on extra-musical aspects of a concert—the lights and show biz—as secondary at best, distracting at worst. When Metallica's lead singer took a swig of beer and belched into the microphone, twice, to a cheering crowd, I was not the type to let it go lightly. It became the lead in my review. By nature, metal bands tended to degeneracy on stage, and I frequently took them to task.

I acquired a reputation as a critic who despised heavy metal. Most of the concerts I reviewed—nearly 90—could be classified as rock, while 33 were country, 30 were heavy metal, and a smaller number were pop, blues, jazz, family, and Christian artists. I appreciated good metal, having grown up listening to Black Sabbath ("Master of Reality" was the second album in my collection thanks to the influence of an older male cousin). The vast majority of metal bands that toured eastern Iowa, however, I considered commercial copycats. I admit I became jaded by what I considered to be their calculated, formulaic, and misogynistic shows, personas, and music. I was harsh in my reviews. Then again, I was subjected to some of the bands repeatedly—by the third time around KISS and Poison tended to lose their appeal, if there had been any initially.

Rereading those reviews after all this time, I see now how I set off the fans, heavy metal fans in particular. Although I was not alone among critics in pointing out the commercial trappings and shallowness of much of that genre, I had strong opinions, and my writing could be unforgiving and scathing, even taking the fans to task for finding the music appealing. It bothered me that these showmen were making a fortune selling their albums, concert tickets, and T-shirts to teenagers, when truly talented musicians were eking out a living as relative unknowns. "What they do verges on audio assault," I wrote of Whitesnake in 1990. "The assemblage of people in the arena is powerless against the force of mega-decibels pounding in their chests. If not for this sheer force of sound, I doubt very much that this music would move anyone." And of Mötley Crüe: "The band appeared to be no more than puppets dangled and operated by the record/concert industry. There was not a feeling that they possessed artistic license or integrity. Someone else designed a spectacular stage show and plugged in Mötley Crüe and its songs calculated to sell millions."

And yet the third and final time I endured a Poison concert, I wrote about a band in tune with its fans: "While there is nothing great to report musically, the overall experience was a good time. And that's about what you should expect from a Poison concert."

* * *

Early on I learned to include crowd reaction so the reader would know that, despite my aversion to a particular concert, the crowd was actually crazy about it. I also adopted a philosophy of judging the music by its own merits—whether it be Bob Dylan or Wayne Newton. I asked myself if the artists accomplished what they set out to do, and of equal importance, if their goal was worthwhile. That way I could point out that while New Kids on the Block were great at doing their thing, that thing lacked originality.

By nature, many of the concerts were slickly produced arena rock, which does not tend to inspire critical acclaim. The morning any seriously negative review ran in the paper, newsroom colleagues would stop by my desk in excitement. Like life, however, most performances fell somewhere in the vast middle ground. Thus, most reviews were a mixture of positive and negative. I sometimes worried that I would run out of ways to describe bands and music. But I never did. It always struck me as a fresh, new experience, and I tried to convey that. Fortunately, I was presented with an astonishing array of artists, from Stevie Wonder to Liberace and everything in between.

In order to meet an 11:15 p.m. deadline for the next day's edition, the reviews generally were written in 30 minutes. Making deadline wasn't too difficult after a show at the Five, which was three blocks from the newsroom. Remote submissions were more challenging. In the mid-80s *The Gazette* purchased several early-model portable computers. The TRS-80 Model 100 has since attained cult status among computer buffs, but I found it clunky and unreliable, especially when filing from off-site. On several occasions it failed, and I was forced to dictate a review to the night desk via phone. And, because the screen was not backlit, it was nearly impossible to use it in a dark arena. There were a few times I locked myself in a Carver-Hawkeye Arena restroom stall—one of the few places with solitude and light—to make deadline before filing the story from a pay phone.

Although I was used to working in a bustling newsroom, it was hard to think and write critically in the middle of an ear-splitting concert venue. To allow me to escape from the party atmosphere at F.B. & Co. in Waubeek, I once was offered a private toilet, where I looked down from an upper-story window onto a sprawling outdoor concert along the banks of the Wapsipinicon River. Next to the throne was a wall-mounted phone, perfect for submitting the story (the editor never knew).

One night after filing a review I announced in the newsroom that they should find a younger rock critic as I turned 30, and they did. At age 31 I switched to classical and jazz reviewing, the assignment for which I was originally hired. Still, I was glad for the detour.

Today, almost 20 years after publishing my last rock review, some people still think of me as my former self. My middle-school daughter had a substitute teacher this year who recognized the last name and announced that her mother "hates heavy metal." A few months later *The Gazette* ran a historical column headlined "Rockers KISS blast review of C. R. concert," recalling a contemptuous note Gene Simmons sent me regarding my review of his band (among other things, I wrote that he was "too overweight to be wearing tight leather pants"). Though it was not fit to print in a family newspaper, I referred to it in a column, thereby giving Simmons precisely the additional publicity he desired. He's still getting it, in *The Gazette* and this publication two decades later—and my family now reminds me that I have become a historical figure.

I had interviewed Simmons prior to the concert (celebrities commonly were motivated to speak with a local journalist in order to sell more tickets). Agents arranged the interviews and at the appointed date and time a handler typically answered the phone in a hotel room somewhere along the tour. Occasionally the outcomes were bizarre, such as when I called Stevie Nicks and was told she was in a bubble bath and would not be available until later.

Rarely did I meet the artists in person. Not only was I on a short deadline after the show, I also wanted to keep my journalistic integrity. An exception was going backstage to meet Stevie Ray Vaughan on his "Soul to Soul" tour. Somehow I also allowed myself to be ushered into Alice Cooper's tour bus parked outside the Five. I left marveling at the show-biz behind this fine-featured, charming man whom I had just observed pulling heads off dolls and parading them on the tip of a sword during "Billion Dollar Babies."

Hey, it was only rock 'n' roll. But I (mostly) liked it.

Just in Case
Alone at Christmas

BY MARIAN MATTHEWS CLARK

2011

I T DOESN'T TAKE a genius to see why Christmas holidays can be dreadful. Friends with families seem shopped out, stressed out, crabby. Those of us without families may feel left out, down and out, scared.

That's how it was for me in 2004 after my father died. For nearly 30 years, I'd hopped a plane in Cedar Rapids to fly to Oregon to spend the holidays with my parents. After Mom died, I focused on Dad, bought him flannel shirts and pajamas from me, and sweaters and books for me from him.

After he died, and I faced the holidays alone, I rationalized what I wouldn't miss. I'd never put up a tree of my own and had no desire to start. I'm not a "Bah Humbug," but I don't like fuss. Even as a child, I disliked rummaging through the cold woods in search of the perfect tree. And I would have tossed the icicles willy-nilly over the branches had Mother not insisted on a tedious one-by-one distribution style. This year it's "Free to be / Without a tree," I told myself.

Yes, there was something to be said for celebrating exactly the way I wanted. I would rent videos, buy take-out Chinese, and open presents from cousins and friends. I'd lined up their gifts in front of my fake fireplace. I'd be fine.

But when my friend Val called a couple days before Christmas and invited me to her place, I bought gifts for Val, her kids, and her granddaughter and drove in record time to her house. There I spent the day playing games with three-year-old Kylie and reading her the same book over and over, as if I were actually good with kids. Val saved my life.

In the ensuing years, Iowa City friends extended the hand of Midwest hospitality and invited me to join them for Christmas dinners and gifts and New Year's festivities. But this year I wanted a change. I wasn't as brave as my friend who was flying off alone for a Greek holiday. But when my friend James told me over our Thanksgiving spaghetti, "This Christmas, I'm having myself a getaway. I'll sit at an unfamiliar bar, check out guys, and not run into anyone I know," I had an epiphany; I'd plan myself a *mini* adventure.

The trickiest part of this getaway plan was what to tell friends. It's one thing to say you'd love to join them if you weren't flying off to Greece, but quite another to admit you're spending the day alone in a motel just up the road. Since the last thing I wanted to do was burn my holiday bridges, I ended up saying, "I'm waiting to firm up plans, but thank you ever, ever, ever so much for asking."

I wish I could say that on that blizzardy Iowa Christmas Day when I arrived at the motel, I encountered a suave older gentleman who said I was the most fascinatingly gorgeous woman he'd seen in years and that he whisked me off on a Caribbean holiday.

But what really happened was this: at the desk, the very, very, very young girl who checked me in was politely efficient as if there was nothing strange about a 60-something woman being alone on Christmas. Maybe she was afraid to pry or simply finished my check-in quickly to get back to texting. Something like: "work til midnite yuc susan here blue scarf and earrings 2 matchy, matchy boring. old lady checking in. gtg."

My first stop after I'd declared my room suitable—I could figure out how to turn on the TV, and the shower handle didn't pass cold on its way to hot—was the hotel buffet. I ate a delicious and mostly peaceful lunch while reading *Don't Let's Go to the Dogs Tonight* (except for a couple interruptions from diners who stopped by to wish me a Merry Christmas). Startled at first, I then noticed I was the only "solo" in the room and wondered how people must perceive me: A pitiful woman, stood up by a dinner partner? An old woman abandoned by kids who couldn't stand to spend the holidays with her?

I thought about my hasty conclusions. Perhaps the very young desk clerk was not hurrying to check me in so she could return to texting. Maybe she was one of her generation's rebels who didn't own a cell phone, wasn't on Facebook, didn't blog. I couldn't imagine it, but then I doubted anyone in the restaurant could imagine I was meeting a lover for a holiday tryst. Not that I was, but you get my drift.

At 4 p.m., I returned to my room, pulled on a swimsuit, covered every inch of skin with a gigantic towel, and headed to the pool. But the door was locked, so I walked to the desk where a young check-in girl said, "Just swipe your room card; it's really easy."

Back at the locked door, I swiped the card in every direction possible. No luck. But I was determined not to return to the desk and admit to kids with "it's really easy" programmed into their DNA that I couldn't get it to work. So after multiple swipes and enough friction to start a grass fire, the green light blinked and I opened the door. There before me lay the pool—calm, green, and beautiful—and empty. Empty, Empty, Empty. I thanked the heavens, removed my towel, stepped into the water, and shivered as I floated on my back, staring at the enormous tube slide that snaked above me.

After a little floating and a few laps, I climbed out of the pool near the slide entrance. I contemplated how glorious it would be, bragging to friends how I'd climbed to the 30-foot ceiling and flown down the 100-foot slide. But the gate was locked to the steps leading to the top. This gave me enough time to come to my senses and to know that some "big brags" weren't worth drowning over. Instead I glanced around and stealthily clambered over the end of the gate. Then I sat on the last stretch of slide and gave myself a mighty push on that slippery tube that shot me into the pool where I sank, surfaced, and floated for several minutes before slogging my way to the hot tub.

As I lay back in the bubbling water, I looked out at the freezing Iowa twilight, settling around the swirling snow. I thanked God for the glory of having the whole place to myself, not having to feel self-conscious in front of a pool full of kids who haven't a clue what it's like, growing old.

And they shouldn't have, after all. It's their time to be the center of things without a chunk of history behind them to analyze or to put things in perspective. It's their time to fly down the full length of the slide, undaunted by consequences, excited about the holidays, the loot they'll get, the fun they'll have doing whatever kids do these days.

But that day, it was my time—to be grateful for the knowledge that I was fine by myself and that next year, if I weren't playing with friends' grandkids or eating spaghetti with James or flying off to Greece, these water jets would be right where I left them, waiting to spray warm, bubbly, comforting water into my ribs. Just in case.

A Common Thread

BY REBECCA SULLIVAN
2012

T HE NEEDLE WON'T pick up the seam that the fabric feed dogs are pushing its way. "What's wrong?" I think, but I growl out loud, mostly because I want to remind my partner that I need to replace my old sewing machine. My growl reminds me of my mother.

While I have warm recollections of her sewing for me—I was particularly fond of the fringes on the plaid miniskirt and poncho that she made—I also recall her audible frustrations when she sewed. When I began mothering a young family, I found myself at the sewing table, daydreaming about the continuities of my life with those of my foremothers. Now, years later, I continue to feel a connection of nurturing and necessity between my mother, my grandmothers, and me.

It seems to me that the proportion of necessity to luxury varied in my grandmothers' lives. My paternal grandmother, Grandma Ostermeyer, actually sewed for a living. Curiously enough, although she certainly had the talent for stitching—and tatted beautiful tablecloths for sale—there wasn't an extravagance in her house. Living in Plain, Wisconsin, this grandmother was known to us kids as the "Plain grandma" as much for her town as for her sensibilities. I imagine the Plain grandma had been too busy clothing her nine children and doing the town's mending to piece together pretty quilts to adorn the many steel-framed beds. During my visits as a child, and often on Sundays, town folks would call or stop by with some hemming or a pattern to be cut out of taffeta. Grandma's front room, an enclosed porch, housed all the tools of her trade: an old, black cast iron machine, a hem marker with a rubber bulb that blew chalk at the designated hem, brittle measuring tapes, and an array of partial spools of thread. The hours I spent toying with that thread were an omen of my taste for the hues and textures of fabric.

I learned the discipline of sewing for necessity when I followed my mother's footsteps into the sewing project of our 4-H club. Inspired by the brown cotton bedspread that Mother had made in 4-H, I went off to the neighbor lady's house every Monday night to learn to sew straight and construct a strong seam. I was proud of the plain blouses and cotton pinafores that I made. These pragmatic skills served me well when it was time to build my first work wardrobe on a budget. When I tried to sew a skirt or vest that I couldn't afford to buy—about two-thirds of my attempts resulted in wearable garments—I thought of my pragmatic Plain grandma who supplemented her meager Social Security check by taking in sewing well into her 80s.

Necessity didn't seem to be such a watchword for my maternal grand-mother. This is the grandmother we called the "goofy grandma" because she enjoyed such frivolities as candy bars and ponies. The one garment that we have from that side of the family is an extravagant, hand-sewn velvet snow suit that Grandma Nesheim made for my brother Michael. I also have two lengths of dress fabric, shiny polished cotton prints of swirls and flourishes, that goofy grandma never cut out. But my prize from the hands of this grandma is two quilt tops that were never backed. My own mother remembers the drive into the country to retrieve these quilt tops from the woman who was supposed to assemble them with fleece and backs. The woman passed away before they were finished, suspending the quilts in the 1940s. A few years ago, I quilted the red and white patchwork top for my mother's birthday. But the crazy quilt top is perhaps more intriguing. Its haphazard, geometric pieces are old silks and elegant knits. I can imagine the Nesheim women wearing these bold prints—tan satins with robin-egg blue spots, jewel-toned velvets, and delicate brocades. Grandma even took the time to embroider around several of the shapes. The luster of the embroidery floss follows her herringbone, feather, and chain stitches across the quilt.

I, too, took up the leisure of this kind of sewing. Equipped with a Montgomery Ward machine that fit my budget, my first project was a 16-square sampler quilt. Its blue and rose hues, popular at the time I was married, now easily date it. When I was no longer a newlywed, I pieced together another patch quilt for daily use. Its rows of simple triangles from discarded scraps in my fabric drawer chronicle the garments and gifts that I have sewn for family members over the years. A third quilt, an Irish Chain of muslin and navy blue, is the product of a sewing circle of friends who gathered at my house on a cold February afternoon. The conversation over that quilt frame was as much of a pleasure as the shared endeavor itself.

But there's another reason that we women sew. Almost 20 years ago, I stitched away the months waiting for our little one to arrive. The resulting quilt, adorned with stars and moons, wasn't a necessity in the winter months. We'd purchased plenty of sleepers and wraps. It served, instead, a purpose that my ancestors may have had in mind when they sewed. Leaning over the quilting frame, I daydreamed of Matthew's quilt as a keepsake more than I imagined him sleeping under it. Like me, I think my goofy grandmother sewed for posterity. Her handiwork records her family life much like photographs and old letters. When our Matthew was baptized, he already owned clothes that were appropriate for the occasion. But I made him a houndstooth Sunday suit in the hope that he would know his mother's care this way—when he found his suit, delicate and aged, wrapped in tissue paper in a trunk.

Looking for souvenirs to display at Matt's graduation, I came across the small houndstooth suit. The fluid drape of the cloth whispers to me this realization: the care and effort put into this little suit have been eclipsed—overshadowed by long nights of swaying and patting, by the daily routine of practicing spelling words, by countless recitals, and by the ongoing negotiation of Saturday chores. I realize that the work of the sewing machine—or any machine—means little to my children. To them, my devotion is apparent in how long I keep at the challenge of restoring our internet connectivity so they can finish their homework. Occasionally, they'll ask me to mend a knee in worn jeans or help them replace a button, but more often they want my attention to talk about the rating of a new video game.

Teenagers would rather die than wear something sewn by their mother. A run to JC Penney or a click online satisfies their clothing needs. They're happy when I sit down at the computer to look up a

Mom's Movie Review as they plead, "C'mon, everyone else is going." If the movie doesn't measure up it's a Netflix instant watch or way too many YouTube videos. On Sunday night, a time for desperate measures, they might invite me to huddle around the desktop to read their essay or help search for acceptable Web sites. If all goes well, we'll get to bed on time so I'm rested for the IT job that helps us prepare for college costs. At the end of the day, much of the work of parenting is keeping an eye on texting habits and peering across the room at Facebook trends. With no time to stitch, I care for my children by helping them navigate their digital connectivity.

Although distanced from the details of daily life, I'll keep the artifacts of my grandmothers' handiwork to remind me of how they nurtured their families. In agricultural economies where new machines made home life easier, one grandmother sewed for keepsakes and the other for groceries. However, in the time I've been a mother, the fabric of family life has changed. My children, who began with board books, now spend their days interacting with digital media. So I teach them life skills for working with bytes rather than bric-a-brac. All the same, I learned a lot from each of my grandmothers—about joy and want, about grace and grit. These lessons provide an enduring thread.

Night Moves at the Riverside Show Lounge

BY DAN EHL

2012

BING-G-G, BING-G-G, BING-G-G.
A young sailor in a cold sweat tightly
grips the control panel while the jarring sound
of his radar grows louder and louder. Flashing green emanations from
the radar screen reveal a growing panic on an otherwise pallid face.
Finally both the maddening din and surreally lit landscape overwhelm
the sailor, sending him stumbling and gibbering insanely from his post.

So ended the early 1970s film I watched in basic training exposing
the dangers of flashbacks. Later in my military career I'd often complain
that I'd never experienced the two-for-one properties of lysergic acid
diethylamide (LSD). Be careful what you wish for. Forty years later
I stood frozen in the grip of what appeared to be a hellish nightmare
originating from some torturous dementia. Amid furious bursts of multicolored micro-novas and weaving death rays stood what could only be
the voodoo reanimated bodies of Agnetha Fältskog, Benny Andersson,
Björn Ulvaeus, and Anni-Frid Lyngstat. In other words—ABBA.

I blame it on Raymond Tinnian, a neighbor and sporadic *Almanac*
contributor. It began with Raymond having a blind date at the Riverside,
Iowa, Casino and Golf Resort—probably through a Russian website,
spam email from the Iowa Correctional Institution for Women at Mitch-
ellville, or a listing in a free magazine from an 1-80 rest stop. He had
reserved shuttle transportation back home to Kalona, but needed the
initial ride to his rendezvous. Giving a buddy a ride is no big deal. It is a
lot to ask, though, when he doesn't want to sit alone until the possible axe
murderer materializes—while being serenaded by disco tribute bands.

Normally I find a night out with Raymond amusing. At times his
whimsical sense of humor can be a bit too much. A lawyer, he likes to
introduce himself as my legal counsel. When someone asks how I am or

what I've been up to, Raymond will interpose, "You don't have to answer that," or, "As your attorney, I strongly advise you to remain silent."

He also is not a good passenger. "What? Are you crazy? Going 55 miles-per-hour is begging to be stopped by the cops. Nobody goes 55. Get it up to 62 mph," he'll rant on the most mundane of drives.

"We're near Kalona. Everyone drives slowly on Highway 1," I'll point out, then threaten to slam his forehead into the dash if he doesn't calm down.

It was with extreme misgivings that I finally agreed to enter the casino for one beer. To reach the show lounge and its free entertainment, one must first wade through "1,156 of the newest and most popular slot machines featuring the latest cashless technology." The incessant ringing is that of a swarm of digital cicadas.

Dominating the middle of the gambling floor is a large circular bar. At its center is an array of built-in TV screens making the drinking area resemble a NASA control room with a very lax dress code. A blue-lit fountain is perched on top. From afar, the bar could be a James Bond set, and all it would take would be a push of a button to send it receding into the floor until only the fountain remained.

Past Mission Control is the less glitzy show lounge bar that shelters a small stage and dance floor from the rest of the casino. It was here that the madness began. The ABBA tribute band was decked out in full disco regalia and garb. Not conversant on style or clothing terminology, I can only note that the women wore sleeves that widened at the cuffs to the point where Agnetha and Anni-Frid looked like giant white and gold flying squirrels—though I suppose they were going for a butterfly look. Benny and Björn were dressed in white leisure suits sporting bell bottoms and buttons that apparently only went halfway up the shirts.

I learned later that the Björn look-alike was bald under his blond wig, a sign of aging not as well hidden by those on the dance floor. Seeing the tribute band was like being caught in a time warp. There in front of me was what appeared to be ABBA from 35 years ago looking and sounding the same as ever. Yet while some in the crowd were in their 30s and 40s, most of those shaking their booties under the flashing mirror disco balls were my age or older. I don't know how to adequately describe a potbellied guy with a receding hairline, wearing bib overalls and striking a John Travolta pose. I was trapped on a cheesy 1970s science fiction set where death rays disguised as colored strobe lights had just transformed a bunch of 20-somethings into elderly beings with thickened waists, sagging tummies, wrinkles, and near senility. Any minute they'd turn to dust.

There was only one hope for saving my sanity. I stumbled blindly to the bar and ordered a beer, from there tightly clutching my bottle as a drowning man would cling to the debris of a foundered ship. Those not dancing stood about me. They seemed normal when not in the context of the stage and dance floor. The second beer began to calm my nerves, and I could scrutinize the scene from Dante's *Inferno* for more than 10 seconds without falling into uncontrollable shaking.

Next to me was a woman close to my own age. She was an attractive and fit woman in her early 60s. We fell into a conversation. For her own safety, I will call her Janet. A majority of those around us, she said, were there almost every weekend at the casino just to dance. At times, Janet continued, it felt as if she were back in high school. Not only because of the music, but due to the catty comments by some of the women. The stinging remarks might be about clothes, hair, fake boobs, or just how the bitch had muscled in on a new dance partner.

The conversation was enough to distract me from becoming completely freaked out when a Bee Gees tribute band next took the stage. It was the first time I'd seen someone dancing to *Well, you can tell by the way I use my walk, I'm a woman's man, no time to talk*—while using a cane.

During this time Raymond had been aggressively circulating through the crowd trolling for his mystery woman, regularly returning to refuel before heading out on another patrol. Raymond spotted me from across the floor talking to Janet. That triggered his highly competitive male instinct, and he almost knocked people to the floor in his rush back to the bar. Introductions were made, and I let Raymond continue the questioning about the evening's social dynamics.

Occasionally Raymond and Janet would wade onto the floor amidst contorting bodies that were either dancing or suffering seizures from the flashing red lights. I didn't follow. In an earlier life my ex and I would join friends for live music at area bars. We'd always end up on the dance floor, and with confidence inspired by a number of beers, I'd rock 'n' roll with abandon, often shouting, "Who says us white boys can't dance?" The women would always answer, "Us white girls!"

A few times through the evening I was asked to dance, but I bowed out, remembering those painful remonstrations from the past.

The evening was ending, and we agreed with Janet to meet again in a couple of weeks—this time when a 60s-style rock band would be playing. From there Raymond and I walked to the exit in search of the shuttle since I had decided hours before to leave my car at the casino and ride home with Raymond. Two casino security personnel intercepted us at the door. They examined us with the unsettled gaze of someone eyeing their dog after it had just rolled in four-day road kill.

"How are you getting home?" they asked while trying not to be too obvious in their positioning between the doors and us. The bartender had most likely passed on the high number of beers Raymond and I had consumed that night. The two appeared unconvinced when we told of the shuttle, though they stepped aside. No doubt they would have called the Washington County sheriff if we'd attempted to leave by car.

Several weeks later we were back at the show lounge. Janet was perched at the bar and we continued our conversation. She would subtly point out the regulars and presented brief histories—who were couples or who had formerly gone with whom. It was quite involved. Some who I assumed were married only got together every couple of weeks for the free casino bands.

A graying man in his middle 60s approached, enveloped in an eye-watering cloud of cologne. He was lean and stood more than six feet in height. This fellow and Janet traded a bit of banter before he went on to socialize with another regular. He was, Janet pointed out, a male strip-per. "Retired?" I asked. She assured me he was still stripping, which left me wondering if AARP booked a lot of parties for the Red Hat Society.

Maybe it was the more familiar rock music. Maybe it was because the surreality had diminished with the absence of disco lights. It could also have been that I didn't fear going into a catatonic fit from the strobes. Whatever the reason, I was getting an entirely different feeling this second time around. I was actually jealous of some of the smooth moves occurring on the floor.

I smiled at one couple. The tall and broad 70ish husband was laboriously crossing the floor with his tiny blonde wife. While he did not look exceptionally thrilled to be on the floor, she gracefully weaved and twirled about him like a bird about a large oak tree. Mellowed by the rock music and beer, I had an epiphany. What a vain fool I'd been. I saw those around me in a completely different light. I'd let my perception of age stand between the dance floor and me while the regulars at the Riverside Casino and Golf Resort's show lounge had not. My peers were enjoying themselves while I sat alone at the bar. These people with their arthritis, bad backs, hip replacements, and hearing aids are the true rock heroes.

I began nostalgically remembering the lyrics of Bob Seger's "(Come Back Baby) Rock 'n' Roll Never Forgets": *You better get yourself a partner, go down to the concert or the local bar.* Copyright laws keep me from quoting the rest, but you know what I mean.

I'm not saying I'll get out and dance the next time I'm at the show lounge, but I might—as long as it's not disco.

I Due

BY LESLIE CATON

2013

A wedding is just like a funeral except
you get to smell your own flowers.
                    —Grace Hansen

Money can't buy you happiness, so
you might as well give your money to us.
                    —Motto of the wedding industry
                    (according to Dave Barry)

MOST OF US HOPE OUR WEDDING will be a once-in-a-lifetime event, a perfect day that provides magical memories for all who attend. Little girls dream of floating down the aisle in a princessy white dress to pledge their undying love to some "perfect" man. Hopefully friends and relatives will be impressed with place settings that include the ever-elegant plate-on-a-plate and napkins that precisely match the bridesmaids' dresses.

Then getting a second job to pay it off.

The average cost of a wedding in the United States in 2012 was between $25,000 and $27,000. If you're thinking, like I was, that number is skewed upward by millionaire couples tying the knot skydiving from a private jet or renting Hawaii, you're wrong. One-fifth of couples married in 2011 spent over $30,000. That's enough to pay for a bachelor's degree at the University of Northern Iowa, build a playground for your local school, or symbolically adopt 600 honey badgers through the World Wildlife Fund.

Thank goodness Iowans are sensible people. The salt of the earth. A decade ago, I was a bridesmaid for a friend I met when I lived in Arizona, just outside of Phoenix. Stacy and I bonded quickly because we both came from Iowa. We knew what kind of snow was best for snowballs and what it felt like to dig in black soil that didn't blow away in a twist of orange powder like the cracked desert ground. We thought the prevalence of breast implants and fake tans among our Phoenix peers was alarming. We were united in practicality.

"I still have real overalls," I confessed shyly, a little drunk at a pool party.

"Me too," she admitted. "And not just because they were cool in the 90s."

"How can you beat that front pocket?" I gushed.

We both eventually moved back to Iowa.

Stacy's Arizona wedding was elegant enough to satisfy her husband's family but not terribly extravagant. I would guess the cost was smack in the middle of the national average, just what I would expect for that poisonous snake/spider/scorpion-and-cactus-filled part of the country, where people irrigate their grass lawns year-round and practicality does not rule. So, if the cost of the average wedding in America could buy you a fully loaded brand new Honda Insight hybrid, what would the cost of an Iowa wedding get you? The same new car minus fake wood paneling and heated seats: the average newly married Iowan spent more than $20,000 on his or her wedding last year. While most couples split the cost between themselves and relatives, the lion's share is often paid by the newlyweds. While that is soothing for parents with kids considering marriage, this is a heavy financial burden for folks who are typically young, often with student loans and first mortgages already on their backs.

The subsequent years of marital bliss will provide all kinds of holes to dig out of without debt from the big day. If there wasn't a large enough nest egg set aside, couples will find plenty of bills in that stack of post-honeymoon mail. What a great opportunity to learn about money management and coping with stress in between writing thank-you notes and cashing in gift cards at Bed, Bath and Beyond. That's what marriage is all about.

If it lasts.

The celebrated union might not last forever, whether or not the couple goes into debt for one phenomenal party. Iowans have a higher marriage rate than the national average, but also have a higher divorce rate. We aren't an unrealistic group; no, Iowans are passionate and eager to commit, yet flexible enough to change our minds. All couples believe they will have a lifetime together (or so one would hope), but it's just not a sure thing.

* * *

Fifteen years ago I tied the knot, and according to our marriage counselor, my husband Michael and I are still married. Our wedding cost $2,500 including dress, flowers, reception, and honeymoon. Sure, I had morning sickness and was trying not to throw up the whole time. My swollen feet throbbed in my high heels. Michael reversed our vows and instead of "I love what I know of you," said, "I know what I love of you" in an accidentally sexy voice; the minister had to wait for the laughter to die down before he could continue. There was no alcohol (I was 19 and pregnant) and no dancing (regret that to this day) but it did the trick. So what if it wasn't some extravagant affair? I was too young to know anything different, and there was little stress. My parents paid for almost everything, for which I am grateful since I would have had our reception at Burger King where Michael could have gotten us an employee discount.

Michael and I were married in the Unitarian Church in Iowa City, the old wood and dust smell familiar from summers I spent playing in the sanctuary while my mom worked as the receptionist. I made the choices that mattered to me: the colors, my dress, the font on the custom printed napkins. My bridesmaids were radiant in silver-blue. I will never forget standing across from Michael while the sun streamed rainbows through the stained-glass windows, the church full of familiar faces smiling at me with tears shining and pledging to share my life with my best friend. Taffeta bows couldn't have made it any better.

A wedding doesn't have to cost as much as building a well for a village in Africa. My sister and her husband were married by a magistrate. I wish she'd had a wedding so I could have been weepy and danced off two pieces of wedding cake, but it worked for her. She and her husband have been married for 10 years, and since she's now an attorney skilled at negotiating divorce, they will probably stay married forever. My brother never married his life partner; they get along better than most married couples I know and have been doing so for 10 years. My dad married my step-mom in a lawyer's office with just their kids in attendance and afterwards, a dinner to celebrate.

Inexpensive weddings can still make an impact. A local wedding singer told me his favorite gig was a ceremony performed on a hay wagon. He and his band sang "Your Cheatin' Heart" among other gems to a bride and groom dressed in overalls and plaid. An afternoon of memorable bluegrass music only cost the couple $250.

If you're starting to think a crazy expensive wedding isn't for you (or your kids), consider the floral arrangements: flowers cost an average of $1,400 to $2,400. Instead of ordering flowers from a florist, plan the wedding for early spring and assign a special friend to pick lilacs and daffodils out of other people's yards the morning of the big day. Everybody loves lilacs. If you'd rather not upset your neighbors, try a cemetery: graves have beautiful, portable bouquets. If that makes you uncomfortable, try your local Hy-Vee like I did. My flowers were reasonably priced, fresh, and lovely. Sometimes, though, there's a downside to buying flowers at a grocery store. While my mom and I stood at the floral counter flipping through a photo album of bouquets, a woman in an electric wheelchair lost control. She smashed me against the front of the counter, pinning my legs. She backed up, apologized, and only ran into me two more times before backing up for real.

If DIY flowers aren't your thing, get some help from your family. Northeast Iowans know how to do weddings. My friend Tracy got married near Waukon, Iowa, a town just west of the Mississippi. Tracy's wedding was fairly typical for this part of the state. The ceremony was in the afternoon, after which she had a few rounds of drinks at a local bar with the groomsmen while her new husband went out with the bridesmaids. They reconvened at an enthusiastic reception in the Monona community center. Iowans invite an average of 215 guests to our weddings (more than any other state), but in northeast Iowa a guest list of 300 to 500 is common. As Tracy and her then-fiancé, Chris, tallied up their guest list, they reached 110 people counting only immediate family and aunts, uncles, and cousins. That's a lot of beer.

How do northeastern Iowans entertain hundreds of guests for less than the national average cost? Iowa practicality. First of all, alcohol is important to blur any imperfections at the reception. Second, a wedding planner is practically unheard of. Why pay someone to tell people what to do when you're going to do that anyway? The bride or the bride's mom assigns tasks before the big day. Everyone gets a job. Aunt Steph cuts the cake, Cousin Dave passes the hat when the beer runs low, and Uncle Jay makes sure the D.J. gets paid. Diplomacy is required to avoid hurt feelings: the guestbook attendant is more prestigious than the punch pourer, who is more important than the chair stacker. Aunts and uncles typically take the gifts back to the house so they don't get stolen. This is important, because the dance after the reception is open to the public. Advertised in the local Market Basket or Penny Saver, wedding dances in rural Iowa serve as a celebration of marriage, community entertainment, and a full-blown high school reunion.

My friend Nick attended a wedding in Manchester with a 29-minute service and nine-hour reception. True to northeast Iowa style, the family pulled together. The groom's father supplied roughly a gallon of beer per guest and the groom's mother provided the food, including three kinds of nacho cheese: plain, venison, and bear.

Unfortunately, community cooperation doesn't guarantee a low-stress event. People in small towns talk, and the pressure to get hitched without a hitch can be nearly overwhelming. At the wedding Nick attended, the groom's parents had endured a difficult divorce. The groom's mom wore a *very* short dress (though Nick says she had the legs for it) and the groom's dad, once he was partway through his gallon of beer, started hitting on Nick's mom. There is stress in every kind of wedding. Your ceremony at majestic Pike's Peak (near McGregor) was perfect until the ring bearer stepped in a nest of ticks; your uncle Steve (on your dad's side) threw up on the limestone terrace at the refined Salisbury House & Gardens in Des Moines.

My friend Flora got married in Cedar Rapids last December, and the ceremony and reception struck a perfect balance between simple and elegant. Their children from previous relationships poured colored sands into a bottle to symbolize blending into a new family, flower girls rolled out a white satin carpet for the bride, and family helped take down decorations after the reception. Flora couldn't wait for the day, not because she was eager for the blissful celebration, but because she couldn't wait for it to be over. All the details to be decided, the calls to make, the cost, the expectations . . . she wanted to be on the other side of the wedding and get on with her (married) life. A lot of brides feel the same—they want the wedding and they want to be married, but the stress distracts them from what really matters.

Standing up next to your friends as they make a lifelong commitment is the ultimate symbol of friendship, but weddings aren't stress-free for bridesmaids, either. Being a member of a wedding party costs an average of $1,500. A bridesmaid buys her dress (specifically chosen to be unflattering), shoes, transportation, and lodging. She buys a gift, a really good gift, because she has the ultimate honor of being part of this milestone event. She supports her friend through wardrobe malfunctions, mother-in-law-drama, arguments with the caterer, and cold feet. It is a privilege to be part of that special day, but the trappings of modern weddings, including the expense and high expectations, make it difficult to focus on the meaning.

Not that I don't appreciate a good party. I like getting dolled up and sitting with a heavy linen napkin in my lap, laughing at awkward toasts, marveling at clever wedding favors like tiny jars of homemade jam labeled "spread the love." There aren't many occasions I can dance barefoot until dawn like I did when my husband's best friend got married. Weddings can be fun. As guests, we get to eat, drink, dance, laugh, and be a part of something wonderful. It just doesn't have to cost a fortune.

If it is important to you to buy your kids a show-stopping wedding, decking out a local winery in flowers and taffeta bows that match the bridesmaid dresses, accompanied by a full orchestra and five-course dinner, knock yourself out. If you and your betrothed have savings you'd rather spend on a wedding than a shiny new car or funding 1,000 micro-loans, go for it. But if you're on the fence about whether you need flowers on each pew or if a couple bouquets are enough, ask yourself why you're considering shelling out a college degree's worth of money for one day. Getting married and embarking on a lifetime of compromise and compassion is enough challenge without setting the material bar uncomfortably high from the get-go. Have a fun day, and appreciate the beauty of what you've got right there next to you, at the altar or in front of a magistrate—with or without the matching taffeta.

The Judge vs. God, Television, and Fashion

BY SHIRLEY MCDERMOTT
2013

M Y FOUR SIBLINGS AND I liked my Uncle Francis, and we had good reasons: candy and money. He wasn't so keen on us, and his reasons were certainly valid: our noise and chaos aggravated his psoriasis to the bleeding point. With his bribes of pennies and nickels clutched in our small paws, we scurried across the alley to the bowling lanes to buy Tootsie rolls, bubble gum, and ice cream cones, reveling in the arrangement.

To which my mother objected strenuously, "Francis, you'll rot their teeth."

"Good, then maybe they won't make so goddamn much noise."

Uncle Frank was the only person in the world Mom had any truck with who swore. In the days when a kid could get his/her mouth washed out with soap for saying "shit," our uncle was as alluring as a circus performer. My mother, Helen Callahan McDermott, was inexplicably loyal to her brilliant brother, who lived in Farley, Iowa, a small town a dozen miles to the north of Cascade, where we lived. Far more grievous to her than his occasional spurt of profanity was that he never went to church! We knew non-Catholics: people who eschewed the one true religion and joined some other, but the only atheist for miles was my uncle. Mom prayed incessantly for the salvation of his immortal soul and sent the priest around frequently, but Francis remained resolutely irreligious. Nevertheless, whenever we traveled to Dubuque to sell the sheep's wool and/or pick up our welfare commodities, Mom would head north on the county gravel, stop in Farley, and visit him. The drive there always featured a lecture. "Now behave yourselves when we get to Francis's—no fighting, shouting, or running in and out. You know how you make his psoriasis flare up."

He lived in a two-room trailer behind Sherrman's Hardware just off Main Street. The trailer was silver outside and a uniform golden brown on the inside as he chain-smoked, never washed the windows, woodwork, or walls, and burned most of what he cooked. Putting potatoes to boil and a pork chop in a pan, he would sit down to calculate a math problem and become totally engrossed. By the time he noticed the smell the spuds were charcoal and the chop shoe leather, so he would meander over to Kramer's Korner Kafé for dinner.

Uncle Frank endeared himself to us somewhat by the late winter or early spring of my eighth-grade year. Dad was dead by then. School had become a trial and a painful tribulation. Everybody had TV, and every day they discussed the latest Mickey Mouse Club adventures of Annette or *Corky and White Shadow*. Unlike parents today who seem responsive to their offspring's every wish and whim, Mom dismissed our pleas for a TV amusingly, mockingly, or truthfully, depending on her mood.

"Now, there's a serious problem—*you* have nothing to say. My dear child, *that* strains my credibility."

Or, "Read a book! Then maybe you'll have something to say that isn't the usual tripe you girls carry on with."

Around the end of the month, Mom would give me a haggard look, run her hands through her gray hair, and groan, "Good Lord, child, I don't know what we will be eating next week, and you want me to spend what little money we have on a TV?"

I quit badgering then and resigned myself to the fate of social pariah. However, one overcast March afternoon, I bopped into the house after school, and like a blue-white apparition of the Blessed Virgin, there was an ethereal glow coming from the corner of the kitchen.

"A TV! You got us a TV, Mom!"

"Rest assured I did not! Sit down and write your Uncle Francis a thank you note."

My uncle fixed TVs in the day when they had tubes and could be fixed. Ours had been in a fire—one side was charred and the owner had given it to Uncle Frank, who didn't want it. With this miracle, I escaped pari-ahhood and became a cheerleader the following year. Our game against Farley was the Friday night before Thanksgiving, and I was standing in front of the mirror ratting my hair when Mom said, "Shirley, you stop by Uncle Francis's and invite him for Thanksgiving."

"Mo-ther!" I howled in my newly adopted exasperated-adult tone of voice. "You have invited him every Thanksgiving, Christmas, and Easter since, when? Nineteen ought two? He wouldn't come here if it was the Last Supper." Mom scowled deeply at the religious dig that I had known beforehand was over the line.

"That couldn't have anything to do with the racket the lot of you make, now could it? Stop and invite your uncle, I said."

Not wanting to tell the other cheerleaders where I was going, I mumbled something about running an errand when we arrived in Farley. I sprinted out of St. Joe's gym, up Main Street, around the corner into the alley, and banged on the trailer door.

"It's open," he called out.

I stepped up into the haze and reek of Camel smoke. More TV sets than I'd ever seen—on the floor, on the counter that formed the kitchen of the trailer, two of them playing Walter Cronkite, all presumably being tested. The ones on the chairs were either fixed or waiting to be. Sitting at the raw wood work-bench in a spot cleared of TV debris was my uncle working a gargantuan algebra problem with a pile of math books and a pad of paper.

Having resolved to be nice to my major benefactor—weird, smelly old atheist though he might be—I grinned, "Hi, Uncle Francis; doing your homework?"

He smiled, and I saw his hair was going gray. It stuck out like Einstein's—that was probably what happened to smart guys' hair with so much going on in their brains underneath, I concluded.

"And how come you're not home doing yours?"

"I am a cheerleader! We're playing here tonight."

More amused than impressed, he shook his head dismissively to which I said, "You got more TVs than a store!"

Again he smiled, and I half expected him to give me a nickel but he didn't. Amazingly, in the tone of voice he used with Mom and other adults, he scoffed, "Ach, I'm inundated, and what's more, some of these drooling, dribbling eejits, dithering cretins, and flaming morons who can't live without their goddamn television sets long enough to bring 'em to town for me to fix are now wanting me to run out to their houses to do it!" He rolled his eyes and shook his head.

"No kidding? You have to go out to their house to fix their TV?"

"'Bout the size of it, girl."

"Uncle Frank, yer a TV doc—you make house calls!" I howled.

He smirked in that deliciously wicked way they all did when my Uncle Walter visited from Chicago. Aunt Agnes, Mom, and their aunts, sparkling with finger rings, pendants, and necklaces, and the great-uncles, their vests draped with gold watch chains, sat drinking long-necked beers in the shade of the elms in our back yard, chuckling, chortling, rolling their eyeballs, and lifting eyebrows. The McDermotts, my father's people, guffawed, gossiped, sang, danced, and drank too much. The Callahans, stylish, educated, and old money (I eventually discovered), were subtle, but I was half and half.

I glanced at the clock. "Oh! I got to get back to the gym. The girls'll kill me if I am late." I pulled my mittens back on and opened the door. "Oh, I almost forgot—Mom says come for Thanksgiving."

He hesitated, "Well, tell her to expect me when she sees me."

"Well, Uncle Frank, we'll expect you when we see you, then." I waved and bolted.

"Bye, kid!" he called as I dashed out, "come again!"

Come again! Flabbergasted, I fell off the trailer step, caught myself, and stood stock still in the mid-winter midwestern dark for a brief moment, frozen in disbelief!

I didn't go again very soon. Now when the car went with the sheep's wool for commodities, it was "the little kids" with Mom. From friends and acquaintances about the countryside, I discovered we were not the only kids whose ructions made Uncle Frank's psoriasis scab, scale, bleed, and creep up his arm like some vigorous forerunner of Ebola. We were the only ones he bribed; the rest he tricked, which made me feel special.

At the pre-dawn of the "information age" (the 1950s in cities, late 1950s and early 1960s in the countryside), many little kids without TVs believed Lawrence Welk and Alice Lon, Bishop Sheen, the Lone Ranger, Roy Rogers, Dale Evans, and Ed Sullivan resided inside television sets, a race of talented Lilliputians, eagerly awaiting the opportunity to entertain us. To young farm kids of rural Iowa, a man who could take the back off a TV set thus liberating the "TV people" was as irresistible as a magician, and they latched on to Francis like schools of lamprey eels. His favorite device for dislodging them was to enlist their aid, holding an "antenna" (of defective wire) he had ceremoniously attached to the TV while they watched and then running as far as its length would allow from where he was working. A friend and his brothers and sisters were discovered "helping" Frank fix the TV long after he had finished the job, eaten the pie, drank the coffee, tossed the toolbox in his rattle trap truck, and driven back to town.

People were amused at his peculiarities, and most didn't take his atheism as seriously as did Mom, but I was totally unprepared for Bobby Locher's assessment at a sock hop one night after a game. We'd been dancing a while, and when the music slowed, he looked at me curiously. "You know, I heard something really interesting about you."

I froze and responded defensively. "Yeah, what?"

"I heard the judge is your uncle."

Relieved it was not some lie a welfare girl's reputation could not fend off, I breathed a sigh of relief. "Nobody in my family is a judge, not even a lawyer."

"No, I mean *The Judge*, Judge Callahan."

"Are you talking about my Uncle Francis across from the bowling alley?" I asked in disbelief.

"Smartest guy I ever met. Wouldn't have passed algebra without him."

Bobby heaped extravagances of praise upon my uncle, who he said helped all the guys in his class, so that the algebra teacher had to start going to him to stay ahead of the class! Good thing we were dancing and he was holding me up because I might have fallen flat on my face. Apparently Farley locals had begun calling my uncle "Judge Callahan" because, according to Bobby, he had been quietly dispensing advice on their dilemmas from his regular table at Kramer's for years—when he wasn't sitting in the trailer working problems mathematicians had been trying to solve from time immemorial or fixing TVs.

I had managed to get myself enrolled in a college that was a bit of a finishing school, the sort of place I was convinced a welfare girl needed.

Late summer before freshman year I stopped in Farley on the way to a shopping excursion. Mom agreed clothes mattered, especially where I was enrolled. Since my existing wardrobe was created on her sewing machine, we decided I needed new. Of course nobody had ever seen Uncle Frank in anything but the khaki shirt and pants he ordered from the Monkey Ward catalog when the previous set bit the dust.

"Well, any time you are going to buy something," he counseled me sitting at the corner table in Kramer's, "consider it and then go home, wait two weeks, and if you still want it go back and look at it or try it on again."

"That's a month, Uncle Francis!"

"Go home and wait another two weeks and go back and try it on again."

"But," I protested, "it will be gone or practically the next season."

"There, you see! You didn't need the goddamn thing to begin with!"

Emperor's New Clothes to the fifth power: He believed that clothes were one of the nefarious ways the human animal had convinced itself that it was "beautiful" and lorded over others. He was ready with facts about cultures where only royalty could wear certain colors and designs, and he delivered them as indictments of the clothes culture. Furthermore, fashion masks ugliness, so it is essentially a lie. Caught between the ethics of my mother and uncle, I returned from my shopping trip with several pieces of material, and I started college that fall in homemade rather than store-bought.

Sometime before I graduated I saw him again, with a handful of guys at the table. He pointed to the change the waitress left before he picked it up, and asked, "See this dime? This quarter? You know what they're made of?"

"Yeah, silver." We replied in unison.

"Not for long. By the time this war is over, there isn't going to be a solid silver coin left on the streets of this country."

"What war?"

"The war in Vietnam," he said. "We've picked up where the French left off, are sending more 'advisors' in there every month, and you can mark my words they aren't going to have any better luck fighting it than the frogs. . . ."

Frogs? Vietnam? Not the first time nobody had any idea what he was talking about. He paused, looking sadly around the table, ". . . and you guys are going to end up fighting it, dying over there."

"Where's Vietnam?"

He explained but most of us had to check a map later.

"So what does that have to do with dimes and quarters?"

"The government doesn't have the money for this war." A glance around the table told him none of us had yet made the connection. "Inflation," he hollered, pounding the table, making the silverware hop. "When the government doesn't have enough money to pay its bills it prints more and mints coins with a lower percentage of valuable minerals."

"How can they do that?"

"Read history! Governments have always inflated their currencies to raise the money for wars they can't afford."

Fatuous and full of civics class propaganda, each of us sat grappling with the concept. Several of the guys found out firsthand where Vietnam was. One returned in a coffin, and a couple others, their health ravaged by drugs and Agent Orange, would have been better off in boxes, I'm sure my uncle would have said.

As happens with many smalltown young people, jobs and opportunities swept us away from the Midwest. I was flying high publishing a medical catalog for Europe; everything I wore was store-bought, my boots Gucci. I did think of my uncle whenever I read an article, heard a lecture or discussion about an idea he espoused or opposed. He was the first person I ever heard use the word "ecology" (though it wasn't the first time he'd used a word I didn't know!). His ruminations on the climatological effects of this or that human stupidity had taken root. I struggled to recall when I'd first heard him fretting over the impact of cutting the great midwestern forest that had once run the length of the Mississippi valley. If not firsthand, second through Mom. When everybody in the countryside was planning on a sleek new automobile, he continued to repair his vintage truck and used it only for work, decrying "driving all over hell's half acre, widening roads, building highways, and taking farmland out of production."

I honestly don't know if he were simply prescient or had a rare source of information. He had taught math at a technical institute during World War II when so many math teachers were drafted, so he had university ties.

Religion, mostly about money, masquerades as spirituality and flatters us shamefully. "If God's only begotten son died to save us, we must really be something, huh?" he asked rhetorically, raising a bushy gray eyebrow. He believed the human race was short on humility and long on vanity, and that the more money you had the more you fancied yourself, and the bigger fraud you were. It began to seem every word he had said had lodged itself in my brain. When a topic arose, his was there to compare with the new idea, but it was years before I could amass the courage to conform my life to his advice.

One summer when my Euro gig was beginning to evaporate, my sister and I were both home and plotting a shopping trip to Dubuque. Mom suggested, "Stop by to see your Uncle Francis. He's not good."

"What do you mean, Mom?"

"Emphysema. Cholesterol. Smoked all those years and ate all that deep-fried restaurant food." She shook her head. A good Catholic woman, steeped in guilt, she still blamed herself for not correcting his lifestyle habits and reconverting him.

When we knocked, we could barely hear him call, as always, "It's open."

We could see he was in bad shape, wheezing and breathing with difficulty. He had quit smoking, too little, too late. The trailer walls had been scrubbed, the windows sparkled, and new curtains hung at them, testimony to my mother's sewing machine and solicitations. There were no TVs now—not having to fix them, he felt no compunction to have or look at one. He was convinced watching television made you stupid because it passively dumped ideas on you without listening to your response.

"Your mom said you were coming home. Hoped to see you, though ..."

"Why wouldn't we come?" I said blithely as we placed the field flowers we'd brought in a jelly jar. We felt overwhelmed with guilt for the times we'd been home and hadn't stopped to see him. At that moment I knew that the handsome, hat-in-hand peasant of a man who was our father was in many ways far less our father than the man whose leonine white mane covered the pillow.

We sat on kitchen chairs in the tiny hallway of the trailer bedroom and chatted. My sister and I intertwined questions about Paul Breen, Bobby Locher, and the others gone to Vietnam and Canada with a happy banter of personal news, family gossip, and European observations which he seemed eager to hear. He was too exhausted to talk much.

He died a couple of weeks later, and though he did not request a priest as she had hoped, Mom gave him a full Catholic funeral. The Knights of Columbus, dressed in their uniforms with the red plumes in their hats, stood guard while most of the townspeople made their way to the parlor, said a Hail Mary! Our Father and Glory Be for the repose of his atheistic soul. We did not bother to object—he would have loved the irony and appreciated their presence anyway.

In his inimitable fashion, he made them really festive. He had left an envelope "To be opened immediately upon the occasion of my Death." Inside was a treasure map showing where he had buried all the silver coins he had squirreled away before they disappeared before the Vietnam War ended!

I eventually moved back to Cascade, to the "homeplace." Mom died, and in the early 1990s I started a newspaper which for a few years covered local city councils and major issues. One day I was selling an ad to Schroeder, the owner of the Farley Main Street bar, when he said, "I heard something very interesting about you."

"This conversation feels very déjà vu."

"Somebody told me you were Judge Callahan's niece." Though he'd been dead by then for almost two decades, nobody had replaced him at the corner table in Kramer's, and he was missed.

"Absolutely true."

"Well, that explains it," he said. "Now I can see why your paper is so . . ." he hesitated, ". . . ah, intelligent, honest."

It also had a reputation for being negative, not surprisingly, as I had committed to what I saw as the "truth." I knew from my uncle it was dangerous: humans prefer lies because they are prettier, and most public institutions oblige.

I often ran into people who remembered my Uncle Francis, but one of them, Bob Sherrman, still confounds me, even though Bob's been in his grave five years. Francis had worked in Bob's hardware store early on. He and I fell into amused speculation on how much time Fathers X, Y, and Z had wasted trying to re-convert my uncle. From there we estimated how many atheists, agnostics, and skeptics Francis had created in his years in the corner at the restaurant.

When we tired of the game, I observed, "He was the only natural-born, organic atheist I have ever known."

"Well, I disagree with that. There is probably no such thing, especially not your uncle. It was Elaine's death."

Flabbergasted, I asked, "Elaine, who's Elaine?"

"Well, I didn't know much about her, but I believe she was from Dubuque and they intended to get married."

"What! Are you kidding me? I don't believe it!"

My Chicago Uncle Walter, the only Callahan left, confirmed this, but he knew even less.

I eventually located a small shred of proof in the family photo album. It is a grainy, deckle-edged black-and-white of a young and handsome Frank Callahan standing in the enclosed upper deck of a baseball stadium or race track with his arm around a pretty young woman with dark, marcelled hair.

Women Who Wore Aprons

BY ANN STRUTHERS

2014

DRINKING A CUP OF coffee, I sit here at my kitchen table where I can see part of my collection of aprons hanging in the back entryway. There is something homey, comforting, and symbolic of the household in their shapes and colors. I remember the women of my childhood who all wore aprons of various styles, women who were hard-working, frugal, practical, down-to-earth, who maintained high standards for the conduct of both children and adults. They knew what was right and wrong; they stood by their values; they required their children to live by those values.

When I was growing up in rural northwestern Iowa, the women I knew wore bright cotton printed aprons over their house dresses. The most popular style was one that I call the Berdelia Lewis apron after the neighbor woman who always wore that over-the-shoulders, tied-in-the-back, almost-as-long-as-her-skirt, one-pocketed garment. She cut off the pattern for my mother. She folded one of her own aprons in half lengthwise, laid it down on a sheet of folded newspaper, and cut around it. Presto, the pattern. My mother was used to city life, and Berdelia Lewis wanted to get her started right.

Mrs. Lewis and other rural Iowa women sewed their aprons from brightly colored printed cotton and inevitably trimmed them with a contrasting color of bias tape. Sometimes the bias tape made the strings that tied in back, too, but most of the time there were same-material sashes because these were easier to tie and untie and didn't get caught in the washing machine's wringer as strings of tape tended to do. I remember my mother putting on a clean apron every morning. Although aprons had to be ironed, a crisp, clean one was a badge of office for them.

Many of the women made their aprons from chicken feed sacks. Chicken feed came in 50-pound cotton bags, and housewives went with their husbands to the feed store to pick out patterns they fancied. To make a dress, it was necessary to get at least two bags of the same pattern, but one sack would make an apron. Usually their aprons didn't match their dresses, but rather provided a vivid contrast both in color and pattern. They could have posed as models for Matisse if he had painted Iowa farm women.

My mother and Mrs. Lewis weren't the only women who wore aprons. All the women I knew wore them. I remember walking to school one fall morning and a group of boys ahead of me started throwing rocks at a squirrel. Mrs. Summers rushed out of her house, scolded everybody within sight, including me. She told us, "Squirrels have a right to live, too." Then she shook her apron at us, shooing us off as if we were a flock of chickens. The women who wore aprons looked after everybody's chickens and children.

The apron was immensely practical. It inevitably had a pocket, even the frilly little half-aprons that brides gave their friends who helped serve food in the church parlors at weddings. Mrs. Jorgensen found out just how practical hers was. One Saturday morning when she was busy picking up everything and cleaning for Sunday, she heard her youngest boy scream. She rushed out to the driveway and found that one of the other children had slammed the car door on his finger, cutting it off. Blood was spurting all over. She ran back to the kitchen, grabbed a clean towel to wrap it in, and drove him to the doctor. While the doctor examined the child's injured hand, he remarked that it was too bad she hadn't saved the fingertip—he thought he could have stitched it back on. Mrs. Jorgensen groped in her apron pocket—and there was the fingertip. She had automatically picked it up! Today Mat Jorgensen has all his fingers, and they all work—because of his mother's apron pocket!

Although most of the country women wore practical clothes, Aunt

Esther always wore her old dress shoes around the house. This was an economy measure with her, but despite the high heels, she always wore the mandatory apron. My brown printed one with a wide white ruffle around it is exactly the kind she wore when serving the threshers dinner.

Not long ago I attended a party where all the talk was of the recent scandals among the highly paid CEOs of American industry—those who were being led off in handcuffs to jail and those who others said ought to be going to jail. I thought to myself, didn't their mothers ever tell them that they could not lie, cheat, and steal? They should have had mothers with aprons, women with sturdy standards, women with no-nonsense characters who made naughty children sit in corners, washed out certain mouths with soap, towered over quarreling kids and without a word broke up their arguments.

Today I collect old aprons and give them to my younger friends as house-warming gifts when they move into a new home. It is fun to search for them at garage sales and church rummage sales, and I always keep a few for myself. Right now my coffee is getting cold while I gaze with fondness at the blue feed sack apron hanging by the range. I slip it on over my office clothes when I come home at night and don't have time to change. It protects me from splashes of spaghetti sauce or the splatter from the frying pan. More than that, it reminds me of those wonderful women of integrity who wore aprons proudly.

The Third King

BY RUSTIN LARSON
2015

Myrrh is mine, its bitter perfume
Breathes a life of gathering gloom;
Sorrowing, sighing, bleeding, dying,
Sealed in the stone-cold tomb.
P. S. Merry Christmas.

M Y MOTHER LIKED TO tap-dance on a pickle barrel when she was five. This was in 1934, in the middle of the Great Depression in a little village in northern Iowa. On Christmas Eve they had a pageant, and all the children received a lunch sack filled with peanuts, hard candy, and one fresh orange. Brimming with *joie de vivre*, my mother tap-danced on her pickle barrel to the tune of "Jingle Bells." The widely known American Christmas song was written by James Lord Pierpont (1822–1893) and published as "One Horse Open Sleigh" in the fall of 1857. It's irrevocably tied to Christmas, but Pierpont wrote it for Thanksgiving. In my mother's day, children costumed as sheep, cattle, kings, and shepherds joined in the revelry, jingling their bags of goodies.

Eventually my mother grew up, married, and had children. I was one of them. With her encouragement, I agreed to be one of the three kings in our church's pageant. I was eight. Two other kings would join me: Sunday school classmates Chucky and Randy.

Randy's mom was our director. She had straight blonde hair she wore in a ponytail. She directed us with her palm held out as if a small bird were about to land in it.

Our church resembled an overturned Viking ship. That was appropriate because many of the parishioners were the descendants of overturned (converted) Vikings. Vikings, it is told, did not convert easily. Those old Norse ways didn't completely leave them. They could not quite get the hang of concepts like original sin, the Incarnation, and the Holy Trinity, so they clung to old practices like the invocation of Valkyries. Becoming Christian was a 200-year-long process. Only when the Germans told them that Christ was a kind of warrior king come to defeat Satan did they start cottoning to the idea.

"We Three Kings," or "We Three Kings of Orient Are" or "The Quest of the Magi," is a carol written by John Henry Hopkins Jr., in 1857. When Hopkins wrote it he was the rector of Williamsport, Pennsylvania Christ Episcopal Church. Singers first performed the carol at a Christmas pageant in New York City. It is still quite popular.

I was selected to be the king bearing myrrh. I was the third king.

> Myrrh is mine, its bitter perfume
> Breathes a life of gathering gloom;
> Sorrowing, sighing, bleeding, dying,
> Sealed in the stone-cold tomb.

By far, those are the song's darkest lyrics. They portend the crucifixion and entombment of Jesus Christ. Chucky was frankincense. Randy was gold. I was the last king to sing a solo verse. The final verse we sang together as a trio.

By the way, myrrh is an Arabic word. Myrrh is a resin historically used as a perfume, incense, or medicine. (Some say it can be drunk by mixing it with wine, but I am by no means encouraging it.)

After weeks of practice in the church basement, we filed into our front row pew on the evening of the pageant. Randy's mom looked as determined as the figurehead of a ship's prow. On with the show. The principal characters—the holy family, the cattle, the sheep, the donkeys, the shepherds, and the angels—all took the sanctuary platform and said their lines. Soon it was time for the kings. The plump pianist sounded her introductory chords, and we journeyed single file onto the scene.

"Frankincense to offer have I," sang Chucky, raspy and a little off key. His dad, who sold recapped tires, smiled uncomfortably. His mother beamed. It was Randy's turn next.

"Gold we bring to crown him again," Randy sang. Randy's mom conducted and nodded, her thin white hand still waiting for the mysterious bird to land in it.

My heart raced. I was next. The piano's chords made a dramatic change in key, it seemed. Could those chords possibly be more melancholy, more minor? Was it possible?

"Myrrh is mine, its bitter perfume / Breathes a life of gathering gloom," I sang, and how was it that my voice became so silver, so pure, so angelic? The song sang itself without cracking; it was a bird of pure silver featherlight blown glass that floated and landed gently in our conductor's outstretched and waiting palm. Her eyes widened; she nodded; she smiled; and by the time I sang "Sorrowing, sighing, bleeding, dying," a single tear was trickling down her powdered cheek.

With our songs completed, the Nativity scene characters took their places again in the pew. I noticed how they were all scrunched together as far away from me as possible, looking through the corners of their eyes and whispering to each other. Randy's mom sat next to me and put her arm around me and whispered warmly in my ear, "That was so beautiful." I felt like a creature perched high in a stone tower. In my mind I could see the lights of the town in winter twinkling in the darkness. In my mind I could hear the bells clang, and I could feel the creature I was suddenly flying.

Things I Didn't Learn in School

BY JONNA HIGGINS-FREESE

2015

WHEN I WAS FIRST learning to speak French, I sat at my desk on the second floor of Frank L. Smart Junior High in Davenport, Iowa. Beyond the trees outside the window, half a mile south of the school, the Mississippi made a wide curve to the west, flowing shallow and brown.

In French class we conjugated verbs and talked about French culture. We imagined sitting at a cafe in Paris, eating crêpes and studying for the baccalaureate at the end of high school, activities so different from my midwestern life of going to the mall for entertainment and eating minute steaks from the crock pot. My friends Chad and Sara recently confirmed that no one told us we were only 150 years too late to speak French right where we stood. No one ever told us that for hundreds of years, people had lived their lives in French—and Ho-Chunk (Winnebago), Meskwaki, and Sauk—in what would become the Quad Cities.

In Social Studies with Mr. Grubbs and Mr. Riedesel, eighth and ninth grade covered early American history, which happened in Boston and Philadelphia in the 1700s. Mr. Grubbs tried to make things fun with a quiz game called "Buzz Box." We walked to the front of the room two at a time, pressed the button when we knew the answer, and whoever answered correctly got to stay.

In my white Reeboks and jeans and heavy sweaters, I could be nearly assured of staying at the Buzz Box at least until Chad came up. We answered questions about the Stamp Act and Shay's Rebellion and the Boston Tea Party, where the colonists protested British taxes by dressing as "Indians." Those Indians showed up again allied with the French for a war, again mysterious in origin.

Much later, I went away to graduate school and lived in the narrow, twisty streets of Boston's North End, near Paul Revere's house. Part of my daily walk to the "T" followed the red painted line of the Freedom Trail. Later my husband and I moved to Concord, and I would think sometimes of how strange it was to live in a place where Important Things had happened, a place so different from the one where I grew up.

In Iowa before the Civil War, there had been a few paragraphs called Prehistory, about when Indians lived here. Some said the state's name meant "Beautiful Land" in the Ioway language, but that seemed too trite to be true. Besides, who'd ever heard of the Ioway? We didn't see any around.

Then, a few years ago, I came across *1491: New Revelations of the Americas before Columbus*, and *1493: Uncovering the New World Columbus Created*, both by Charles Mann.

Following a trail of references and footnotes from these books, I learned that U.S. history had been presented as happening on the east coast, not because nothing was happening in the blank middle of the continent, but precisely because there was so much: a vast, dense Native New World of French and British traders and native hunters, farmers, and business people who controlled land and resources and trade in the center of the continent.

The English settler colonists had been confined to the eastern seaboard for hundreds of years because they weren't in charge elsewhere— they didn't have the technology or social networks required to survive travel through the Great Lakes or up the Mississippi without indigenous guides and chaperones.

How could I have missed learning about this fascinating "middle ground," where there was conflict and violence and resistance—yes, but also cooperation, trade, friendship, marriage, and families?

One weekend as my husband and children and I drove from Iowa City to the Chicago suburbs to visit family, we passed Algonquin Road, Sauk Valley College, Fox Lane. We'd traveled this way many times before, but this time, I saw. I knew now the Algonquin referred to a group of related languages and peoples who, in 1491, had lived in territory spanning from the St. Lawrence to the western Great Lakes. I knew now that the Sauk were the Sac, of the Sac and Fox tribe. They have land now in Oklahoma,

Kansas, and Nebraska, but from the late 1600s to the 1820s they lived in Illinois and Wisconsin. I no longer assumed that the Fox River was named for a small red mammal, but knew that it might well refer to the Fox, or Meskwaki, who had lived in the area until the Fox Wars of the early eighteenth century.

Once I connected the names with the history, I began to see them everywhere: Dubuque, Joliet, Marquette, LaSalle, Black Hawk. Especially Black Hawk: Black Hawk College, Black Hawk State Bank (with Black Hawk's profile as the logo), Black Hawk Road.

Black Hawk lived when the middle ground of marriage and indigenous control of the land was giving way to something else. In the late 1820s, when the Sauk returned from their winter hunts to Saukenuk, a town with wood-framed homes laid out along streets and open squares where Rock Island, Illinois, now stands, they found United States citizens living in their homes and planting their fields. The U.S. government said the Sauk had ceded the land by treaty in 1804, with the provision that the tribe could continue living there until the land was wanted for Anglo settlement. The Sauk denied ever having ceded any land north of the Rock River. Each spring they turned the Americans out of the homes and fields they had taken. But every year when the Sauk returned from their winter hunt, there the Anglos were again.

The Sauk protested. They talked to George Davenport, a well-connected former army officer and fur trader at Rock Island. And they talked to Antoine LeClaire, the army interpreter at the fort, who was the son of a French Canadian man and a Potawatomi woman. His wife, Marguerite LePage, was the daughter of a French Canadian and the granddaughter of the Sauk chief Acoqua. Davenport and LeClaire advised the Sauk to not return to Saukenuk (Davenport would later buy 3,000 acres of this land from the federal government). About two-thirds of the Sauk, led by Keokuk, believed it was futile to confront the Anglo settlers. They had seen what the U.S. had done to the tribes which had resisted the invasion of the Ohio country and to the Winnebago who resisted the taking of their land in 1827 in Wisconsin.

But Black Hawk, a quiet, traditional man, wanted to return to Saukenuk, the center of his people's world, where many of his ancestors were buried on the ridge above the river. He was encouraged by many of the women, who wanted to return to the fields the tribe had cultivated for a hundred years. Their sisters and cousins, who had broken new land in Iowa, told them how difficult it was to till the new fields and harvest enough crops to feed the children through the winter.

And so, in April 1832, Black Hawk led a thousand or more men, women, and children back across to the eastern side of the Mississippi.

I never studied the Black Hawk War in school, although Smart Junior High stood on Fifth Street, which had been called Chippewa Street until the Davenport city council changed the street's name in 1840. The other east-west streets downtown—Sac, Fox, Ottawa, and Potawatomi—also were changed to numbers. (Davenport's north-south streets are still named for the U.S. military leaders from the conflict: Clark, Gaines, Brady, and Scott.) Instead, we memorized the Preamble to the Constitution until Sara and I could, for entertainment, recite it to each other at breakneck speed, while we waited in the cold for the bus.

As an adult, then, I learned that the Sauk won early battles in the war and succeeded, temporarily, in emptying parts of three states of European settlers, who fled their farms and took shelter at some 30 forts. General Atkinson was willing to avoid a fight if possible, although he was thwarted by the Illinois governor and the volunteer militia, who mostly wanted only to kill Indians. Twice Black Hawk's band attempted to surrender. But by the end of July, Black Hawk's people had traveled hundreds of miles up the Rock River and back down the Wisconsin. They had lost men, women, and children to fighting, hunger, and illness. Even their horses were dying. They set out to escape back west, across the Mississippi (into Iowa) just below the Bad Axe River. By pure chance, some U.S. soldiers and militia picked up their trail. On the east bank of the Mississippi, on a hot August afternoon, the Sauk once again tried to surrender to an armed steamboat on the river. Their offer was ignored. Trapped between the steamboat and soldiers on the bluffs above, hundreds of men, women, and children were butchered. One escapee swam across the river with her baby wrapped in a blanket held in her teeth. The Battle of Bad Axe could only be classified as genocide.

What had changed? What altered conditions to devolve from a time of marriage and negotiation to one of intense racial hatred?

After some time reading an academic history of "settler colonialism," I concluded that the explanation rested in the fields at Saukenuk: The

Americans who arrived in the 1820s were settlers, not traders as the British and French had been. They wanted the land. Settler colonists pretend to themselves that the land is an empty wilderness, available for the taking. The settlers wanted Saukenuk not because it was an empty wilderness, but because Sauk women had cultivated it for a hundred years. It was more fertile and easier to work than new fields hacked into the sod (especially before 1837 when John Deere invented the steel plow).

Our teachers and the textbook authors must have thought we shouldn't learn about the Meskwaki villages that had stood just steps from Smart Junior High on Chippewa Street. We shouldn't learn about the Sauk fields our ancestors wanted as well as the Meskwaki and Winnebago lead mines north of us at Dubuque and in Wisconsin and Illinois. We couldn't learn about the hundreds of years when the French and British traders who married the Sauk and Meskwaki, or of the armed soldiers who murdered women and children just upriver from us, because that wouldn't have fit with the story about justice and the blessings of liberty. Learning that history would have complicated the story and opened the possibility that things could have been different then—or that we ought to do something different now.

As William Faulkner so famously said, the past is never dead. And for me, it was constantly erupting from the landscape of my daily life. I drove on Dodge Street to an office on Scott Boulevard. I lived in Iowa City, whose location has everything to do with the three prominent Meskwaki villages that stood here in 1839, as well as the land speculation and cessions that followed the Black Hawk War.

I didn't blame the Europeans who wanted the Indians' land—well, some of them I did. The more I learned about George Davenport, the more reprehensible he seemed. (In addition to buying the Sauks's land after advising them to stop fighting for it, he had two children with his stepdaughter, who was 16 when the first was born.)

But the people who bought that land from Davenport were, I thought, not so different from me: just trying to feed their families and keep a roof over their heads. The farmers and small business owners who fought in the militia came from families like mine and those of the kids I attended school with at Frank L. Smart. They had nothing much in the world but their ability to work and the opportunity to do so, whether on a farm in 1832 or the John Deere or Oscar Mayer factory in 1982. I wasn't sure

I'd have done anything different from what they did—wasn't sure I was doing, in effect, anything different from what they did. When I listened to NPR in the morning driving to work, and heard about millions of refugees fleeing their homes in the Middle East, I knew that was partly about the gas in my car. I wasn't less implicated because I wasn't carrying a gun.

I couldn't stop thinking about the Sauk woman swimming across the Mississippi under gunfire, with her baby in a blanket in her teeth. I've always been afraid of water, and when I wake from a nightmare, as often as not, it's of a child slipping from my hands under the surface of a lake or river. I could feel her terror and the courage that comes from having no choice. Systematically, legally, violently, the Indians had lost their land and their homes, likely at the hands of my great-great-grandparents.

But I wasn't interested in seeing the Indians only as wise, environmentally conscious, peaceful victims, burying their hearts at Wounded Knee, either. I remembered hundreds of years of negotiation and conflict and marriage, of creating a middle ground between what the Indians thought right and the Europeans wanted. The Indians, too, had been violent and cruel. Though they had lost their land, though they'd been clearly wronged, they were wronged as people, as whole and complicated human beings. And though they'd been wronged, they had not vanished. As Johnathan Buffalo, a Meskwaki, writes, "In 1721, the French King signed a decree commanding the complete extermination of the Meskwaki. Nevertheless, the Meskwaki remain. Neither New France nor its French monarchy exists anymore."

I didn't want a fairy tale or a horror story, but something more real, more like my own mundane life, than any romantic visions of Paris or an idealized Indian past. Learning to read the names that remained in the landscape brought history into the present in a way that was, for me, complex and layered and satisfying.

Living with complexity—which is, after all, the real condition of all of us whose lives are built on fossil energy and slave labor—seems better than the alternative, better than turning Chippewa Street into Fifth Street and pretending the past was orderly and safe.

I don't know if anything would be different if I had learned these things in school. I learned recently about Unsettling Minnesota, a group of non-Indian people working in solidarity toward decolonization in

Indian homelands. I haven't found a group called Unsettling Iowa, and part of my privilege is the possibility to decide that I might not care to engage in uncomfortable work as an ally to native people in their struggle. Having done some activist work in the past, my excuses are that I'm not good at it and that it's unpleasant. Not as unpleasant as being shot at in the river, of course, but less pleasant than a leisurely canoe trip on Black Hawk Lake.

But I can hear now more of what the landscape around me is saying. I can try to weave it into stories that will make sense of it. And so can you.

I've nearly always lived in places where the Sauk and Meskwaki used to live, so as one ridiculously trivial gesture toward allyship and unsettling, I'll send the payment from this essay to the Meskwaki Museum and Cultural Center in Tama, which I know now was named for Taimaj (1790–1830), a Meskwaki man who led villages near present-day Burlington, Iowa, and Gladstone, Illinois.

Editor's note: The writer would like to thank Catherine Reinhardt of the Special Collections Department at the Davenport Public Library for her tedious search through early city council minutes. Also, Chad V. Holtkamp and Sara Tietjen Jones for help with details of the curriculum at Frank L. Smart Junior High in the 1980s, to say nothing of their decades of friendship. And finally she would like to thank all the teachers of the Davenport Community School District for instilling a love of learning.

The Naming of Birds

BY GLENN FREEMAN
2015

To name something is to wait for it in the place you think it will pass.
—Amiri Baraka

MY NECK HURTS FROM staring straight up for so long into a clear May sky. We've seen the movement but can't find the bird. Then we get a glimpse of the tail—black and white—but we can't see more. A brief glimpse of orange—a redstart perhaps?—then the bird is gone, and we crane our necks farther back, slowly spinning and stumbling in tight circles waiting for movement or a flash of color. But the bird is hidden at the top of a 40-foot canopy, thick with wood and young leaf and brilliant sun. If I were a better birder, I'd be able to make something out of this clue: a bird which forages at the very tips of such tall trees. But then it flies through the foliage and lands in a new spot, one less dense, one with better lighting. I catch a silhouette. Orange on the breast and shoulder. I should know it by now, but I don't—definitely something I haven't seen before, but I can see it in my mind's eye from the book, some bird I know I've run by in my attempt to identify other birds. But I don't have my book. And the bird has flitted into shadows again.

This is my kind of hunting, to seek out and find a new bird on its own terms. I can see it moving in and out of foliage above my head, but it's

mid-day, and the sun only obscures its features. Eventually the bird drops
down a few limbs away from the sun. So close to solving the puzzle, but
it eludes me. Only when it seems to have had enough of this game and
turns straight toward me with its brilliant orange chest and streaked head
am I able to name it: my first Blackburnian warbler. There are birds that
over years of birding become almost mythical; you've heard the name,
seen the images, but you get to where you will never see one. Over 20
years of birding, and I have now seen one Blackburnian. But I will always
know this bird, and the next time I get a flash of that particular orange
I will know it. How I love that moment when you finally uncover what
you're looking at and can name it, can add it to your list.

For decades, my Aprils and Mays have been lost in the search for
these neotropical migrants. As the juncos head north mid-April, the first
kinglets arrive from the south, tiny nervous birds that blend into the still
leafless woods except for their occasional tiny but extravagant flash of red
(or gold, depending on species) at the crest of their heads. I know where
to find them, and so I keep watch, and once I see my first, the woods
seem to become alive with them in their jittery, revealing-yet-secretive
dance. And then they come with their showy displays: the tanagers and
orioles, the warblers and vireos, buntings and grosbeaks, the oranges
and yellows and blues, lively painted ornaments in the newly green
woods. You walk watchfully, aware now of different habitats of dead
brush or small streams, the edges of woods, bog, or fence line. You listen
for the familiar strain of a song among the multitudes, attune yourself
to the ones closest; you scan the woods looking for the flash of color or
shadowy movement.

This is an accessible wildness. We may think of the birds as tame since
they will come to the feeders in our yards, but songbirds are still wild.
But we do not need to be adventurers to find them. A stroll through the
local park with the desire and the right kind of attention is all you need
to find the exotic, the wild.

Birding has always seemed to be a kind of spiritual practice: you narrow your focus, and the world disappears around you. It flits from the
brush, perches on a nearby branch, and you find yourself staring, eye to
eye, with a brilliant little bird who has just returned several thousand
miles from the wilds of Costa Rica or Panama or some other lush, exotic
land to the south. As you gaze through your binoculars, you are lost in

that moment. You are not thinking of tomorrow's meeting or the bills, or even the world around you. The sun is warm and you can hear all the songs, but for one moment you are focused only on this one bird. You look forward to seeing them like old friends and always hold out the hope of meeting a new one. One of the pleasures of watching the birds is knowing that at any second you can be completely surprised, a moment when a sudden beauty drops into your vision, a bird unknown right in front of you, the surprise of my first orchard oriole that landed in the brush across a pond as I tried to watch a yellow warbler, or the rare hoary redpoll that showed up at my feeder one frigid winter day.

I see scarlet tanagers on occasions in my ventures, but I'd hardly call it commonplace. But recently I was walking through Squaw Creek Park in Cedar Rapids when I realized that I was suddenly surrounded by them, at least a dozen flitting through the brush by a tiny stream. I sat stunned by their beauty, the splashes of deep red and black against a muddy background. I love the spectacle, but such sightings also remind me of the everyday—all those birds I know so well at my feeders—the cardinals and finches and juncos—are just as gorgeous. I know there's some metaphor here for how we attune ourselves to our everyday world, finding ways to remind ourselves how beautiful it is to be here at all.

But birding can be a double-edged sword. On one hand, birds connect us to a natural world that we all can feel disappearing. They remind us of that world and its preciousness. Anyone who pays attention to birds can see how the baseline is quickly changing: the range of birds I have known in my life is already diminished. What I knew as a child will be a different world from that the next generation will know: What birds will come to feeders? What species will people be able to experience? A common sighting now may be a rarity in the near future. It reminds us of how vital and beautiful this world is and keeps us in touch with something that we ultimately fear losing. On the other hand, birding can do the opposite. It's easy on a sunny day in early May, walking through some urban woodlands, to feel that things are good: you see dozens of species of magnificent color and song; you will see birds hunting in the shallows of river or lake, flocks of warblers high in the canopy, creepers pecking at the base of trees or towhees scratching at the dried leaves on the forest floor. It's easy to walk from the woods and feel that things are

still in balance. But these are not our grandparents' woods; this is not the same ecosystem they would have seen just a hundred years ago. To bird is to be in tune with the ecosystem and to fear its loss. To bird, you must learn habitats and habits. Which feed on the ground? Which high in the canopy? Which seek berries, which tiny insects? Which follow the fence line, which the deep forest? Which chatters, which sings? Birds are, like spirit, in this world but not quite of it. Remember, they are mere ephemera and will disappear as quickly as they arrive. It is easy to think of birds as simply cute, but birders know all too well that the hawk they've been watching is also watching that flock of finches for dinner; the herons are spearing frogs and fish with those magnificent beaks; and most of the migrants won't make it back another year to their hunting grounds. Birding is a way to see the world as it is, with its own rhythms and its own beauty. I don't know what evolutionary drive had made us connect with birds, but I do know that come spring we can feel as if we are part of that flock. Who knows where in our genetic past that feeling arises, but any birder knows that it's there. Birds live in that liminal space between our normal lives and the unknown. I can feel connected, but I am not. It doesn't matter how far into the woods or wilderness I go, there is always a kind of veil beyond into which I cannot go, the tree or brush a world where I can only live at the edge. Birds are a kind of mediation between the human and the natural, the urban and the wild. The wild things will come to the edge of my world and reveal themselves but just as quickly disappear, returning to their wild state that I can see only from without—I am always on the outside of their world looking in. Yes, humans too are nature, but we are of a different order. I have had birds come to me, to enter my domain—a hummingbird for instance who lands on my finger—but they are still of a different world into which I can only glimpse. But for that brief instant—a splash of color, a fragment of song, the gleam of a tiny black eye looking my way—
the wild steps out and sings for me.

Seeking Asylums

BY JANE PURCELL
2017

I WENT TO THE Independence State Hospital hoping to give my Anamosa grandfather a voice. Ever since then I've been hearing voices.

Although the 144-year-old building is routinely listed as one of the 10 most haunted places in Iowa, I didn't hear footsteps and whispers on the grand stairway or in the cavernous corridors. I didn't see apparitions of former staff and patients in the buildings and on the grounds. The voices didn't begin until I was back home again.

One of the most strident voices asks, "How can a state which ranks first in literacy rank 50th in number and availability of psychiatric beds?" It's not a rhetorical question, and it deserves a more thoughtful answer than the obvious conclusion: Iowa cares about reading books more than it cares about *crazy people*.

Crazy people. Does the label make you cringe? Good. It is meant to make you uncomfortable. I borrowed it from Ron Powers, who used it in the title of his 2017 book *No One Cares about Crazy People*.

Powers took his title from a 2010 e-mail written by Kelly M. Rindfleisch, the deputy chief of staff to Scott Walker, then serving as Milwaukee County executive. At that time Milwaukee County Hospital was in the news for allegations of mismanagement of its mental health complex, and Walker was concerned the scandal would be an issue in his campaign for the governorship. "Don't worry," Rindfleisch wrote. "No one cares about *crazy people*."

But enough about Wisconsin.

We have our own problems right here in River City—more so, perhaps, than in 1930, when my grandfather died at Independence. In his day, we might have known a lot less about the science of *crazy people*, but we did seem to care more about them—enough to keep them off the streets and out of prison, anyway.

Grandpa Ownis's story is a short one. He wasn't mentally ill when he died at age 32. Nor did he die of pneumonia or "serious lung trouble," as reported in the local paper. In 1930, there were many reasons a person might find himself in a locked ward, but pneumonia wasn't one of them. A state hospital was where patients suffering from any of the 100-plus diseases now listed in the *Diagnostic and Statistical Manual of Mental Disorders* (DSM) were housed along with a mish-mash of drug addicts, geriatrics, dipsomaniacs, and women who had lost interest in domestic pursuits or rejected their infants.

Grandpa was one of the dipsomaniacs—a "drunk."

Yes, alcoholism is a disease, and I should retire the word "drunk" with the word "crazy," but during Prohibition the definition was not so refined. An alcoholic was simply a person who drinks alcohol, not someone with a medical ailment. During the years Grandpa was drinking whiskey out of a barrel with a ladle, enjoying alcohol was a crime.

Today's definition of alcoholism first entered the lexicon with the formation of Alcoholics Anonymous in 1935. When Grandpa bit the dust three years before the death of Prohibition, the word they used was "dipsomaniac." His official cause of death was "delirium tremens."

While Grandpa Ownis's newspaper obituary featured a photo of a handsome young man in an army uniform, his hospital records tell a different tale. At intake he was 5'8," but weighed a mere 115 pounds.

However, his heart was "fine" and his teeth were "good." His complexion was "fresh," and his eyes were "blue." His chest was "well-formed and symmetrical." I glean that he had drinking buddies from "cause of habit: associates." I suppose the note reading "Heredity: Good" bodes well for me, although I'm not aware of the criteria used to upgrade or downgrade one's heredity—not that I don't personally know folks whose genealogy I privately consider "unfortunate." And not everyone can boast of a "well-formed and symmetrical chest."

With these few facts and a bit of imagination, I conjure the image of a dying man (of good heredity and with my mother's blue eyes) confronted with indignity and loneliness in his last moments.

I find it more difficult to imagine what his wife felt at the end for the man who had won her heart despite her parents' disapproval—the man who had fathered her three young daughters, as well as the one kicking in her womb. Perhaps, all things considered, she felt some relief. And, of course, she was embarrassed.

Any death in the State Hospital brought painful stigma to the family. My grandmother outlived her husband by 63 years, with her marriage more or less redacted from her history. The only time I heard her speak of him, it quite literally wounded me.

"Would you like this cameo?" she asked. "My husband gave it to me."

I didn't realize it was a pin, until it pricked the palm of my hand and drew a small drop of blood. I still have the cameo, but that's both the beginning and the end of that story.

My grandmother's silence grieved and infuriated my mother, who was only four-and-a-half when "Daddy died." Mother desperately wanted a father who was more than the granite slab in the cemetery where she often visited him over the years, sometimes taking a picnic.

Whereas it is strange and in many ways wonderful that the community followed my grandmother's lead, and the four children heard nary a word about their father's intemperance. Those familiar with the interconnectedness of small towns will not find it strange that my father's father's signature is prominent on my mother's father's commitment papers. As Deputy Sheriff, Grandpa Ray played Andy to Grandpa Ownis's Otis— only in the TV series Andy never drives Otis to the State Hospital to die.

But at least there was a state hospital to take him to and a bed to lay him in. In the 1840s, the first generation of American mental asylums was founded largely due to the efforts of Dorothea Dix, who pestered state and federal legislatures into building 32 federally funded state psychiatric hospitals—four of them in Iowa.

The Iowa Lunatic Asylum in Mount Pleasant opened in 1861. Four years later it was already overpopulated, so the state legislature made it a priority to build a second hospital in Independence, expending $845,000 to see that it was done right. The Clarinda State Hospital (1884) and the Cherokee Lunatic Asylum (1902) completed a plan to provide services in each quadrant of the state.

In contrast, even though additional inpatient beds are urgently needed, Iowa's Governor Branstad closed the Mount Pleasant and Clarinda facilities in 2015. He responded to criticism by predicting a wave of privatization that hasn't happened and won't help those without health insurance.

Branstad has gone to China, of course, but there's so far nothing to suggest that Governor Reynolds will veer from her predecessor's "Iowa as a business" model. Apparently it's no longer the business of the state to provide services just because they are badly needed and it is the right thing to do. Which begs the question: what is the purpose of state government if not to do exactly that?

There was a very different philosophy of state government behind the funding of the four Iowa mental health hospitals. The legislature knew it was paying for Kirkbride Hospitals, named after another prominent mental health reformer, Thomas Kirkbride, a doctor who advocated a philosophy of Moral Treatment. Kirkbride conceived of large palatial buildings in secluded areas with expansive grounds designed to make patients feel important and valued. They were to be sanctuaries for the mentally ill, with long rambling wings staggered so each room received maximum sunlight and fresh air.

The Independence facility, for instance, was set on more than 1,000 acres. Able-bodied patients maintained large floral and vegetable gardens as well as entire farms. Cherokee prided itself on its apiary. This agrarian treatment wasn't a new idea. As far back as the fifth century B.C., Hippocrates pioneered treating the mentally ill with techniques focusing on changing the patient's environment.

My pondering of the healing power of nature is interrupted by other voices—this time accompanied by sirens and tambourines. It's 1966, and my friends and I are singing a new and very popular song. Perhaps you remember it:

> They're coming to take me away ha-ha
> They're coming to take me away ho-he hee-hee-ha-haaa
> To the funny farm
> Where life is beautiful all the time
> And I'll be happy to see those nice young men
> In their clean white coats
> And they're coming to take me away ha-haaa

The lyrics parody the ideals of the Kirkbride model where life is beautiful on a farm, tended by nice young men in clean white coats. The next verse includes a call "to the happy home with trees and flowers and chirping birds."

Remembering the song made me wonder how much of my thinking about mental institutions is influenced by media, including films such as *One Flew over the Cuckoo's Nest* (1975), *Rain Man* (1988), *Girl, Interrupted* (1999), and *Shutter Island* (2010).

A good friend, a psychiatrist, scowls and waves her hands dismissively when I mention these films: "The media portrays *everything* about mental illness wrong," she says. "Shows such as 'Law and Order' perpetuate the myth that the mentally ill are dangerous and more prone to violence. In actuality, they are much more likely to be the victims of violence. Mental wards are not often pleasant places even under the best of circumstances, but neither is living on the street or in prison."

In her 20 years working within the VA and in other mental health treatment settings, my friend never met anyone remotely like Nurse Ratched. And yet, the popularity of *Cuckoo's Nest* replaced the stereotype of the nice young man in his clean white coat with a sadistic, man-hating, large-breasted control freak.

My recent attempts to make friends and influence people by pontificating on the history of mental health care in Iowa were often interrupted with questions about lobotomies. My audience obviously wants me to get to the good part . . . the macabre part . . . the truly barbaric.

Lobotomies are indeed a sticking point (pun intended, but hardly funny) in my argument that patients might have had it better "back then." Many treatments were performed that are regrettable by modern standards, but lobotomies are arguably the most heinous.

In fact, Nurse Ratched is a ringer for Florence Nightingale when compared to the real-life duo of Drs. Walter J. Freeman and James Watts who, in 1936, performed the first prefrontal lobotomy in the United States. The good doctors went on to pioneer the less invasive, but still horrific transorbital lobotomy also known as an "ice pick lobotomy." They also coined a host of euphemisms for the procedure.

I couldn't resist testing out one particularly charming example on an angst-ridden friend:

"How would you like to reduce the complexity of your psychic life?" I ask.

"Sign me up," she says.

"Okay, there's a bit of a waiting list because the doctor is really famous, but once he monkeys about in your frontal lobe with an ice pick inserted first in one eye socket and then the other, you'll be a lot less emotional. In fact, assuming the procedure doesn't kill you, it's possible you'll be rid of emotions forever."

"Monkey about?" she asks.

"Stir. Swish. Fiddle—call it what you will."

"Ah," she says, "I think I'll stick with yoga."

One of Freeman's most public failures occurred at the Cherokee site. While performing a lobotomy in front of an audience, Freeman stepped back to accommodate a photographer, causing the ice pick to slip too deeply into the patient's brain, killing him. It both horrifies and saddens me to know that many of Freeman's clients were parents who wanted better-behaved, less obstreperous children. His youngest patient was only 11.

To be fair, most families would have made this awful choice out of desperation. Their loved ones were clearly suffering, difficult to handle, and sometimes a danger to themselves and others. At the time there were no effective treatments for schizophrenia. So, did relief from pain and the debilitating effects of severe psychosis outweigh the considerable drawbacks? In some cases I'm sure it did—which is why Egas Moniz, the Portuguese neurologist who pioneered the procedure in Europe, was awarded the Nobel Prize in 1949.

In 1967, Freeman performed his final transorbital lobotomy—also ending in the patient's death. All these years later, however, the procedure still fascinates people. The lobotomy room is the most popular exhibit at the hospital museum in Independence, and comedian Tom Waits's deadpan assessment of the surgery, "I'd rather have a bottle in front of me than a frontal lobotomy," is a favorite of modern-day dipsomaniacs.

The word "lobotomy" also crops up in the most unexpected places. Hurrying through the Denver airport last summer, I was stopped in my tracks by a billboard-sized advertisement for a local distillery.

"Distilling vodka one time is giving it purity. Five times is giving it a lobotomy."

I still don't get it.

And what about electroshock therapy? That was pretty awful, too, right?

Actually, and perhaps "shockingly," electroconvulsive therapy (ECT) is still a viable treatment for severe depression. ECT is done under general anesthesia; small electric currents are passed through the brain, triggering a brief seizure that can quickly reverse symptoms of depression. So no, ECT is *not* the second most horrific chapter in Iowa's mental health history. That chapter was written early in the last century by the Iowa State Eugenics Board.

I have a brother-in-law (soon to be ex-brother-in-law, praise the Lord) who preaches eugenics—most often when the only parking spaces available are marked "Handicapped" because "those people shouldn't be driving anyway" or when he hears of an infant born seriously premature or handicapped. "You know in ancient Greece they would throw those babies off cliffs," he says. "That way they don't become a burden to society." By the way, this man is a doctor!

Jim lives in Texas, but Iowans aren't in a position to cast stones. In 1911, we became the ninth state to pass a law allowing for the sterilization of "criminals, idiots, feeble-minded, imbeciles, lunatics, drunkards, drug fiends, epileptics, syphilitics, moral and sexual perverts and diseased and degenerate persons." By the early 1960s, nearly 2,000 people in Iowa (the majority being female) had been sterilized. The board remained active until 1977.

As a national movement, the popularity of eugenics decreased after World War II. In Iowa, however, sterilizations increased, due in part to the activities of Birthright and the Human Betterment League. The Iowa chapter of the latter was established in the 1940s to educate the public on the benefits of sterilization, including the elimination of poverty.

Even though lobotomies and sterilizations were still being performed in the 1960s, antipsychotics and lithium were found to effectively treat many types of "insanity" that would have previously forced institutionalization and surgical intervention. A movement toward deinstitutionalization (the "movement's" word, not mine) spread across America, wherein mental health services were moved into the communities where people lived, giving them access to treatment while allowing them to live with the general population.

Generally a move in the right direction, deinstitutionalization occurred largely in response to a series of legal cases brought about because of egregious conditions in some state mental hospitals.

One new law prohibited the mentally ill from working on farms or in kitchens, or sewing or engaging in any activities considered rehabilitation unless they were paid wages. Another guaranteed the right to a "least restrictive environment," which was often conveniently determined to be "not in an institution." Across the nation, states, Iowa included, saw an opportunity to lower costs by shifting responsibility to local community health clinics that were supported primarily through federal block grants, not the state.

Filmmaker Barry Morrow won an Oscar and an A-list reputation for *Rain Man* in 1988, but he was already a celebrity in Iowa for his first film, the autobiographical *Bill* (1981).

Morrow was inspired by his friend Bill Sackter who at the age of seven began a 44-year stint at the state hospital in Fairbault, Minnesota. Sackter wasn't mentally ill; he was mentally challenged—a "slow" child from a poor family. He was diagnosed as "likely to become a burden on society." As a college student Morrow crossed paths with a deinstitution-alized Sackter, and when Morrow accepted a job at the University of Iowa School of Social Work in 1975, Sackter joined him in Iowa City. In an old classroom near his office in North Hall, Morrow helped Sackter set up a modest coffee service. His customers stopped by not only for a 25-cent cup of joe, but to hear the "barista" play his harmonica. Sackter died in 1983, but Wild Bill's Coffee Shop in North Hall is still going strong (although the coffee could be stronger) as is its spinoff Uptown Bill's and the Extend the Dream Foundation.

Outside support made all the difference in Bill's becoming an inter-national hero for people with disabilities. A little friendship and atten-tion transformed his life, but his story isn't typical. The sad truth is, the mentally ill sometimes wear out their welcome with friends and family, and the policy of deinstitutionalization has left fewer places to serve people with mental illnesses. In addition, many of the community mental health services that were meant to replace institutions have been closed due to lack of funding. In consequence, nationwide one-third of the homeless population and half of the total prison population have a diagnosable mental illness, and they are the fastest-growing segment of the prison population.

* * *

Historically, the advent of Christianity was a bad time for the mentally ill. Epilepsy, hysteria, and forms of psychosis were often equated with possession by evil or satanic spirits. In the modern world, these ideas have been, for the most part, excoriated—but that doesn't mean the church has no function in mental health care. The original mental hospital movements in both England and America were faith-based. The first superintendent at Mount Pleasant began his inaugural report with this verse: "Inasmuch as ye have done it unto the least of these, ye have done it unto me" (Matthew 25:40).

Today, priests and ministers, especially those in rural communities, provide one of the main sources of services for the families of the mentally ill.

Take this situation, for example:

"Remember that kid who killed his football coach?"

"Yeah, I do. The one up in Parkersburg, right? Around 2009? It was in *People Magazine*. Terrible thing. I blame the parents."

"How can you blame the parents? The kid was schizophrenic."

"True, but they knew that. They should have gotten him some help. Kept him away from guns at least."

I wasn't sure what to expect when I met Joan Becker for dinner last spring. Joan is the mother of Mark Becker, who did, indeed, kill his football coach during an episode of psychosis. Mark didn't hate the coach. He loved the coach. The whole family loved the coach. The whole town loved the coach. In fact, Coach Ed Thomas played cupid for Joan and her husband Dave when they were just kids at the same high school their three sons later attended.

When Mark began hearing voices, one of the most persistent demanded that he kill Coach Thomas. Is he sorry? Yes! Horrified? Yes! Could the tragedy have been avoided? YES. Only after Mark Becker was sentenced to life in prison did he get the treatment he needed despite *years* of advocacy by his parents. The system let them down. As for the gun. . . . In the United States anyone who wants a gun can get one. Easily. But that's another story.

Joan credits her Christian faith for helping her to survive the tragedy. Members of the same church, the Becker and Thomas families have prayed together and have supported each other since the day of the tragedy. Before that Coach Thomas had prayed often with Joan and Dave as they struggled to understand how their middle son had become so lost as a young man.

Perhaps even more impressive than having God's car, Joan Becker finally got Governor Branstad's ear for a 30-minute audience. Branstad, however, was not a good listener. Well, that's not fair. Joan said he listened respectfully and without interruption, but he didn't *hear* her. If he had, I don't think he would have concluded the interview with, "Well, let's face it, Joan, it's so much cheaper to get them the help and supervision they need in prison."

It's true that Mark, now 29, has found treatment where too many mentally ill people do—in prison. He's doing well at Oakdale, in one of the 1,956 beds for the mentally ill in Iowa's correctional system. Joan's point, however, was lost on the good governor: PRISON should not be the typical solution!

"Law enforcement officers spend days trying to place those who need mental health services, spending millions of tax dollars every year locking up Iowans with mental health issues instead of treating them," she said.

Joan believes God wants her to share her family's story as a means of reaching out to other families coping with paranoid schizophrenia. To that end, she gives talks around the state and, in 2015, published *Sentenced to Life: Mental Illness, Tragedy and Transformation*, the last chapter of which is written by her son, Mark.

Joan is no longer able to help Charla Nicholson from Bondurant, Iowa, however. Charla's 20-year-old son Chase shot his mother, father, and sister to death last April after the family had been unable to find a hospital that would let him stay for more than 24 hours. Chase turned himself in to police almost immediately. Like Mark Becker, Chase hadn't wanted to kill anyone. But the voices...

When I say to someone (as I did recently, to someone I like and respect): "Did you know Iowa is 50th in the nation for access to psychiatric beds?" And his response is, "Well, someone has to be 50th. Why does it matter which state?" I get mired in trying to answer the question. But he's right, in a way. The problem is nationwide and fixing it shouldn't be a competition. Still the ranking should, I think, be cause for shame and an incentive to improve.

Over the years, our understanding of the brain—how it works, what goes wrong when it is injured or diseased—has increased dramatically, and yet the stigma of mental illness remains. Even though mental health professionals and most of the rest of us no longer routinely reference lunatics, drug fiends, moral degenerates, imbeciles, and the feeble-minded, until we put our money where our mouth is, it is clear: In Iowa, not enough of us care about crazy people.

Author's note: I learned a great deal about the four Iowa mental health hospitals from David Rosheim, who in 2015 published *The Four Sisters: A History of Iowa's State Psychiatric Hospitals.* A book-seller by day, Rosheim is a mental health activist in his own right, working to help people understand that such institutions still have a place, and that closing them does not save money but simply shifts the burden to county officials, jails, and state prisons.

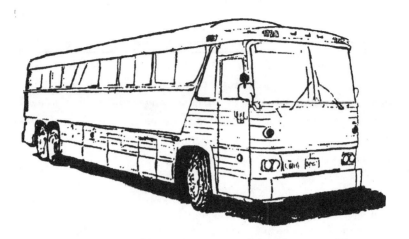

Christmas Found on a Trailways Bus

BY KELLEY JON DONHAM

2018

RETURNING TO IOWA CITY from Chicago on the bus, I noticed a man sitting across the aisle from us—seated alone. He was a small man, maybe five foot six at best, thin, 140 pounds at most. He looked to be in his mid-60s. He wore a white straw cowboy hat, a white denim jacket, and blue jeans. His cowboy boots were shined, as were their silver tips. He carried a rolled-up blanket, tied with a leather thong on either end with a slack in the line so that it could be carried over his shoulder. Seeing it recalled for me the saddle rolls of cowboys in old western movies. This was the extent of his luggage. From his looks and dress, I surmised he was from the Mexican cattle country of the state of Sonora.

I found myself wondering, why was he there? How did he get here amongst the denizens of the many Americans by choice or necessity who cannot afford more comfortable and more private travel? Was he an immigrant? Was he an illegal immigrant? I had to caution myself as I was starting to profile this little man and perhaps develop a negative perspective about him,

Our first stop was Naperville where we paused for a few minutes, and then we were back on the road again west bound on I-80. My wife, Jean, and I settled back and relaxed to the humming of the tires on the pavement—contemplating a nap. However, I could not get settled, as I noticed the small man across the aisle begin to fidget. He turned to me and gave me a nervous smile, flashing two gold front teeth.

He asked, "¿Dónde está Naperville?" It was obvious that he could not speak English. Well, I did understand what he was asking, barely penetrating the cobwebs of my neglected college Spanish. I replied, "Pasamos Naperville 50 millas de regreso" (We passed Naperville 50 miles ago). His smile disintegrated to sadness, contorted with fear. Concerned by his changed affect, I asked, "¿Cómo te llamas?" (What is your name?). "Mi nombre es Jesús," he said (My name is Jesus). He spoke again, saying something I could not get this time. He took out his billfold and pulled out a piece of paper. On it I saw a phone number and a name. Through my very rusty Spanish and our back-and-forth exchanges with exuberant gesticulations, I understood that he had relatives in Aurora. He was supposed to get off and meet them at the Naperville stop. Of course he could not understand English, so he had no idea that we had stopped at Naperville and then moved on. He showed me his ticket—to Naperville! I looked at the phone number. It was an Illinois number for the Aurora area. He had no phone. I called the number with my cell phone. No answer. I suspected that the number I called was a land line for his relatives. They were probably now at the Naperville bus station waiting for their husband? grandfather? uncle? brother? friend? or?

I approached the bus driver and explained what apparently happened. He looked back at the sad and frightened little man. The other passengers were now aware of the drama unfolding. The driver turned his eyes back to the road, shook his head, stared straight forward, and continued westward. After a few minutes the driver pulled out his cell phone. He motioned for me to go sit down in my seat. Moments later the driver got off his phone and called me back up front. He explained that he had arranged a rendezvous with a bus coming down from the north, bound back east to Chicago, and that bus would meet our bus in Dixon. They would deviate to Naperville on the way and take Jesus back to where he was supposed to meet his people. Our bus and the rescue bus would each suffer up to an hour delay. I went back to Jesus and explained as best I could what was going to happen. His expression changed from one of fear and sadness to a broad gold-toothed smile.

The bus driver turned onto the exit ramp for Dixon and stopped at a gas station. On the loudspeaker he explained that we would have at least a 30-minute delay. The driver didn't have to explain the delay; the passengers had figured it out. They knew the delay was for the sake of Jesus. Nobody got upset. Everyone just settled back. Some got off the bus and went inside to get something to eat. I looked at the old man and asked, "Tienes hambre?" (Are you hungry?). He responded, "Un poco" (A little hungry). I went inside and bought him an egg salad sandwich and a bottle of milk, which he consumed con mucho gusto.

Soon the driver called the passengers back on the bus. The old man, clutching the remains of his milk and sandwich, slung his bed roll over his shoulder and walked out of the bus as the others got on. The rendezvous bus arrived.

As we pulled away, I looked back to see the little man standing, with his bed roll strapped over his shoulder, ready to board the east-bound bus. As he tipped his white cowboy hat, a broad grin spread across his face. He was going to see his family, with a little support from 50 friends and a special bus driver.

The gift here was that the driver demonstrated sympathy for the old man, risking protest from other passengers and rebuke from his bus company boss. The gift also included the 50 passengers who understood they were going to be late because of this one small elderly Mexican traveler in a foreign country with a language that he did not understand. But that delay in time was not as important as seeing him united with family. The gift was also to me, as my initial profiling and prejudice (is he an illegal alien?) faded to realize he is a human being with immense courage, humbleness, thankfulness, grit, and desire to connect with his relatives. I assumed he was an immigrant. This led me to think that there is something about our current immigration policies (the effort to stop "chain immigration" for example) that does not consider the humane side of the equation. I wish more people did.

Jean and I frequently take the bus. Yes, it is cramped, uncomfortable, and not private. You may be sitting next to someone carrying their belongings in a garbage bag. You may be sitting across from a woman with three children under the age of four, and one or more of them are crying—most of the time. You may sit across from an Amish couple who carry their lunch in a tied-up cloth feed sack. These are people of lower socio-economic status stigmatized by much of the middle class and the one percent. However, they are a group rich in culture, lacking in hubris, and open to the greater good of "their people." Different I think from the "me first" culture, more common in the upper socio-economic echelons of society.

I have learned important lessons from bus rides. On a different bus ride, again returning from Chicago, I experienced another gift. It was just a few days before Christmas. I had given a talk in Chicago and was excited about getting home and being with family for Christmas festivities. About 20 miles outside of Moline, Illinois, the bus started to slow down, eventually to about 20 mph (not a safe speed on I-80). The driver pulled into a rest stop. He got out, lifted the engine cover, and was greeted by a cloud of blue smoke. Getting back on the bus, after a phone call to base, he informed us that a rescue bus would come to fetch us.

Thirty minutes later the rescue bus arrived. We boarded and headed for Moline. The new driver informed us that his bus was headed south to St. Louis, and we west-bound passengers would have to wait about two hours for another bus to take us on to Iowa City. So, I—along with 50 other passengers—waited. Some with plastic garbage bags as luggage, some with small children who were getting tired and anxious, but patient. Finally, after about three hours the substitute bus arrived. We all boarded, calmly, happy to be on the road again. Now we were about four hours behind schedule. I am sure everybody on that bus had holiday plans they were eager to get on to—not just in Iowa City, but others on to Omaha, Lincoln, North Platte, or other cities on west to Denver, the run's final destination.

As the sun set and it grew dark on the bus, someone started softly singing "Silent Night," alone. Soon another joined in. When they had finished, someone started "O Holy Night," and then others followed with the more joyful songs of "Rudolph the Red Nosed Reindeer" and "Jingle Bells." Soon the entire bus was reveling in festive singing, with feeling! As I got off the bus in Iowa City, the fading tune I heard as the bus pulled away was "I'll Be Home for Christmas" (I hoped they would).

Bus rides have taught me a lot about not making prejudged social generalizations. Perhaps my interest and desire to "stay in touch" with people of different socio-economic classes is owing to my history. I grew up poor. I did not live in a house with running water (except for me running a bucket to the house from the windmill 100 yards away) or plumbing until I went away to college at age 22. Water would freeze in the winter in upstairs bedrooms of the house our family lived in. My sister and I would make Dad drop us off three or four blocks from school as we rode in the back of our old cattle truck sitting on bales of hay. We were ashamed of what our classmates might think of us. "They are country hicks; they are poor and stupid."

Now I live in a house with all of the middle-class amenities. I have worked over 40 years as a professor, with colleagues who have had vastly different upbringings. I am aware of the social stigma and prejudice often acted out by the most socio-economically privileged. One example I'll offer recounts how I witnessed differences in social behavior by comparing bus passengers to those using a different mode of travel—air this time.

I was traveling home by air from Montreal. Somewhere in the air nearing Detroit, a goose hit the plane's windshield, cracking it. The pilot announced we would have to make an emergency landing at a small airport. We landed safely. People got off the plane, grumbling. In the waiting area the agents tried to keep the delayed passengers apprised of the situation, saying they had to wait for another plane to come in to continue our flight. An hour later a plane arrived, but it was much smaller than the original plane.

The agent informed us that only half the passengers could travel on this flight. The rest would have to wait another hour. Further, the agent said, "Those of you willing to give up your seat and wait for the second plane, please approach the desk." Nobody got up (me included). Then the agent said, "O.K., those who absolutely must get on this flight please approach the desk." There was a rush to the desk like junior high boys racing to the cafeteria at lunch time. People fought for position near the front of the line, elbows flying and bodies shoving like basketball players fighting for a rebound. Angry language spewed forth, verbally assaulting the agents. "I have to get to blank, blank, and blank today!" "I am a doctor, and I have to get to blankety blank tonight. . . ." "I am going to sue you and the whole damned company you work for."—Nasty!

The bus people may lack the wealth of those on the plane, but the social justice wealth of the bus people surpassed by far that of those on the plane. Jim Wallis, founder of *Sojourners Magazine: Faith in Action for Social Justice*, wrote in a recent article (I paraphrase) that nothing distracts more from social justice than economic success.

When I can, I will take the bus and recall fondly the spirit of giving, the "do it for the greater good" experienced on past rides. Not the hubris and "me first" vibe I witnessed on that plane ride.

County Fair

BY DOUGLAS MCREYNOLDS
2018

O F ALL THE WORDS THAT conjure images of fairyland before the bright eyes of rural midwestern childhood I think there is none so powerful as "Fair," and no phenomenon binds us so securely to a place and time we call ours as the annual County Fair. The State Fair is more famous, but it's way over in Des Moines, and it's mostly about things like butter cows and politicians having their pictures taken and fried food served on sticks. The County Fair belongs to us, actually comes to us; it is an anchor for our lives as well as an extension of them. The gratification we find here is enduring and, as if in some time machine, we return year after year: to this same place, these same colored lights, same carnival rides, and same livestock exhibits long after we have ceased to show our own animals. Here is even the same peeling gray paint on the same wooden screen behind which the same tattooed magician exhales kerosene flame and swallows glowing fluorescent tubes before the wide eyes and gaping mouths of children as awe-struck as we were when first we watched him do it 40 years ago, 50 years ago. Nothing has changed.

The damp August night itself is the same, and the cicadas. The throb of stock car races over at the west end of the fairground rises and falls and rises again as drivers slide into and accelerate out of the grandstand track's curves. On the Midway, pink cotton candy being spun in stainless steel vats tonight was spun for us when we were children, and we taste it, and the fibrous, airy sweetness of it collapses on the tongue and melts into nothing as it always has. In the dance pavilion, the same caller is calling out the same squares. Around this corner we'll take a little peek; now back to the center and . . .

The carny barkers have not changed, nor has the canned calliope music blaring from underneath the Tilt-a-Whirl. The shills' games are the same, and we know we cannot win, but, well, somebody is lugging around an oversized teddy bear, and maybe this year it will be our turn to get lucky. After all, each game still costs only a dollar to play, and the sign still says a prize is guaranteed.

Nor has the mingled smell altered that is part trampled grass and feedlot filth and popcorn, part stale beer and cotton candy and exhaust fumes. It is, as it was when we were young and for uncountable years before that, an admixture of incongruous aromas so perfectly balanced with this time and this place as to be compelling. We test it, and as the lungs are filled with air, the mind is filled with time stopped. There is no world but this world, and this one is world enough.

Such excitement! Marvelous Hampshire hogs nearly as big as cows, longtailed black stallions, glossy and nervous, which must have come straight out of *The Arabian Nights*, Percherons with knotted manes and tails, shampooed Hereford and Angus steers to be shown in the morning by the 4-H'ers asleep beside them now. We stand amidst an unimaginable wealth of pampered livestock, each animal a gleaming champion. And the rides, the noise, and the carny games: no detail, however trivial, has been overlooked. All is the same as it has always been, and so it will remain. This is a land that lives, like Brigadoon, for one short week in August and then disappears among the vapors of time and memory.

It is not that the Fair transports us back to some dreamed childhood, some Neverland fantasy. The Fair is not an escape into the imagined past or an evasion of life-as-it-is in favor of life-as-it-ought-to-be. The youth showing the steer peers forward into an adulthood as green as the childhood we remember, and the children watching the sword swallower belch fire can only guess at what strangeness the future is apt to hold. No, the Fair is outside of time; it points forward as well as back. Brighter far than that circling shaft of searchlight which advertises it across the whole county, the Fair illuminates our potential, drawing its power from the dynamo that is our past.

Once, caught up in the excitement of a Saturday night grandstand concert, I let go of an item I had wanted to keep, and I did not think about it until I was home some hours later. I determined to go back to the fairground at daybreak and look around on the off chance that it was still where I'd left it.

But when I arrived the Fair was gone; it had simply disappeared in the night. Oh, there were ghosts of it all around me, and I stood among them in awe, reminded sharply of my own mortality. The Fair's essence lingered in the air in the smells of dewy grass, manure, and last night's beer, but the carnival and the crowd had vanished while I was sleeping. Where did it all go? I couldn't imagine. I supposed there must be people and animals asleep in the closed barns, and I knew that beribboned displays of cut flowers and quilting, baked goods, and garden vegetables remained, locked away in the great exhibit hall that dominates the fairground, but these would be only relics either for retrieval or for consignment to the landfill; the Fair itself was gone.

I walked slowly through the grandstand, watching and listening as empty cups and popcorn boxes blew about in the early morning breeze. I was glad of the scraping sound they made, for I had suddenly realized I did not want to be alone in this place. The item I sought was not surprisingly gone, but its not being there scarcely seemed important to me now. My original purpose in coming was nothing more than an afterthought in the presence of this, this lack of a Fair, this hole in space where a Fair had so recently been.

I walked down in front of the grandstand, out onto the wooden stage where garish, reverberating music had lately been played, for there was no security guard left to tell me not to. An empty pizza box and half a dozen Coke cans attested to the technical people who had torn down last night's sound system after the last musician had played his last encore; nothing more, and nothing was all around me.

I stood there for a few minutes, then walked back through the grandstand and out into what had been the carnival Midway. I could not even tell where each ride or carny booth had been, though I tried; I could not imagine anymore just how it had all looked. It might have been a dream, the kind that eases away just as you reach for it in coming to morning consciousness and leaves you with no more than the vague remembrance of its prior existence, its precise shape gone forever. Once a noise startled me, but as I turned toward it there was only the wind, scattering orange ticket stubs down along Franklin Street.

Wapsipinicon

BY JOHN PETERSON

1989

WAUBESSA PINNE-AC, white potato, swan apple,
Edible root of *Sagittaria.*
The Sac-Fox named you for the practical thing,
Starchy root of arrowhead growing in the wet places.
They came to gather along your banks and backwaters,
Up your tiny tributaries,
From spongeland prairies in the north
As far south as the Mississippi,
For even the smallest of you has its backwaters.
                              Imagine the watershed.

Rain drenches the prairie,
Draining into lowlands.
Drops pool at the tops of carbonate ridges,
Cutting by weak acids through the graveyard of algae,
Bryozoan, brachiopod, coral, and crinoid,
Rock of living eons,
To recharge aquifers that are the hidden source
                              of your powers
Trapped in Silurian limestone,
And spill through tiny cracks.

Follow these waterways; they take us down
Past each water-deflecting rock stratum
To the smallest crumbly particle

Beneath the richness of prairie,
Down hillsides into your winding basin,
Through moist ravines where blue cane of blackberry
                                        bars the way,
Over otter-slick banks, cut banks, point bars,
And onto the smooth surface of open water, your river,
East Branch, Middle Branch, Little Wapsipinicon.

ON THE gloomy morning of the Solstice I watched
A heron step off the rim of splintering ice
And drag its butt in the steaming water
As if it hadn't the slightest care.
I talked to it in a lunatic's soft voice,
"Why are you here so late, crook-necked devotee
                            of little waters?"
Alongside ice in the weedy shallows
Where frogs and stranded fish
Fattened it in the glaring summer of the drought,
It lingers with its yellow bill angled over black water,
Stalking chubs or shiners.

Now the river freezes shut,
Giving up the ghost.
A dour wind blows off the freeze-burned landscape
                            of striped fields
And shoots right through the bark of hickory on the ridgetop
Into the hard straight heartwood shaft.
Only the dance of sharp deer hooves can break the icy crust.
And on the water there's a death march
In the heron's slow step.
For winter here will kill it, yes it will.

Then thaw, split and muck, trees in bloom,
Trees in leaf, catkins hanging thickly.
The river chainlinks murk and clarity and a million tiny eyes.

HOW MUCH of the unbroken prairie and wooded floodplain
Abides in this new river,
Still supple in its slow gait
Despite the bitter lesson of farming,
The farmer in love with land,
Resentful when the river claims its portion?

On the disturbed banks, nettles and ragweed grow dense
Above half-submerged junked cars
Dropped along the outside bends to break the water's force,
Revetment, riprap, broken chunks of concrete,
Reinforcing rods poking crazily into air.

Who remembers when the Wapsipinicon ran wild
                          over glacial rubble,
The genius of its continent,
And the deep pools simmered with pike
Even through farm country,
Before marginal land was planted,
And fields sprouted stand pipes,
And a tile line ran to every ditch?

They would ditch the Wapsie.
It's what they really want;
Not everyone, but most.
                     Think of it simply as arterial.
After rushing off its fields, silt slows down.
It tumbles into its places,
Fits into its point bars, pieces of a puzzle,
Mechanisms of a lock. It ticks together, a sign of time,
                                        a clock.
At some spots the channel is choked to a muddy sheet;
Or else it staggers
Like a drunk from bank to bank, dropping its load.
A canoer knows it needs the good flushing of a flood.

FOR TWO hundred and twenty-five miles,
Past the Minnesota line, where so many of Iowa's
                                rivers start,
Pure rivulets through clumps of grass,
To the Mississippi, fat and dirty at the end,
The Wapsie does a humble job,
Reducing upland elevations, hauling them as far
                                as they will go.
Past Frederika, Sumner, Fairbank,
Tripoli, Littleton, Independence,
                    Quasqueton,
Troy Mills, Central City, Waubeek,
Stone City, Anamosa,
Olin, Oxford Mills, Massillon, Toronto, Folletts.
Past storm sewer pipes, too, hauling grease and garbage
From their streets,
And pipes from their sewage treatment plants.
Past the table where the farmer earns and spends
A million dollars before breakfast, and is always broke,
Past fields where anhydrous pierces
The clean white of a farmboy's eye,
Past the straight-row sameness that disorients,
Past rural ghettos, the timbered dark
Where deer are shot by flashlight and coons hate full moons.
Past the coiled stink of piggeries,
And river-terraced trampled hillsides
Where cattle drool like idiots and break down fence
                                to get to shade.
There's effluent from the factory
That makes the water shine
An instant only, and then it wraps inside
                    the steady brown.
There's a leak up a ditch somewhere that's killing fish,
But only for half a mile or less.
There are nitrates, ammonia, chloride, phosphates,
                        fecal coliform bacteria,
Arsenic, barium, lead, and zinc.

There are still the springs that join it, from caves
                        and secret dens.
There are wild turkeys, ruffed grouse, wood ducks,
And pileated woodpeckers, if you know how to look,
And a few river otters.
Back to the scene of extermination,
Night-hunting watersnakes, crayfish, and frogs.
And mostly there are fish that feed by touch and taste,
Carp, suckers, bullheads, catfish moping under rocks,
But also walleye, crappie, pike, bluegill, bass
                  —fish that brighten water,
And the brown silt billows when fish dart off.

WATER, OF all inanimate things, dreams.
It's true.
It has animal anticipation and memory.
At the flat interior wetlands of its source
It dreams its salty destination.
It dreams its whole course, beginning, middle,
                         and end.

And even to a more profound beginning,
It dreams when its course was born
In a river under the glacial sheet,
Where water gushed from tunnels under ice,
Roaring in a marvelous voice,
Ice that became the pump of heart,
Equalizer of river destinies,
Parent of those close sisters,
The Cedar, Iowa, and Skunk.

Imagine what we see and know
And what it may become, and what it was.
Gone are the pound of turbine wheels,
The rumble of burr runs grinding wheat.
But imagine them, imagine

Jay Sigmund picking his path along the bank,
Choosing his "fellowship of streams," his "tipsy eddies,"
The quarry master J. A. Green, Grant Wood,
                 who dreamed of order,
George Matsell, big city cop who became the perfect
Backwoods host on his hills of hickory, ironwood, and oak.

The people who built the fish traps
And who came to pull the root of arrowhead from the muck
Are longer gone, but hold a faster claim,
     Waubessa Pinne-ac, Wapsipinicon.
So let's have no more nonsense
About Princess Wapsie and her lover Pinicon.
What we need are river practicalities,
To get our water lives in order,
Slough, bank tangle, limestone jumble,
And on a warm night clouds of caddisfly,
Healthy haunted river in its gloom or brightness,
Where the living are just a kind of water,
Die and are pulled into the current,
Lodged against an underwater stone
Until the current nudges them free.

Let us be joyful in its faultless trickle
To join the water that makes the world.

Filling the Cumberland Gap

BY FLOYD PEARCE

1988

I RETURNED TO Iowa five years ago after an absence of more than 35 years. Strange how the brief years of childhood permeate our entire lives. Strange, too, how during those many years living in other places, I always thought of myself as an Iowan. I'd lived more than half my life in San Francisco. I love San Francisco, and I know the city better than I know Iowa.

After graduating from high school in Atlantic, I left Iowa (except for irregular visits to my father in Marne and the two years I spent at the University of Iowa). During my years of "exile," I remembered my childhood more or less accurately, but I'd idealized small-town life—glossed over the numerous shortcomings.

Feelings of alienation and loneliness have always formed a large part of my conscious life. I've attributed this partly to my parents breaking up when I was a child, partly to being the only boy in a family with three girls. But I've come to think that some of us naturally house more space than we can put a name to. Some of us are inherently restless. I know that when I left, I felt a conscious need for intellectual and artistic nourishment. I went West.

I was a "culture vulture." An abiding concern during my maturing years was "Who were the great geniuses of Western Civilization and what had they done?" How immense a trip I was taking! At that time I was pretty certain I couldn't find the answers in the small towns of Iowa or in its cornfields. (I'm much less certain of this now.) Since then, I've spent a considerable part of my life in the theaters, museums, libraries, concert halls, opera houses, and the great parks of three continents. I've acquired enough "culture" to learn that one lifetime is too brief a period to do more than tap the glorious achievements of which man is capable.

During my "exile" I sometimes felt that I might one day return to live in Iowa. Then the death of my father somehow set me adrift. It left me with no reason for going home. (My mother had died years earlier in California.) The childhood I'd never really come to grips with seemed more remote than ever. Is there a balm and is there a Gilead? Can you ever go home again? Is it folly to try?

The risks were great. I think single people place a greater value on friendship and relatives than those who marry and have children. I was single and launched full-sail into middle age. I had reached an age when two close friends had already died. Did I dare leave friends of 25 and 30 years? (And very dear and loving friends they are.) I expected it would be difficult to make friends in middle age. In a small town, certainly. People aren't prepared to disrupt long-established relationships. I knew one doesn't pick up high school friendships where they broke off 35 years earlier.

For financial reasons, it was necessary to settle in a *very* small town. Property values are considerably higher in Atlantic—17 miles away. I visited all seven of the smaller towns in Cass County. On Main Street in Cumberland, population 315, I found a handsome brick building waiting for me. I bought it for considerably less than what a year of San Francisco rent would cost. After remodeling, insulating, rewiring, adding equipment to what I'd brought with me ... *voilà*! Within two years I had the printing shop of my dreams.

While working on the building, I'd crisscrossed the state several times making numerous contacts and acquaintances. Several of these have developed into fine friendships. I began to relax—perhaps I *could* make a home here. This was the first of my two great discoveries. The second was that I found, and was shown, a veritable hotbed of fine poets in the state. A renaissance is happening here, and I seemed to be the only person to recognize it. There must be 10 to 15 poets here who deserve national reputations. Incredible! I saw a local job that had to be done. Get these poets in print! There is a need for me here, and it's good to be needed.

* * *

But what's it like living in a small town? Above all, day-by-day living is much more convenient than in a large city. Main Street in Cumberland fails miserably in its attempt to be two blocks long. The post office is across the street; the bank is a block away; the garage is across the street; the Farmer's Co-op (with UPS) is a block away. There are no lines, no traffic, no parking problems. Frequently, you can see more rabbits and squirrels on Main Street than people. Certain places, like the post office, the feed store, and the telephone office, are closed during lunch hour. I find this direct response to a basic need unspeakably wonderful.

It's quiet. So quiet you can hear the birds. For a couple months in the fall, you can hear the low sound of the elevator running 24 hours a day. Generally the air is clean. (This spring there was considerable dust because of dryness and the winds.) It is May, and last night the air was indescribably soft and sweet with the green freshness of sprouting things. The town is fragrant with lilacs now, peonies later. There will be garden vegetables all summer—with pears, plums, and apples in the fall.

Social life is built around the churches and clubs and fraternal organizations. There are three churches, and near as I can tell, there must be about 15 clubs. A tavern occupies the back of the café (which is half a block away, across from the store), and it can be reached either through the café or a door around back.

The social structure is rigid. Wealth and "old families" hold precedence. Americans have always had an inordinate reverence for money. There's a quaintness and gentility that attends "established families." At any gathering in a large city, a standard conversational ploy is "where you from?" City populations tend to be highly fluid and especially on the West Coast. Granted, many cities still have their "old families" but they seldom carry the force they once did. In cities you *are* what you do and how much you earn. I've always been involved in social groups populated with creators, consumers, and purveyors of "the arts." Small towns place little value on these activities. My being an impoverished printer of modern poetry places me very low on the social scale. My honors come from elsewhere. I will, when pressed too far, remind the local arbiters that my family arrived in this county in the 1850s. Unfortunately the fact that they settled 20 miles away places them in another world.

I had to return to remember why I left.

Much of the business of running a small town is done through clubs and volunteer committees. Clubs don't interest me, but I've done considerable committee work. I helped with fund-raising for the new Community Building. I'm active on the Cass County Arts Council, and have served a term on the Family Living Committee—both in Atlantic. I spent a three-year term on the Literature Advisory Panel of the Iowa Arts Council. Recently I was on a 12-person state-wide task force addressing any shortcomings in the way the Iowa Arts Council functions. (I represented poets and private presses, and I was the *only* person who represented Iowa's thousand small towns!) My statement is that in some ways a person has the opportunity to live a much more complex and varied life in a small town than in a city.

So much has been written about the loneliness of small towns that I won't go into it except to say it's true—in spades. People who say cities are lonely places have never lived in small towns. If you are in any way different, you are isolated and highly visible. It's a rare person here who is interested in anything outside his very limited experience. Talk is limited to farming, the weather, and sports. Women worry about shopping and children. Everybody talks about what they ate for dinner. You can be sure it will include at least four of these items: meat, potatoes, white bread, artificial butter, and gelatin in some form. Since everyone knows everyone and everyone has the same experiences, much of the men's conversation centers around dirty stories and memories. The stories are generally stupid, sexist, racist, and *familiar*—but everyone laughs. The memory stories tend to be about high school escapades or tales of travail from the 2nd World War (40 to 50 years ago!). They are rehearsed with a gusto that suggests the incidents happened only yesterday. It's sad to consider that those times may have been the most memorable for the ones who tell the tales.

Few people read or go to the theater. In a word, almost no one does anything that takes him out of his everyday experiences. Most are full-time participants in the national distraction—watching television. Cute situation comedies and a heavy dose of football can hardly be called soul food. When will it be obvious that the emotions and the intellect require wholesome nourishment every bit as much as the body?

There's a horrible tyranny in small towns that dictates you cannot disagree with anyone about issues. Even worse, you can't *discuss* issues.

A general belief persists that if you disagree with someone it means you don't like that person. If you disapprove, you must remain silent. If you speak at all, you must be careful and *not* say anything important. Everyone knows everyone (and is probably related—at least by marriage), so anything you say is bound to get back to the person whose opinions you are discussing. There's the conviction in small towns that expressed disagreement on issues will somehow blow the town wide open, make it inoperative. After seeing some of the damage this sort of thinking causes, I'm convinced it creates more problems than it solves. (But I'm still the new face on the block. How could I know? *That's* one way to ignore criticism!)

I've had my run-ins with the library board; I've locked horns with small-town religiosity and have looked the beast square in the face; I've even defended the mayor on some issues. . . . There may still be a few people in town who like me. It's possible that given another year I'll have offended everybody. I hope not. I think I like it here.

Of course humor is dangerous and must be used with considerable caution, and irony not at all. Don't make waves. Guard your emotions. In far too many things only a deadly mediocrity is encouraged. It is no wonder so many of the best and brightest leave. Is it any surprise that self-esteem is so low in small towns? Hell, "If you were any good, you wouldn't be here!"

Well, I *am* good and I *am* here. I think the Iowa malaise is a weak ego—and this is not to be confused with genuine modesty. (I knew I was a resident and no longer a visitor the day I started criticizing.) I think it would help if all Iowans took a thorough course in Iowa history. We all know that Iowa is the nation's cereal box and its corn and pig producer. We know about the work ethic and quality craftsmanship. The Mormon Trail and the Underground Railroad are but two elements that tie Iowa into the fiber of the nation's destiny. There has been a continuous chain of fine writers since Hamlin Garland—over 100 years ago. Iowa has far more excellent institutions of higher learning per capita than any state in the country. Developments in hybrid grains and livestock made in Iowa have had an incalculable effect on agriculture world wide. Iowa has produced an ample list of international personalities that includes: Herbert Hoover and Henry Wallace, Billy Sunday and Elsa Maxwell, Grant Wood and Meredith Willson, Buffalo Bill and John Wayne. Then

there's Bix Beiderbecke, John L. Lewis, "Dear Abby," and on and on. . . .
The state is fertile and beautiful, the climate moderate.

The only good thing lacking in Iowa is Iowa's good opinion of itself.
Again and again (and this is most important) I have seen and experienced
a deep warmth, a concern, and a fundamental humanity here that put
the lie to all that's trivial and twisted in the small-town psyche.

One day (over a beer) a local farmer told me, "Farming is the only
occupation that *creates* wealth. Other occupations manipulate what
already exists." I like the pride in that voice. (I didn't suggest that this
is also true of the artist.) Farming produces wealth—and nourishes life.

I stand here before my press with both feet planted firmly on the
(metaphorical) sod. I have printed fine poets with national and international reputations. I am occupied now printing poets of genius—Iowa
poets—their poems growing (not metaphorically) from the rich soil. I
know this will be the most important work to come from my press. I
work, and I expect the daily miracle because I know it happens.

When I ran for city councilman, a woman here mentioned she hadn't seen
any campaigning in the newspaper. A couple days before the election,
I asked Barb (who runs the café which, in summer, has the best fresh
fruit pies I've ever tasted) if she thought I should provide the town with
free coffee on the morning of the election. She looked at me with a faint
and wise small-town smile, "Why don't you do it the morning after the
election?" That's what I did. There's profound virtue in a town with a
sensibility that knows it's better to say "thank you" than "please."

Editor's note: The good citizens of Cumberland elected Floyd to the city council
position. We've not heard how the coffee party turned out.

Wapsipinicon
ALMANAC

No. 17 ~ Route 3 Press ~ Eight Dollars

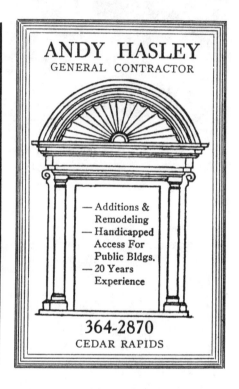

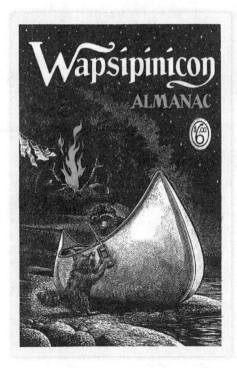

TALK OF THE TOWNSHIP, 2010–2018

I'm planning a garden party of sorts. We'll celebrate the season on a family farm in a southern township of Delaware County southwest of Hopkinton. I'll invite Iowa's governor and his lieutenant as well as our state Secretary of Agriculture. And for good measure, the CEO of the Iowa Pork Producers Association shall receive one of my engraved invitations.

Our setting belongs to an acquaintance I've come to know through the world of vintage tractors. I visited his farm recently to pick up a part for my tractor's wheel bearing assembly. He's farmed this tract for most of his life and has always worked jobs in town. Lately, as he approaches retirement age, he's rented the crop ground.

Several years ago a Confined Animal Feeding Operation (CAFO) appeared nearby in his township's fairly flat terrain. Well, O.K., but then more of the stench factories began to pop up like poison mushrooms. Now his rural setting is burdened with 14 CAFOs, all within one mile of his house. When you're surrounded with these "operations," it really doesn't matter which way the wind blows; you will never escape that biting, aggravating Wall-of-Misery odor.

This fellow's grounds and buildings are well maintained. His roofs are good, all the siding is painted, and you don't walk over or around piles of junk to move from place to place. One glance at his workshop hurries me home to clean and organize.

So there we'll sit on a sunny, late May Saturday afternoon. Terry and Kim and Bill and Rich as well as my tractor man and I will sip lemonade while sitting in white vinyl chairs by a round patio table large enough to hold my friend's photo albums and scrapbooks. We'll page through those yellowing pictures of grandparents and great-grandparents who worked so hard to farm and pay for these acres. Perhaps we'll leaf through news clippings highlighting various blue ribbon 4-H calf or sow awards.

Good local stuff. The patio table's large green umbrella will shield this middle-aged gathering from the late afternoon sun.

Fourteen CAFOs within one as-the-crow-flies mile. Goodness. There could be conversation concerning how "ag" sure has changed, the importance of "keeping up with the times" or how voluntary soil nutrient retention policies are "beginning to show promise." But what I'm ready for, what I'm anticipating, is this: as the late afternoon breezes settle and the untenable stench of thousands and thousands of pounds of pig shit dampens the merry tinkle of ice cubes clinking in glasses—I want to closely observe Terry. Terry's Big Ag buddies do indeed oppose any notion of local control when it comes to siting CAFOs. And how many of his appointees to Iowa's Environmental Protection Commission enjoy strong ties to the hog industry? I want to watch as Terry's trademark 'stache, smarting from that smell, goes twitchity, twitch, twitch. . . .

Anamosa has emerged as a destination for motorcyclists. Big rigs thunder through town and on nearby highways throughout the riding season. Their owners spend a lot of money here. The twice annual hill climb event draws crowds and fills taverns, but the bigger draw is the National Motorcycle Museum now housed in a former Walmart store near the four-lane highway.

I marvel at the hordes of Harley Davidson riders and their impressive mounts. On some weekends I almost picture this as some kind of cattle trail drive post—with hundreds of faux outlaws dressed in their period garb inhaling that liberating air of the open road, rumbling through in a jaunty parade of freedom.

But wait a minute. Somebody is working long hours in an office or factory to pay for those machines and leather outfits. I'm told a new full-bore "dresser," the largest Harley (which we used to call the "hog"), now costs between $23 and $30 thousand dollars. The leaner "Sportster" will set back an adventurer at least $8,000. And the big 3-Wheeler numbers, increasingly popular among the more senior riders, check in with a price tag between $38 and $48,000. A huge market for riders now involves the accessories angle. I understand that a Harley rider can easily drop $10,000 on fancy pipes, seats, wheels, handlebars, etc., and the labor involved to attach these things.

To me it makes more sense to send off to Netflix to rent "Hells' Angels 69" or the "Glory Stompers" or any of a number of bad, bad late 1960s biker movies.

I'll confess. When I hear in the distance that weekend roar from Highway 151, I know that the brothers are off to new adventure and that I'm only wasting away my short life by hoeing these potatoes and painting that shed. Then it's time to drop the tools, lose the straw hat, unbutton my shirt's top button, and mount MY rig, my own two-wheeled trail to that sound of a different drummer. "What the hell," I mutter as I crawl onto my steed, my ticket to the open road. I kick-start that beast, gingerly finger the throttle, and cruise east down dusty Shooting Star Road toward that highway away from this old farm and its endless demands.

I should point out that my mount doesn't roar like a Harley or even purr like a Gold Wing or a big Kawasaki. It sort of whines like a middle school girl because it's a Honda 50, circa 1965. Its motor would fit in your lunch box, and 80 cents worth of gas would probably get me as far as Milwaukee, or Green Bay with a good tail wind.

The fact that on this thing I look like a French guy buzzing around Paris in some 1967 psychological drama film doesn't bother me in the least. The kids in town love this motorcycle (or is it really more of a scooter?), and they always wave and smile.

An artist friend of mine acquired it years ago for $1 from a neighbor who wanted it out of his shed. I didn't even give a dollar for it. It required a bit of TLC but now I can blow into town (strictly on the side roads) and show those big rig leathered and painted-up outlaws just what's what.

⚌➤◦◄⚌

I wandered recently into a Saturday night blitzkrieg of a performance by Dubuque's own "Fast Clydes." Their rockabilly howling nearly blew out the walls of the Voices Gallery in that town's old warehouse district. What a good idea: transform ancient industrial warehouse real estate into a huge space for gallery events, some of them way too much fun.

The Clydes, a fairly new three-piece combo, rock most any joint with their electrified renditions of such 1950s blasters as "Tear It Up" and "Rock This Town." If some part of your body is not tapping to this kind of music, then you have been clinically dead for at least 20 minutes.

A couple I know arrived quite near the end of the show. They'd just attended a performance of the Dubuque Symphony Orchestra. These people were dressed to the nines and were full of wonder, having absorbed an evening of the Russian masters (Tchaikovsky, Rachmaninoff, etc.) at Dubuque's classy Five Flags Theatre. This was opening night of yet another fine symphony season.

What a great culturally diverse smorgasbord these small midwestern cities can offer: only a mile or so from the dignified coat and tie highbrow venue to the sweating strains of "Baby, Let's Play House."

———※·◦·❦———

Yes, many midwestern small-town main streets have been gasping for resuscitation for a good 25 years. The heavily populated Saturday night shopping bonanzas on those main streets have been only memories for even longer. Consumers in these towns drive to cities now to shop unless they find what they need in a "local" Walmart.

And why did Saturday night shopping/socializing fall by the wayside? The late Clarence Mitchell from Oregon, Illinois, offered one of the most convincing opinions I've encountered. In his 2004 memoir, *The Diary of a Journeyman—The Life and Times of the Past Century*, the old printer claims the Saturday nights in town ended in the 1950s because the farmers all stayed home to watch "Gunsmoke" on TV. That long-running western, he says, kept those shoppers away. That's a mighty valid observation.

———※·◦·❦———

Former drinkers I know often dispense words of wisdom at no charge. All of them I know are men, and I'm glad they've quit drinking because I like them, and they'd be dead had they not changed their ways.

One sage mentioned, "I was never as handsome or charming as I thought I was while I was drunk." Another revealed, "I had to hustle to find things to do when I finally quit drinking. Suddenly you have a lot of time on your hands when you're not at the bar every night."

Offering some defense for his past, one wag confessed, "I've only been drunk twice in my life. Once for 12 years and once for nine years."

———※·◦·❦———

I felt a bit sentimental as I watched my Ford Escort disappear down the gravel as he took his final road trip perched atop the salvage yard trailer.

I bought that car 10 years ago for a very reasonable price. A 1996 very quiet silver model, it was about as simple a car as you could have purchased in America: stick shift, small 1.9 motor, no air-conditioning, roll-up windows, manual locks, etc. With only 48,000 miles on it, I hoped it would last a good while. It did. And the car delivered admirable gas mileage—usually 40 or more mpg. One critic thought it "mighty sporty," and something I'd bought "just to impress women." I countered with the facts: this car was about as exciting as an afternoon in Peoria. The Escort may have wanted to be cool, but he was ultimately a nerd. I christened him "Glen."

The elements and road salt caught up with Glen. His body succumbed to cancer, and he began to suck dust and fumes too readily. Mr. Reliable's days were finished. What I find annoying is that car manufacturers, both here and abroad, don't seem to want to produce such a simple, solid no-frills ride as Glen. Consumers wanted cars with more "pep," and that's what they got. They also got poorer mileage.

I suppose the car thing can translate into lifestyle evaluations. Do you strive for good mileage and reliability or are flash, noise, and gadgetry your thing? You know, we'll all someday head down that gravel road atop the salvage trailer.

———◆———

There I sat down by the little creek on our farm. Perched in a shady grove, I enjoyed my sandwich on a fine fall noon. I noticed movement across the waterway from perhaps 50 yards west of my spot. Here he (or she) came into full view, that hearty figure of an adult lone coyote loping along without a care in the world.

I watched as the coyote crossed the field, not 100 feet from me. It never saw me, but I admired the critter in all its wild grace. Its coat was rich and luxurious, and it held its head high. There I sat squeezing in a bit of lunch before heading back to the shop for more work. That lucky dog, I'm assuming, eats when he's hungry and drinks when he's dry.

Later I recounted my sighting to a neighbor. He'd been raised in the 1940s and 50s on a typical small diversified northeast Iowa farm. Having grown up around calves, lambs, and hens, his reaction was "too bad you didn't have a rifle."

Yes, it's all fangs and claws out there in the real natural world, but that doesn't detract from its beauty.

—————⇒∘⇐—————

I enjoyed a pleasant encounter last mid-spring on an eastern Iowa trail. There I was, strolling at a leisurely pace through this heavily wooded tract, and who should round a bend headed my way, but two probably mid-20s women. Each carried a bag, and they told me they were collecting gooseberries. That product was in its green stage, but they claimed the recipes they planned to employ called for not-yet-ripe gooseberries.

These were perhaps the first young women I'd seen in two years not holding and operating a hand-held device. We traded berry tips and moved on. How nice.

—————⇒∘⇐—————

I snuck away with a lovely companion on a weekday afternoon during the third week of October and headed for a timber bordering a rapidly moving river. Managed to find honey mushrooms, cottage mushrooms, and the remnant of a hen-of-the-woods specimen. Tell me of anything better than the Iowa October woods, a sunny blue sky day, a leaf show to die for, and all of our insect friends tucked away somewhere far out of mind.

What is fine printing? Fine printing involves an esthetic dedication. It is an expression of the human spirit which, through the arrangement and presentation of the printed word, reaches toward order, harmony and beauty.

◊ JOSEPH BLUMENTHAL ◊

WAPSIPINICON
ALMANAC

ROUTE 3 PRESS   NO. 25   NINE DOLLARS

Contributors

WINSTON BARCLAY publicized the arts during his career with the University of Iowa. Now he splits his time between Iowa City and South Dakota.

DAN BRAWNER, a native of Mount Vernon, Iowa, has painted houses for many years. A published novelist, Dan also contributes a weekly column to the *Mount Vernon Sun*.

MICHAEL CAREY is a poet and teacher who for many years farmed in far southwest Iowa near Farragut.

LESLIE CATON of Cedar Rapids is working toward a degree in marriage and family counseling.

CARMEN KRAEMER CLARK grew up and raised kids in Iowa, surrounded by generations of pigs, cows, and cornfields. To this day, she stands for civil rights and economic justice, tells her stories, and cheers as new crops of progressive Iowans ripen once again.

MARIAN MATTHEWS CLARK of Iowa City enjoyed a career as an academic adviser at the University of Iowa.

MELVIN CORSON (1916–2002), a native of Littleport, Iowa, was a proud member of the Cedar Rapids Collins Radio team assisting with the 1969 moon landing.

OSHA DAVIDSON is a widely published journalist and the author of several books. He now resides in Arizona.

BETH CHACEY DeBOOM, a former *Cedar Rapids Gazette* journalist, is the Cedar Rapids go-to person regarding historic preservation.

KELLEY JON DONHAM taught for 40 years as a professor in the Department of Occupational and Environmental Health at the University of Iowa.

DAN EHL now lives in sunny Arizona following many years as an editor for small-town Iowa newspapers. Striking novels continue to emerge from his prolific pen.

GARY ELLER is a writer from Amcs. His recently published novel *True North* is drawing good reviews.

RACHEL FALDET of Decorah recently retired after a long career of teaching at Luther College.

TIMOTHY FAY is a letterpress printer and publisher living near Anamosa, Iowa.

GLENN FREEMAN teaches English at Cornell College.

ANNIE GRIESHOP is a piano tuner and technical writer living in rural Melbourne, Iowa.

STEVE HANKEN, a Vietnam vet, grew up on a rough-and-tumble farm near the Maquoketa River in Jones County. Now retired, he keeps a close eye on civic happenings in his town of Monticello.

JONNA HIGGINS-FREESE of Iowa City works for the University of Iowa. She's just finished writing a novel about Frances Perkins and the passage of the Social Security Act.

MIKE KILEN formerly wrote for the *Des Moines Register*. He's now living and writing in Arizona.

RUSTIN LARSON of Fairfield has witnessed the publication of several books of his poetry.

VERL LEKWA, a true expert on Iowa towns, taught for many years in Iowa schools. He lives in Columbus Junction.

DAVID MANNING lives in lovely rural Maquoketa, Iowa, on Bluestem Farm. He worked before retirement as the Jackson County zoning administrator.

STEVE MARAVETZ of Mount Vernon formerly worked as a DJ for public radio in Iowa. He retired recently after many years of writing for the University of Iowa Hospitals and Clinics.

SHIRLEY MCDERMOTT has worked in many countries throughout her teaching career but now, perhaps reluctantly, calls her native Cascade, Iowa, home.

J. HARLEY MCILRATH of rural Grinnell is the celebrated author of *Possum Trot*, published by Ice Cube Press in 2010.

DOUGLAS MCREYNOLDS was the Bissell Professor of English at Upper Iowa University of Fayette. He's now retired and living in Cedar Falls.

BETTY MOFFETT taught at Grinnell College. Her collection *Coming Clean* appeared in 2018 from Ice Cube Press.

ROBERT NEYMEYER of Waterloo is affiliated with Waterloo's Grout Museum District. He also lectures on Iowa history at the University of Northern Iowa.

FLOYD PEARCE (1927–2019) was a printer, poet, publisher, and the mayor of Cumberland, Iowa.

MEL PEET (1922–2007) was for years a college professor of history, literature, and religion. He spent his final years in his hometown of Anamosa.

JOHN PETERSON lives in Kansas City, where he continues to produce interesting fiction and poetry. John formerly worked as a marketing writer.

JANE PURCELL has returned to the Midwest after a long academic career in California.

DEE ANN REXROAT formerly worked as entertainment writer for the *Cedar Rapids Gazette*. Dee Ann now writes for her alma mater Cornell College in Mount Vernon.

MICHAEL ROSMANN farms near Harlan in southwest Iowa. He formerly ran a psychiatric practice that specialized in assisting farmers and other rural folk.

NORMAN SAGE (1910–2001) lived for years on the shore of Lake Macbride near Solon, Iowa, where he pursued his lifelong love of printing and design.

LARRY STONE has written about and photographed Iowa's wild and natural landscapes since the 1960s. He's currently heavily involved in northeast Iowa's Save Bloody Run battle against a massively large and ridiculous feedlot operation.

ANN STRUTHERS of Cedar Rapids finished her teaching career at Coe College. Ann is a widely published poet.

REBECCA SULLIVAN of rural Decorah recently retired as a teacher at Luther College.

RAYMOND M. TINNIAN (1960–2020) worked for the Office of the State Archaeologist in Iowa City and later in his own private law practice in Kalona, Iowa.

Bur Oak Books